YALE HISTORICAL PUBLICATIONS

David Horne, Editor

MISCELLANY 79

*Published under the Direction of
the Department of History*

German
Social Democracy
1918-1933

BY RICHARD N. HUNT

NEW HAVEN AND LONDON
YALE UNIVERSITY PRESS
1964

FOR MARGERY

Preface

The German Social Democratic Party stands today as the left flank of Germany's emergent two-party system, and has traveled a long road from the classical Marxist socialism of its early years. The Bad Godesberg Program of 1959 no longer explicitly demands, for example, national ownership of the major means of production but limits itself domestically to a number of economic and social reforms within the framework of contemporary capitalism. The movement away from traditional socialism has not been a sudden volte face, but a long process beginning formally with the Görlitz Program of 1921. Indeed, many characteristics of the Social Democratic Party in the first decade of the Bonn Republic were already clearly noticeable in the Weimar period: the general aging, ossification, and bureaucratization of the party, together with its inability to break through the "one-third barrier" to win an electoral majority. These characteristics were the distinguishing features of a long period of metamorphosis through which Social Democracy has passed, and from which it appears now to be emerging, as a different kind of party, in the 1960s. The purpose of this book is to study certain aspects of that great metamorphosis.

In the years before World War I, the German Social Democratic Party was the acknowledged and admired model of the world socialist movement. Its ideological pre-eminence and imposing million-member organization made it the backbone of the Second International. Within Imperial Germany the SPD (from the German initials of the party, Sozialdemokratische Partei Deutschlands) had established itself as the primary representative of the industrial proletariat. By 1912, after a half century of irrepressible growth, it had become the largest single party, expressing the fundamental opposition of over four million voters—one-third of the nation—to the existing political and economic system. In their ebullient optimism, prewar Social Democrats believed it only a matter of time before the party would be swept into power by a triumphant majority. Then they could carry out the major socialist aims of the movement: the complete democratization of the German state, national ownership of the means of production, and the elimination of economic and social inequality.

These optimistic expectations were upset, between 1914 and 1919, by a series of monumental events: World War I, the Bolshevik Revolution, the defeat and collapse of the Wilhelmian Reich, and the creation of the Weimar Republic. These events, together with certain internal developments, seriously altered the political prospects and outlook of the Social Democratic Party, changed its role in German society, and initiated the period of transformation which is the subject of this study.

In 1917 the more radical antiwar wing of the movement broke off from the conservative majority, a schism that resulted (after an involved process of regroupment) in the permanent division between the Communist and Social Democratic parties. The departure of the radical wing left the conservatives in complete control of the old organization and enabled them to revise the party program in accordance with their reformist beliefs. In the Görlitz Program of 1921 the SPD officially renounced revolutionary socialism in favor of a gradualist approach within the framework of the democratic state. In the years of the Weimar Republic, between 1918 and the advent of Hitler in 1933, the German socialist movement was divided, and the now officially reformist SPD had to function for the first time with a more radical party on its left.

At the same time there occurred a reversal in the traditional Social Democratic attitude toward the state. More than any other party, the SPD had been responsible for the creation of the new democratic republic. After 1918 the Social Democrats could no longer stand off in "pure opposition" to the state, nor did they want to. They gave full and enthusiastic support to the Weimar Republic and sought to share governmental responsibility whenever possible. Thus they provided the young democracy with its first president, Friedrich Ebert, and three chancellors—Philipp Scheidemann, Gustav Bauer, and Hermann Müller. Perhaps equally important was the stable administration the Social Democrats gave to Prussia. Otto Braun and Carl Severing led this crucial *Land* government (with jurisdiction over two-thirds of Germany's population) almost without interruption from 1920 to 1932. The advent of the Weimar Republic transformed the SPD from an opposition party into a government party.

This period brought important internal changes as well, changes within the SPD that will form the particular focus of this study. First, the party organization suffered increasingly from bureaucratic and oligarchic tendencies which all but inundated its original democratic forms. These tendencies produced in the leadership a group of entrenched, aging, and unimaginative officials who seemed quite unequal to the enormous tasks thrust upon them in the Weimar years. Second, the long and seemingly inexorable expansion of the SPD came to an abrupt halt after 1919, and the movement was faced with stagnation. Electoral support did not widen, and the party was not able to recruit enough young people to replace its aging membership. Third, the SPD became less clearly a proletarian class party: its social composition shifted noticeably as it lost working-class support to the Communists and attempted to attract new backing in the lower middle classes; even its proletarian supporters seemed affected by a gradual infiltration of middle-class standards and values.

All three of these internal developments reinforced the increasing conservatism of Weimar Social Democracy, and they were accompanied by a mood of profound discouragement as it appeared more and more likely that the party would never win an absolute majority or achieve its major socialist aims but was doomed to remain nothing more than a permanent minority party—a kind of parliamentary lobby for German labor. These attitudes go far to explain the lack of aggressiveness so evident in Social Democracy as it fought the losing battle against Nazism in the early thirties.

While internal developments clearly affected the political behavior of the Weimar Social Democrats, it lies beyond the scope of the present volume to analyze this external political activity comprehensively. The primary focus of the study is inward: on the evolution of the party organization, on the sociological characteristics of the movement, on its interconnections with the trade-union movement, and on its internecine factional struggles. The organization is in part chronological but mainly topical. The concluding chapter integrates the various findings and points out their relevance to the general metamorphosis of German Social Democracy.

PREFACE

I would like to acknowledge a profound indebtedness to Hajo Holborn for his kindly and expert guidance and for his unfailing encouragement. He has seen the book through from beginning to end. The late Sigmund Neumann graciously gave me the benefit of his unparalleled knowledge of German parties, and lightened my work in other ways. It was Robert A. Bone who first awakened in me an understanding of the importance of party organization. I would also like to thank Leonard Krieger and Harry R. Rudin, who have read the manuscript and offered valuable suggestions. John L. Snell has generously permitted me to use some of his manuscript data on the SPD Reichstag fraction. Ruth Drescher skillfully prepared the graphs. And to Yale University I am indebted for the financial assistance granted during the course of my research.

R.N.H.

Pittsburgh
August 1963

Contents

CONTENTS

ILLUSTRATIONS

Tables

TABLES

Abbreviations

ADA	Allgemeiner Deutscher Arbeiterverein	General German Workers' Association
ADB	Allgemeiner Deutscher Beamtenbund	General German Federation of Civil Servants
ADGB	Allgemeiner Deutscher Gewerkschaftsbund	General German Trade Union Federation
AfA	Allgemeiner freier Angestelltenbund	General Free Federation of Salaried Employees
BVP	Bayrische Volkspartei	Bavarian People's Party
DDP	Deutsche Demokratische Partei	German Democratic Party
DNVP	Deutschnationale Volkspartei	German National People's Party
DVP	Deutsche Volkspartei	German People's Party
KPD	Kommunistische Partei Deutschlands	Communist Party of Germany
NSDAP	Nationalsozialistische Deutsche Arbeiterpartei	National Socialist German Workers' Party (Nazis)
SAJ	Sozialistische Arbeiterjugend	Socialist Workers' Youth
SAP (1869)	Sozialdemokratische Arbeiterpartei	Social Democratic Workers' Party

xvii

ABBREVIATIONS

SAP (1931)	Sozialistische Arbeiter-partei	Socialist Workers' Party
SPD	Sozialdemokratische Partei Deutschlands	Social Democratic Party of Germany
USPD	Unabhängige Sozial-demokratische Partei Deutschlands	Independent Social Democratic Party of Germany
VSPD	Vereinigte Sozialdemo-kratische Partei Deutschlands	United Social Demo-cratic Party of Germany
Z	Zentrum	Center (Party)

1. Introduction: the Evolution of the Party Organization

At the birth of the Weimar Republic the Social Democratic Party possessed the largest and most elaborate party organization in Germany, as well as one of the oldest. Its continuous history stretched back over half a century to the period preceding national unification. If we are to understand the internal affairs of Weimar Social Democracy we must first understand how the party evolved from a tiny sect in the mid-nineteenth century into a great mass movement embracing, in 1919, a million dues-paying members and over eleven million voters (38 per cent of the electorate). The political history of the party has often been recounted[1] and will enter our narrative only where it plays a crucial role in the structural growth.

1. The standard work covering the entire prewar history of the party is Richard Lipinski's brief and official *Die Sozialdemokratie von ihren Anfängen bis zur Gegenwart* (2 vols. Berlin, 1927–28). For the early years there is the classic study of Franz Mehring, *Geschichte der deutschen Sozialdemokratie* (4 vols. in 2, Stuttgart, Dietz, 1897). Carl E. Schorske has presented a first-rate history of the party in the period leading up to the great schism in *German Social Democracy, 1905–1917* (Cambridge, Harvard Univ. Press, 1955), while A. Joseph Berlau treats the years of war and revolution in *The German Social Democratic Party, 1914–1921* (New York, 1949).

1

The Dual Heritage: Lassalleans and Eisenachers

Like most European socialist parties, German Social Democracy was an offspring of the industrial revolution. It began as a movement of the urban proletariat in those regions that first saw the introduction of modern industry. The movement grew organizationally, as in part politically, out of German liberalism; both antecedents of the modern SPD derived from workers' clubs sponsored by the Progressive Party. The Lassalleans and the Eisenachers, the two rival socialist groups whose merger created the Social Democratic Party, stood in sharp contrast to each other, not only in their politics but in the forms of organization they chose. They left a strange dual heritage to the later party, which helps to explain some of its paradoxes.

The Lassallean group came into existence in 1863. It was formed by the joint effort of a number of workers' educational societies (Arbeiterbildungsvereine), organizations established by the Progressive Party which, in theory at least, were nonpolitical and devoted to the technical and general education of the working class. The more radical members of the societies were dissatisfied with this nonpolitical orientation, as they were with the Progressive Party in general. Early in 1863 they invited the gifted if somewhat erratic young socialist orator, Ferdinand Lassalle, to advise them in setting up a new political organization to be devoted primarily to the struggle for universal suffrage. Lassalle enthusiastically approved the plan and, at its founding convention in May 1863, became the first president of the General German Workers' Association (Allgemeiner Deutscher Arbeiterverein, ADA).[2]

2. Mehring, *Geschichte*, 2, 8–17, 53.

The ADA quickly assimilated the political ideology of its president. Lassalle considered the cardinal purpose of the new organization to be "a legal and peaceful but untiring, incessant agitation for the introduction of universal and direct suffrage."[3] Only in this manner could the masses of the population break out of the poverty imposed upon them by the so-called Iron Law of Wages (the doctrine that real wages could not possibly improve under capitalism). Once universal suffrage brought the poor into political power, the economic resources of the state could be used to establish producers' cooperatives. These cooperatives would in time come to dominate the national economy, thus in effect "socializing" the means of production and supplanting capitalism. Apart from his socialist views, Lassalle was also an ardent German nationalist and looked to Prussia to achieve the unification of the fatherland.[4]

Organizationally, the ADA was constructed on highly autocratic and centralistic lines. The leadership of the group fell upon a president and a twenty-four-man executive. While executive members were elected annually, Lassalle managed to have his first term set at five years. Moreover, executive members resided in all parts of Germany and could meet only infrequently, thus leaving the president in personal command the bulk of the time. Lassalle also disposed of the party funds, named his own vice-president, and appointed a deputy for each city to preside over the meetings of local comrades, acquainting them with the leader's wishes and keeping their finances in order.[5] Lassalle's organizational conceptions are revealed with embarrassing exactness in

3. Quoted ibid., 2, 25.
4. Ibid., 2, 17–25; Berlau, *Social Democratic Party*, pp. 20–22.
5. Wilhelm Schroeder, *Geschichte der sozialdemokratischen Parteiorganisation in Deutschland* (Dresden, Kaden, 1912), pp. 8–9, 60–63. Schroeder has reprinted here all the SPD statutes from 1863 to 1912.

3

one of his letters to Bismarck. He enclosed a copy of the ADA statute, referring to it as "the constitution of *my* empire," and commented: "From this miniature picture you will be able to see clearly how true it is that the working classes are instinctively inclined to dictatorship, if they can be justly convinced that this dictatorship is exercised in their interests."[6]

The geographical structure of the ADA was designed to circumvent the Association Laws, which forbade political organizations from having branches. Every member of the ADA, regardless of his residence, belonged to the Leipzig organization. For legal purposes no locals existed, and the comrades of any given city were governed by a deputy of the central Leipzig organization. Once a year each city chose delegates to attend a national assembly, the principal function of which was to elect a new executive.[7] By means of this organizational arrangement, the ADA could operate efficiently as a legal political group, but at the cost of losing all local autonomy. Similarly, the concentration of dictatorial power in the presidency gave the party able and energetic leadership but precluded any genuine intraparty democracy.

Lassalle died the year after the founding convention, but his post was soon taken up by another authoritarian leader, Jean Baptiste von Schweitzer. Although the party suffered many adversities, including internal wrangling, Schweitzer was able, by superior administrative and financial methods, to set the organization on the road to healthy expansion. Its membership grew from 5,500 in 1865 to 16,538 a decade later.[8]

Not all the workers' educational societies had joined the

6. Gustav Mayer, *Bismarck und Lassalle: Ihr Briefwechsel und ihre Gespräche* (Berlin, Dietz, 1928), pp. 59–60.

7. Schroeder, *Parteiorganisation,* pp. 7, 60–63.

8. Berlau, *Social Democratic Party,* p. 34.

ADA in 1863. Those remaining outside Lassalle's group merged with other workers' organizations the following year to create the Union of German Workers' Societies (Verband der Deutschen Arbeitervereine) under the leadership of August Bebel. Politically, this union was under the influence of the liberal-democratic Saxon People's Party. But Bebel himself moved rapidly leftward in the next few years, and succeeded in pulling the organization along behind him. By 1868, at its Nuremberg congress, he had persuaded the union to join the Marxist International Workers' Association and adopt the International's program as its own. The following year, at Eisenach, Bebel consummated his work. The union dissolved itself to form—along with some Lassalleans disgruntled by Schweitzer's personal dictatorship—a new political party to be called the Social Democratic Workers' Party (Sozialdemokratische Arbeiterpartei, SAP).[9]

The program adopted at Eisenach reflected in its theoretical section the Marxism of the International; but the immediate demands of the new party scarcely differed from those of the ADA. They included a call for democratic government and state-aided producers' cooperatives. What really divided the Eisenachers from the Lassalleans were two quite different issues: first, the SAP was composed almost exclusively of Middle and South Germans who, in contradistinction to the Prussian-led ADA, rejected the Bismarckian Reich and advocated the "greater German" approach to national unity. Secondly, the SAP opposed the authoritarian and centralist organizational form of the ADA, choosing for itself a fully democratic structure based on autonomous local units.[10]

The Eisenachers' statute provided for a yearly congress

9. Mehring, *Geschichte*, 2, 177, 192–94, 242–44, 273–76.
10. Ibid., 2, 193–94, 275–76; Berlau, *Social Democratic Party*, pp. 29–31.

5

representing the local units, which was empowered to pass binding resolutions on "all questions concerning the party." An annually elected executive of five persons led the group between congresses. Its chairman, unlike the ADA president, possessed no special or far-reaching individual powers. The work of the executive had to meet the approval of the congress and was further supervised by an independently chosen control commission, to guard against "arbitrariness."[11]

In organizing their party horizontally, the Eisenachers faced the same legal restrictions as had the Lassalleans. But their circumvention of the Association Laws took a radically different form. Instead of complete centralization, the SAP was constructed of many autonomous locals, connected to the national leadership only informally by Vertrauensmänner (literally, "men of trust"). For legal purposes each local constituted a separate political association. This informal federal structure left a great deal more authority in the hands of the rank-and-file membership.[12]

The ultimate sovereignty of the membership was further strengthened by a provision requiring that all resolutions of the congress regarding program, statute amendments, and levies be ratified by a plebiscite of the entire party.[13] This painstakingly democratic organization was undoubtedly more fragile than the ADA, yet it proved viable. The party showed a modest growth, after the initial loss of its liberal periphery, from 6,255 in 1871 to 9,121 by the time of unification in 1875.[14]

From its outset the German labor movement had a dual heritage in organizational as well as in political matters. The Lassalleans and the Eisenachers provided two sharply

11. Schroeder, *Parteiorganisation*, pp. 66–69.
12. Ibid., pp. 16, 20, 66–69.
13. Ibid., p. 67.
14. Berlau, *Social Democratic Party*, p. 34.

contrasting models of organization: the one authoritarian, rigidly centralized, efficient, and disciplined; the other ultra-democratic, loosely federalist in structure, and lax in discipline. In the subsequent history of the Social Democratic Party, one can follow the interplay of these two clashing conceptions of organization.

From Illegal Sect to Mass Party

In 1875 neither party was more than a sect. The ADA outweighed the SAP with 16,538 members as against 9,121. In the elections of the previous year the Lassalleans had received 180,319 votes and sent three deputies to the Reichstag; the Eisenachers captured 171,351 votes and had five deputies. But both parties together accounted for a scant 6.8 per cent of the total vote.[15] There had been several attempts to unify the two groups. Increased harassment by the police had pushed them closer together, and the ouster of Schweitzer as president of the ADA removed a large obstacle. All realized that in the long run only a unified organization could achieve the radical goals of the socialist movement. The ADA and the SAP merged at Gotha in 1875 to form the Socialist Workers' Party, somewhat later renamed the Social Democratic Party of Germany (Sozialdemokratische Partei Deutschlands, SPD).[16]

The Gotha unification represented a compromise, but whereas the Lassalleans preponderated in ideological and tactical matters, the Eisenachers preserved the main elements of their organizational structure. This victory of the SAP stemmed chiefly from the fact that the Prussian police just prior to the congress had officially dissolved the ADA in that state. The authorities no longer found the ADA cir-

15. Ibid., pp. 34, 348; Schroeder, *Parteiorganisation*, p. 21.
16. Ibid., pp. 19–22.

7

cumvention of the Association Laws legally acceptable. Thus the Lassalleans were willing to adopt the major components of Eisenacher organization: the five-man executive, the control commission, local autonomy, and the decentralized system of Vertrauensmänner. The seat of the executive was strategically placed in Hamburg where the local Association Law permitted much more latitude in political activity. From the Lassallean organizational legacy the united party chose to retain the superior methods of financing and the stricter conception of discipline.[17] The new organization, however, lasted only three years, until Bismarck dissolved it with his Anti-Socialist Law in 1878.

In terms of modern political repression this law seems mild. It permitted Social Democratic candidates to stand for election and to speak and vote freely in the Reichstag, but it proscribed the SPD as an organization, forbade all meetings attacking the state or private property, banned the publication and distribution of socialist literature, and sanctioned the exile of "professional agitators."[18]

The dissolved party soon adapted itself to the new situation. Underground groups sprang up at the local level in factories and in the innocuous form of card clubs, smoking clubs, and the like. By 1880 it was possible for these groups to send delegates to a party congress held safely beyond the reach of the German police at Wyden Castle in Switzerland. This congress set the structural forms for the illegal movement: the leadership of the party would be assumed by its Reichstag deputies; congresses would be held abroad at least once every three years; a new party organ, *Der Sozialdemokrat*, would be published in Switzerland and smuggled into Germany.[19]

17. Ibid., pp. 23, 69–73; Mehring, *Geschichte, 2,* 354.
18. Schroeder, *Parteiorganisation,* pp. 31–32.
19. Ibid., p. 33; Mehring, *Geschichte, 2,* 430–31.

Within the Reich, agitation went on much as before—clandestine meetings were held, funds collected, and illegal literature distributed. Before elections the comrades of an electoral district would meet secretly to nominate a candidate and plan the campaign. Above the local level no formal organization existed except, of course, for the Reichstag fraction, the immune parliamentary leaders, who directed the national policy of the movement.[20] This absence of any formal structure made it necessary to conduct party affairs chiefly by personal contact and ensured thereby a great intimacy between the leaders and the led—all of which was fondly recalled by later critics of the party's bureaucratization.[21]

Bismarck's repressive legislation failed to curb the expansion of the German socialist movement. The party's popular support grew relentlessly from 493,258 (9 per cent of the total vote) in 1877 to 1,427,298 (20 per cent) in 1890 when the legislation was finally permitted to expire.[22]

The new SPD statute of 1890, following the lapse of the Anti-Socialist Law, set up the basic organizational structure which lasted—though modified and rationalized—down to 1933. An annual congress, composed of delegates elected by the locals, constituted the "supreme representative institution of the party." As the "legislative" body of the organization, it "enacted" the party program, determined the broad policies to be followed, decided the form of organization, and elected the "executive" and "judicial" bodies. The party executive, composed of two chairmen, two secretaries, and a treasurer, directed the affairs of the movement between congresses. It

20. Schroeder, *Parteiorganisation*, pp. 35–36.
21. Otto Jenssen, "Von der Revolte zur Massenorganisation," *Die Organisation im Klassenkampf* (Berlin, Marxistische Verlagsgesellschaft, n.d. [1931]), p. 23.
22. Berlau, *Social Democratic Party*, p. 348.

was required to submit an annual report for the approval of the congress. A seven-man control commission, the "judicial" branch, was empowered to oversee the executive and to act as a court for complaints against that body.[23] The local organizations chose the party's candidates for the Reichstag and put them up for election. Social Democratic deputies were expected to vote as a disciplined body according to the party program and congress resolutions. Every year the Reichstag fraction submitted a report to the sovereign party congress and received instructions from it. Between congresses, the only connection between the national leadership and the locals remained the Vertrauensmänner, as the Association Laws continued in effect. The selection of these men was left up to the locals, as were matters of local organization. Such, then, were the structural elements of the growing party.[24]

Shifting for a moment to the political development of Social Democracy, we may observe a leftward movement toward an openly revolutionary position during the period of illegality. At the Wyden congress the phrase in the party program "by all legal means" was shortened to read "by all means." The outlawed party would continue to participate in elections, but only "for agitational and propagandistic reasons."[25] This radicalization of the SPD found theoretical expression in the new Erfurt Program adopted in 1891. The analysis and prognosis of German society contained therein gave a mirror image of undiluted Marxism: capitalist economy tends toward monopoly, with ever greater exploitation of the working class and proletarization of the middle class-

23. In the 1890 statute the control commission was formally included within the executive, apparently out of legal considerations (Schroeder, *Parteiorganisation*, p. 45). By 1900 it had reappeared as a separate body.
24. Ibid., pp. 73–76.
25. Mehring, *Geschichte*, 2, 430.

es; the process is abetted by periodic crises and ultimately will culminate in the seizure of power by the proletariat and the socialization of the means of production. Thus the new program affirmed the revolutionary aspirations of the Social Democratic movement.[26]

But German society in 1891 did not appear to be on the brink of collapse: the economy was healthy and expanding, the government stable and powerful. In view of this situation, many comrades felt it necessary to work in parliament, for the time being at least, to achieve lesser goals within the framework of existing institutions. Consequently, a second section of the program, following the theoretical analysis, put forth a list of immediate demands: proportional representation in the Reichstag, referendum and recall, progressive income tax, eight-hour day, extension of social insurance, and so forth.[27] The Erfurt Program embodied a synthesis of revolutionary long-range objectives and reformist demands for the here and now, thus satisfying both the more radical and the more moderate elements within the party.[28]

The developments of the next years seemed to bear out the moderate point of view. In a dynamic and prosperous Germany each election brought fresh voters and more mandates to the party, culminating in the overwhelming electoral victory of 1903, when the SPD captured 3,010,472 votes, or 24 per cent of the total, and 81 seats in the Reichstag.[29] The parliamentary tactic seemed vindicated. By centering its efforts on election winning, the party could become a

26. *Erfurter Programm*, reprinted in Paul Weidmann, *Die Programme der Sozialdemokratischen Partei Deutschlands von Gotha bis Görlitz* (Hamburg, Kellinghusen, 1926), pp. 26–29.

27. Ibid.

28. Schorske, *Social Democracy*, pp. 4–6.

29. Berlau, *Social Democratic Party*, p. 348.

strong and positive force to improve the political and economic condition of the working class even before taking over governmental power. Moreover, it appeared only a matter of time before an absolute majority of the voters would rally to the socialist cause.

The success of the parliamentary tactic could not fail to influence the organizational development of the movement. In 1905 the party congress, prompted by the recent victory at the polls and by the repeal of the Association Laws, undertook to rewrite the party statute. Three alterations of major consequence ensued. First, the basic unit of the SPD was changed from the local organization (Ortsverein) to the electoral district organization (Wahlkreisverein).[30] The old locals which had grown up organically—and therefore haphazardly —with the labor movement were replaced by new, artificial units based on the electoral constituencies. This change presupposed that winning elections was the prime function of the party apparatus and thus reflected the shift in tactics since the years of persecution.

Secondly, the informal Vertrauensmann system (no longer legally necessary) was abandoned for a more rational pyramid structure. Between the new district organizations and the executive were to be created either Land or regional organizations,[31] having their own executives and congresses, and serving to connect administratively the top and bottom rungs. Formerly each local could express its opinions directly to the executive; now it became necessary to go through

---

30. Schroeder, *Parteiorganisation*, p. 81.

31. Ibid., p. 81. Owing to the peculiar structure of the Reich, Land organizations were not everywhere suitable. Whereas they generally were used in the south, Prussia had to be divided into several regional organizations (Bezirksverbände), usually corresponding to the provincial divisions. Saxony likewise used the latter units (Schorske, *Social Democracy*, p. 121).

a Land or regional intermediary. Social Democracy had created official channels! And as the close contact between the top and the base of the pyramid disappeared, important decisions tended more and more to be made at the summit.[32]

Finally, the 1905 reforms mark, for all practical purposes, the inception of the party bureaucracy. For the first time a uniform system of financing was established, with 20 per cent of all dues collected going to the national executive. The party's income had been growing apace: 58,763 marks in 1876, 249,582 marks in 1900, and 810,917 marks by 1906.[33] Annual reports covering agitation, membership, and finance now had to be made by branches at all levels. The vast paper work created by these measures obviously could not be handled on the old volunteer basis. The executive itself acquired three more paid secretaries between 1904 and 1906. More important, it was invested in 1904 with the power to appoint paid secretaries at all levels of the organization. By 1909 virtually every one of the forty-three Land and regional offices had such an employee, as had sixty-two of the nearly four hundred district offices.[34] Since these secretaries (though nominated by the branch concerned) were appointed and paid by the executive, they tended to reflect its viewpoints, and as professionals they soon acquired considerable influence in their branch organizations, all of which greatly augmented the power of the executive within the party.[35]

Thus the German socialist movement evolved, within the space of twenty-five years, from an illegal sect to a great mass party of three million supporters. From the minimum

32. Ibid., pp. 127–28.
33. Ibid., p. 119; Schroeder, *Parteiorganisation,* p. 100.
34. Schorske, *Social Democracy,* pp. 120, 125.
35. Fritz Bieligk, "Die Entwicklung der sozialdemokratischen Organisation in Deutschland," *Organisation im Klassenkampf,* pp. 75–76.

of formal organization possible under the Anti-Socialist Law, the party had built up a formidable and smoothly functioning machine for winning elections.

The organizational history of Social Democracy contrasts markedly with that of the bourgeois parties of Germany. The latter developed in the nineteenth century as Honoratioren-parteien, "parties of notables," run by their parliamentary leaders without mass organization or even a clear concept of party membership. Local organizations characteristically contained only the "notables," or prominent local backers of the party, who hand picked the candidates for their constituencies. Financially the organizations depended on large contributions rather than regular membership dues. And between elections they lay dormant; there was no program of continuous agitation and few if any ancillary organizations.

After 1890 the bourgeois parties made some efforts to build out mass organizations. The Conservatives and Center began to make use of ancillary organizations,[36] while the liberal parties even instituted regular party congresses, although these congresses had no formal—much less effective—control over the Reichstag deputies who still made party policy. All the bourgeois parties endeavored to expand their apparatus and modernize their electoral agitation, but in general their organizational structure continued to reflect their predemocratic origins: "The most important characteristics of an Honoratiorenpartei, independence of the local leaders in putting up candidates, at least a relative preponderance of the 'natural' leaders over the led, and the in-

36. For the Conservatives, the Bund der Landwirte (Farmers' League); for the Center, the Volksverein für das katholische Deutschland (the Catholic German People's Club).

dependence of the fraction . . . remained in all the [bourgeois] parties until 1918."[37]

This organizational dissimilarity between Social Democracy and the bourgeois parties was not unique to Germany but followed the standard European pattern. Most socialist parties resembled the SPD—some, in fact, had been modeled on it, since it was the oldest, largest, and most efficiently organized party in the Second International—and these socialist parties all differed in much the same ways from the bourgeois parties in their own countries. In part the dichotomy reflects the generally later dates of origin but, more importantly, it appears to be rooted in ideological disparities which affected the very purpose of party organization.

The following suggest themselves as the primary reasons for the organizational variance between the SPD and the other German parties. To a large extent they would hold true for other continental countries. First, the SPD was explicitly created as a mass party. It had the aim of infinite membership recruitment among the masses of the population, and as the party grew it became physically necessary to build out an ever larger administrative bureaucracy. The bourgeois parties traditionally were not interested in recruiting the masses to membership but only in enlisting the support of prominent notables, so their organizations remained largely decentralized and prebureaucratic.

Second, the SPD organization rested upon democratic principles. Recognizing the sovereignty of the membership, the Social Democrats created the party institutions requisite

37. Thomas Nipperdey, "Die Organisation der bürgerlichen Parteien in Deutschland vor 1918," *Historische Zeitschrift, 185* (1958), 550–602 (quotation from p. 602). Nipperdey's full-length study, *Die Organisation der deutschen Parteien bis 1918* (Düsseldorf, 1961), appeared too late to be used in this study.

to democracy: a representative congress, an elected and responsible leadership, a judicial body. The bourgeois parties did not possess these features because they lacked the fundamental democratic conceptions underlying them. Their leadership remained oligarchic, co-optive, irresponsible.

Third, the SPD had extraparliamentary origins and purposes. It did not begin in parliament as a coalition of like-minded deputies but as a socialist agitation group for which winning elections was only one of several activities. Aimed at the total reorganization of society, the Social Democratic Party carried out important educational tasks independent of elections and stood ready to lead mass demonstrations and political strikes, ultimately perhaps to lead a popular revolution against the semi-autocratic German state. This being the case, it was natural to subordinate the Reichstag fraction to the party as a whole: it was the task of Social Democratic deputies not to make policy but to carry out in a disciplined manner policies decided upon by the democratically elected congress. The bourgeois parties were in the main formed for purely electoral purposes by parliamentarians who became their natural leaders, and who retained thereby a large degree of individual independence, both from their backers and from the relatively undeveloped party machines. These antithetical types of organization, then, reveal discordant conceptions of the very purposes of political activity.[38]

Party Organization and the Great Schism

Increasingly after 1905 the Social Democratic party organization became the arena of struggle between opposing fac-

38. On these general points, see the excellent discussion and categorization of Maurice Duverger in *Political Parties, Their Organization and Activity in the Modern State*, trans. Barbara and Robert North (London, Methuen, 1954), pp. xxiii–xxxvii, 1–3, and passim.

tions within the movement. Indeed, so bitter did the conflict grow that ultimately, in World War I, the factions could no longer be contained in a united organization. Social Democracy split into two, and then three, separate political parties. We cannot, therefore, understand the further evolution of the organization without taking into consideration the emergence of a new revisionist and a new revolutionary wing on either side of the party center.

The forces of reform in the German socialist movement were manifest even before the turn of the century and flowed from two primary sources. The Free Trade Unions,[39] growing even more rapidly than the party, pressed the SPD to give up its revolutionary pose and concentrate exclusively on present-day reforms, acting more or less as the parliamentary lobby for organized labor. Similarly inclined were South German Social Democrats, who needed a more moderate program to appeal to the predominantly agrarian population of their region. Furthermore, because of the stronger democratic and parliamentary traditions in the South, they were among the first to advocate positive work within the existing political system.[40] Eduard Bernstein gave intellectual form to these reformist currents. His revision of Marxism rested on the view that German society would not undergo any great crises in the foreseeable future but, on the contrary, would continue to expand and prosper. Consequently, Social Democrats should work in the political and economic fields for gradual reforms. Slowly but inevitably, socialism would come about through the combined effect of these piecemeal

---

39. The development of the Free Trade Unions and their close relationship to the SPD are discussed in chapter 5. They chose the name Free Trade Unions to distinguish themselves from company unions and other nonsocialist unions.

40. Schorske, *Social Democracy,* pp. 7–16; Harry Marks, "The Sources of Reformism in the Social Democratic Party of Germany, 1890–1914," *Journal of Modern History, 11* (1939), 334–56.

improvements.[41] The official rejection of Bernstein's Revisionism at the 1903 party congress did not abate the swelling influence of the reformist forces within the movement.

On the opposite side of the party center a new radical wing emerged in the social ferment of 1905. Economic recession and intensified labor unrest in Germany combined with enthusiasm for the Russian Revolution to produce a fresh wave of radicalism, particularly among the unorganized workers of the larger cities.[42] Rosa Luxemburg, the intellectual leader of this tendency, reaffirmed the orthodox Marxist expectation of impending economic collapse. Viewing the coming period as fraught with social unrest and revolutionary possibilities, she called upon the party to seize the opportunity by adopting a new tactical weapon—the general strike.[43] But the radicals were no more successful in altering the tactic of the SPD than the reformists had been in modifying its theoretical foundations. At the Mannheim congress of 1906 the general strike issue was consigned to oblivion.[44]

In 1909, however, the radicals scored a modest organizational victory by securing more adequate representation at party congresses for the large, usually radical urban branches. Hitherto each district organization—regardless of size—had sent three delegates; thus a single delegate might represent anywhere from 25 to 10,000 members. Such a system loaded the congress with rural and small-town representatives and pushed the political fulcrum to the right. Under the new scheme adopted in 1909, districts with up to 1,500 members sent one delegate; up to 3,000, two; 6,000, three; 12,000,

41. Eduard Bernstein, *Die Voraussetzungen des Sozialismus und die Aufgaben der Sozialdemokratie* (Stuttgart, 1899). Also see Peter Gay, *The Dilemma of Democratic Socialism* (New York, 1952).

42. Schorske, *Social Democracy*, pp. 29–38.

43. Rosa Luxemburg, *Massenstreik, Partei und Gewerkschaften* (Hamburg, 1906).

44. See Schorske, *Social Democracy*, pp. 49–53.

four; 18,000, five; and over 18,000, six. Still far from complete proportionality, the reform constituted a significant
gain for the left wing of the party.[45]

Between the reformists and the radicals lay the party center, composed of traditionalists and the bulk of the Social
Democratic leadership. The political position of this group
can best be defined by reference to the Erfurt Program.
Whereas the right-wingers wanted a revised theoretical section to harmonize with the moderate immediate program,
and the left-wingers pushed for a revolutionary tactic to
match the Marxist theory, the centrists stood solidly behind
the Erfurt synthesis. They desired to abandon neither the
traditional Marxist heritage of ideas nor the moderate parliamentary tactic that had proved so successful. Thus they could
side with the radicals to defeat Revisionist doctrine in 1903
and then back the reformists against the general strike in
1906.[46]

Placed strategically between the two extremes, the centrists held the decisive balance of power within the party organization. Although given a leftish appearance by their fight
against Revisionism, the underlying tactical conservatism of
the centrists quickly revealed itself after the emergence of
the new radicals. Increasingly after 1905 they viewed the
Luxemburg group as posing the greater threat to the party's
traditional politics, and consequently aligned themselves with
the right wing against this danger.[47] There is a corresponding
and ironic reversal in the positions of the radicals and reformists on organizational questions. Initially the radicals,
feeling the weight of the party apparatus on their side, pressed
for greater discipline and centralization to keep the reformists in check, while the latter were advocates of greater doc-

45. Ibid., pp. 138–39; Schroeder, *Parteiorganisation*, p. 88.
46. Schorske, *Social Democracy*, pp. 6, 183–87, 196.
47. Ibid., p. 196 and passim.

trinal tolerance and regional autonomy. By 1912, however (and from then on), the situation was reversed: right-wingers enjoyed the support of the party machine and sought to curb the influence of the leftists, who themselves had suddenly become champions of intraparty democracy.[48]

In the view of the radicals, the executive had badly compromised itself in the Morocco Crisis of 1911,[49] and they set about to shorten the leash on its independence. Their reform efforts were adroitly diverted, however, by the politically more sophisticated reformists, so that in the end the executive emerged with an even longer leash than it had previously possessed.[50] Traditionally, the work of the executive was checked by the control commission, a body in which the left wing enjoyed heavy representation. In fact, since the nineties the control commission had acquired customary rights far exceeding the provisions of the statute. It exercised an "active participation in the leadership" (mitleitende Tätigkeit), advising the executive on all important questions.[51]

After the complicated reform maneuvers of 1912, the control commission was strictly confined to its statutory functions, while a new party council (Parteiausschuss) was created to "deliberate jointly with the party executive on important political questions affecting the party as a whole."[52] The critical clause in the revised statute stipulated that the party council be composed of members co-opted by the Land and regional executives. Since their creation in 1905 the Land and regional organizations, particularly in the South, had become strongholds of right-wing power. For them to select council members was therefore to guarantee a reform-

48. Ibid., pp. 24–25, 203, 221–23.
49. See ibid., pp. 197–205.
50. For a detailed account of this maneuver, see ibid., pp. 213–20.
51. Ibid., pp. 213–14.
52. Schroeder, *Parteiorganisation*, p. 103.

ist majority in the new body.[53] The executive itself, over which the whole controversy had started, came out without any changes whatsoever and now possessed "an impressive rubber stamp."[54]

Gradual alterations in the composition of the executive further strengthened its alliance—ultimately, its complete identification—with the reformist wing of the party. The appointment of two more paid secretaries (bringing the total to seven) in 1911 gave the bureaucratic element a clear majority over the five other members of that body.[55] Old Bebel's death and replacement by the career bureaucrat, Friedrich Ebert, in 1913 accentuated the rightward drift.

Meanwhile the movement continued to expand in every direction. The 1912 elections brought the Social Democrats their biggest victory yet, with 4,250,329 votes, or 34.7 per cent of the total, and 110 mandates. With a third of the nation behind it, the SPD was now the largest party in the Reichstag. By the beginning of 1914, membership had passed the million mark.[56] The Social Democratic press, including 90 dailies, reached 1.4 million subscribers. The party boasted a flourishing women's movement and youth section, an elaborate adult education program, even a special school for training future party officials. The various undertakings of the SPD were worth, in capital assets, 21.5 million marks and gave full employment to 3,500 people.[57] As the party acquired more and more ancillary organizations, employees,

53. Ibid.; Schorske, *Social Democracy*, pp. 127–36.

54. Ibid., p. 220.

55. The remaining five included two chairmen, a treasurer, and two "associates" (Beisitzer); the last were added in 1900 and were tacitly permitted to be Berliners, a concession to the powerful Berlin organization (ibid., p. 205; Schroeder, *Parteiorganisation*, p. 46).

56. Berlau, *Social Democratic Party*, p. 348.

57. Lipinski, *Sozialdemokratie*, 2, 281, 228–55.

property, and income, it found itself ever more enmeshed in existing society. Like the German working class in general it now had more to lose than chains.

The Social Democratic Party's stake in existing society became public knowledge on August 4, 1914, when the Reichstag fraction, convinced that Russia's mobilization against Germany justified self-defense, unanimously voted for war credits and agreed to a domestic political truce—the Burgfrieden. These acts of support to the imperial war policy came as a surprise only to those who were unfamiliar with the internal development of the party, particularly the rightward drift of the leadership and center in the years leading up to the war.

At the fraction caucus on August 3, fourteen members had opposed a majority of seventy-eight in the crucial decision, but they voted with the majority on the Reichstag floor in accordance with the traditional policy to vote as a unit. This opposition grew slowly and became bolder as the war progressed. On December 2, 1914, Karl Liebknecht broke fraction discipline to vote publicly against war credits. A year later he was joined in his rebellion by nineteen other deputies. This intraparty opposition controlled the central SPD organ, *Vorwärts,* as well as several provincial newspapers, and found swelling public support for its antiwar stand after the bitter "potato winter" of 1916–17.[58]

The majority leadership reacted to these developments by tightening party discipline and leading forays against the opposition press. In November 1914 an opposition newspaper, the *Schwäbische Tagwacht,* was seized by the majority, and its editors were dismissed. This proved a prelude to

58. Eugen Prager, *Geschichte der USPD* (Berlin, Buchhandlung "Freiheit," 1921), pp. 26, 33, 43–47, 87–88; Schorske, *Social Democracy,* pp. 308–12.

the famous seizure of *Vorwärts* from the leftists two years later.[59] In January 1916 Liebknecht was expelled from the Reichstag fraction (but not from the party); two months later the rest of the opposition deputies received like treatment. Finally the majority leadership instituted a thoroughgoing purge of the entire party, expelling all opposition members. On January 16, 1917, the great schism was consummated.[60]

Representatives of the expelled comrades met on Easter Sunday, 1917, in Gotha to create the Independent Social Democratic Party (USPD). The new party contained a hodge-podge of divergent political viewpoints, held together only by common opposition to the prowar policy of the Majority Social Democrats. On the right stood a few Revisionist intellectuals, including Bernstein himself, who were separated from the main party only by their principled internationalism and rejection of the war. The bulk of the USPD consisted of internationalist or "left" centrists, who rejected the policy of August Fourth because they viewed German war aims as annexationist, and because acceptance of the political truce precluded traditional domestic opposition to the imperial government. Equally alien to Revisionists and left centrists alike were the conceptions of the Luxemburg radicals, now called Spartacists: they wanted to use the unrest created by the war as a vehicle for social revolution.[61] The Spartacists remained in the USPD only until the November Revolution, when they broke away to form the Communist Party of Germany (KPD), thus completing the three-way schism.

59. Ibid., pp. 298–99; Prager, *USPD*, pp. 116–20.

60. Ibid., pp. 129–31.

61. Arthur Rosenberg, *The Birth of the German Republic, 1871–1918*, trans. Ian F. D. Murrow (London, 1931), pp. 117–22; Schorske, *Social Democracy*, pp. 314–16.

Within the Majority Party the war years had other effects besides the tightening of discipline. Activity at the lower levels of the organization came to a standstill; the political truce barred agitation for usual Social Democratic objectives, and the discontinuance of Reichstag elections removed the primary raison d'être of the party apparatus. The membership was slashed to one-quarter of its prewar size by military conscription. For the duration of the war this truncated organization existed in a state of suspended animation.[62]

The SPD leadership, on the other hand, enjoyed an importance and prestige never before possible; this was the positive side of the truce. Top-ranking Social Democrats now attended ministerial policy discussions; they visited the front on parliamentary tours; to a limited extent they could even mix socially with the traditional ruling circles. As the party leaders drew closer to the old regime they became more independent of their own followers. With the outbreak of hostilities in 1914 the annual congresses were suspended sine die, and only one such gathering met during the war period. Not only did this suspension remove the most important form of membership control over the leaders, it also extended indefinitely their terms of office. Such were the portentous effects of World War I on the party organization.[63]

Between 1905 and 1918, then, we have seen the development and consummation of the great schism in Social Democracy as well as a continuation of the general organizational trends previously described. These trends, which characterize the entire pre-Weimar history of the SPD, may be summarized as follows: (1) the transformation of the party from a close-knit, revolutionary agitational group into a vast apparatus for capturing votes; (2) the elaboration, rationaliza-

---

62. Ibid., pp. 297–98; Berlau, *Social Democratic Party*, p. 348.
63. Schorske, *Social Democracy*, pp. 292–94, 298.

tion, and bureaucratization of this party apparatus; (3) the concentration of decision-making power into the hands of an executive relatively immune to pressure from below; (4) the gradual growth and ultimate predominance in the whole structure of the reformist wing of the party. Not without reason has it been said that, next to the Kaiser's army, the Social Democratic Party was the most Prussian institution of the Empire.

2. The Weimar Organization

The SPD in the Weimar Republic

The Second Empire did not survive its military defeat in World War I. The popular revolution of November 1918 destroyed the old regime and set up in its place the Weimar Republic. The Social Democratic Party was primarily responsible for the creation and character of the Republic and remained its backbone of support down to the debacle of 1933. The internal development of the party must be understood in the context of this crucial political activity, which of necessity can be recounted here only in its barest outline.[1]

1. No first-rate political history of Weimar Social Democracy exists. Evelyn Anderson's brief account, *Hammer or Anvil, The Story of the German Working-Class Movement* (London, Gollancz, 1945) treats both the Social Democrats and the Communists and is critical of both. The most knowledgeable presentation can be found in the broader work of Carl Landauer, *European Socialism* (2 vols. Berkeley and Los Angeles, 1959); Landauer devotes some 400 pages to the Weimar SPD and ably defends its policies. More critical, but thin and rather disappointing, are the relevant chapters in vols. 4 and 5 of G. D. H. Cole's *A History of Socialist Thought* (5 vols. in 7, London, 1953–60). Friedrich Stampfer, *Die ersten 14 Jahre der deutschen Republik* (Offenbach/Main, Bollwerk–Karl Drott, 1947) presents a leading Social Democrat's view of the Republic, with much material on the activity of his own party.

Late in the summer of 1918 the German High Command realized that the war was hopelessly lost and decided to create a democratic government for the purpose of negotiating with the Allies. Prince Max of Baden became chancellor of a new liberal coalition pledged to conclude peace and initiate constitutional reforms. The Majority Social Democrats shattered another party tradition by accepting responsibility in Prince Max's cabinet. This decision marked the second major step —the vote of August 4 was the first—in the transformation of the SPD from opposition party to government party. The ensuing succession of constitutional amendments, bringing responsible parliamentary democracy to both the Reich and Prussia, helped the Social Democrats justify their action. Additional justification was found in Germany's critical military situation. Friedrich Ebert, particularly, argued that the party must stand by the fatherland in its hour of defeat and take on the unpleasant burden of making peace with the victors.

The SPD went into the revolutionary period as a government party, loyal to the existing regime and wanting above all to maintain order against the growing wave of popular discontent. Despite their professed republicanism, the Social Democratic leaders sincerely tried to preserve the throne for William II or, failing that, to preserve at least the throne itself. Far from desiring a revolution, they did their utmost to prevent one.[2]

Their efforts proved inadequate. War weariness, the near

2. The role of the SPD in the Revolution and in the creation of the Weimar Republic is treated in A. Joseph Berlau, *The German Social Democratic Party, 1914–1921* (New York, 1949). For the Revolution in general, see Ralph H. Lutz, *The German Revolution, 1918–1919* (Stanford, 1922), a standard account; Hermann Müller, *Die November Revolution* (Berlin, 1931), a Majority Social Democratic version; and Rudolf Coper, *Failure of a Revolution* (Cambridge, Mass., 1955), a recent left-wing critique.

starvation imposed by the blockade, and the full realization of Germany's defeat had engendered a bitter mood in the masses of the population. As the armistice talks dragged on into November and the Kaiser steadfastly refused to abdicate, this mood turned revolutionary. A sailor's insurrection at Kiel on November 4 provided the necessary spark. One by one the large cities of Germany were taken over by revolutionary workers' and soldiers' councils in a spontaneous and nearly bloodless seizure of local power. On November 7 the Independent Social Democrat, Kurt Eisner, proclaimed a republic in Bavaria. Street demonstrations in Berlin grew more and more ominous, threatening the central government and placing the SPD in an extremely awkward position.

Not until the morning of November 9 did the Social Democratic leaders, fearful of losing all popular support, associate themselves with the extraparliamentary pressure for abdication. But by now it was too late to save even the institution of monarchy. While Ebert negotiated frenetically with Prince Max to take over the chancellorship, his second-in-command, Philipp Scheidemann, took it upon himself to proclaim a republic. The Social Democrats had become revolutionaries in spite of themselves, assuming illegal authority solely to prevent the Independents or, worse, the Spartacists, from being lifted to power on the wave of mass discontent.

Once this irreversible step had been taken, the SPD leaders bent every effort to rein in the forces of revolution. The next day, November 10, a six-man provisional government was formed, basing its authority upon the Berlin soldiers' and workers' councils. The Independents were not to be denied parity representation in this body, nor did the SPD oppose this, since the Independents were less dangerous as partners sharing responsibility than as a revolutionary opposition. In the Majority Social Democratic view, the provisional government was charged only with caretaker functions: to bring the armistice negotiations to a successful conclusion, and at home to maintain order and protect property until a democratically elected National Assembly could meet to determine the nation's future. The SPD leaders refused to carry out left-wing demands for immediate socialization and government by councils. The mandate of November 9, they argued, had been for peace and democracy, not socialism and proletarian dictatorship.

The Free Trade Unions manifested their accord with this conception of the revolution by concluding an agreement with the employers' associations on November 15. The unions won the eight-hour day and recognition as collective bargaining agents but agreed by implication to the continuance of private ownership.

As the revolution developed, the SPD increasingly turned for help to the representatives of the old regime. The party found itself in an alliance with the authoritarian Right against the radical Left. If the task of the provisional government was to preserve order, and the threat to order came from the left, it seemed only natural to seek assistance from the old governmental apparatus. The civil service and judiciary could help maintain the authority and efficiency of the young Republic, while the army could protect it against the danger of a "second revolution." Near the end of December the Social Democratic leaders were forced to make a final choice between their military allies on the right and their Independent coalition partners on the left. When they chose the former, the Independents resigned from the provisional government. Ebert and his lieutenants were now left a free hand to rule in concert with the forces of reaction.

From the outset Ebert had anticipated a violent showdown with the Spartacists and left-wing Independents, who wanted to push the revolution further in a socialist direction. Understanding that he was the Kerensky of the German

29

Revolution, Ebert feared a parallel fate, and vastly over-estimated the strength of the small and disorganized extremist groups.[3] It was this fear which had prompted Ebert, as early as November 10 to enter a partnership with the old High Command for the purpose of combating "bolshevism." When the conscript field army, brought home from France, proved an unreliable instrument for this task, Ebert sanctioned the creation of volunteer *Freikorps*. These new organizations attracted the most violent and reactionary elements from the vanishing Imperial army. By the beginning of 1919 the Social Democratic provisional government had shelved its earlier half-hearted attempts to create a republican militia and now placed its full confidence in these professional soldiers of the old regime.

The conflict with the extremists soon reached a climax. In January 1919 the radicals in Berlin rose in protest over the dismissal of the sympathetic USPD police chief. Freikorps units quickly smashed this insurrection and brutally murdered the two Spartacist leaders, Luxemburg and Liebknecht. From Berlin, Freikorps troops were sent all over the Reich suppressing the radicals wherever they seemed a threat. By May 1919 all was secure, but the government now depended for its existence upon an antirepublican military force—a menacing omen for the future.

Meanwhile the SPD proceeded with its positive task by calling for the election of a National Assembly to furnish parliamentary government and draw up a new constitution. On January 19, 1919, the German electorate returned the prorepublican parties with a landslide majority of 85 per cent. The National Assembly emerged shortly with a document providing Germany with the most advanced parlia-

3. On this point see the recent works of Eric Waldman, *The Spartacist Uprising of 1919* (Milwaukee, 1958), and Walter Tormin, *Zwischen Rätediktatur und sozialer Demokratie* (Düsseldorf, 1954).

mentary democracy in Europe. The Social Democrats supported the basic features of this constitution, which included a bicameral legislature, a responsible cabinet system of government, and a popularly elected president. Having suffered most from the inequities of the old constituency elections, the Social Democrats were instrumental in creating a system of proportional representation for the Reichstag. They also insisted on provisions for popular initative and referendum. They would have preferred to dispense entirely with the federal structure of the old Empire, but satisfied themselves instead with a strengthened Reich government. The party also endeavored, unsuccessfully, to keep the presidency an essentially ceremonial office.

Most clearly Social Democratic in inspiration were the unique social and economic clauses of the Weimar constitution. The workers' councils that had carried out the revolution were denied any political role in the new state, but Article 165 provided for factory councils to look after the social and economic interests of the employees. The revolutionary council movement was thus rendered harmless and became an adjunct of the trade-union apparatus—a solution that was eminently satisfactory to the SPD. The constitution also made possible the socialization of private enterprises with compensation to the owners. It put natural resources under the supervision of the state, guaranteed the right to earn a livelihood, placed mothers and children under special protection, and promised a comprehensive system of social insurance.

A modern democratic welfare state—this was the aim and accomplishment of Social Democracy in the November Revolution. The accomplishment was in many respects impressive. Yet underneath the promising constitutional forms remained governmental and social structures hardly compatible with stable democracy. The reluctant revolutionaries

31

did not dismiss reactionary elements from the civil service or judiciary, or create a politically reliable army. They did not nationalize any great industries or break up the Junker estates. The social and political forces thus left intact became the principal enemies of the SPD in the following years and contributed more than a little to the downfall of the Weimar Republic in 1933.

Once the elections of 1919 had taken place, the provisional government resigned in favor of a permanent one. The National Assembly elected Friedrich Ebert as Reich president, while Philipp Scheidemann became chancellor in the first republican cabinet based on a majority of the Assembly. With 38 per cent of the popular vote, the SPD was the largest single party, but it could not govern alone. Scheidemann therefore formed a coalition with two other prorepublican parties, the left liberal German Democratic Party (DDP) and the Catholic Center Party (Z). (The Independents declined to join any cabinet that included bourgeois parties.) This alignment of forces, known as the Weimar Coalition, continued to rule Germany for most of the next four years, although the chancellorship passed from Scheidemann to Gustav Bauer, then to Hermann Müller, and then out of Social Democratic hands. Later the SPD participated in two other cabinets, one during the national emergency of 1923 and the other, led by Hermann Müller, lasting a remarkable twenty-one months, from 1928 to 1930. These latter were Great Coalitions which included the right liberal German People's Party (DVP) as well as the DDP and Center. In sum, the Social Democrats shared power for approximately five of the fourteen years of the Weimar Republic.

Far more stable and pervading was the Social Democratic influence in the administration of Prussia. This crucial state, larger than all the other Länder combined and containing two-thirds of Germany's population, was governed almost without interruption from 1920 to 1932 by the SPD-led coalition of Otto Braun and Carl Severing. Although Prussia no longer occupied a privileged position in the Reich, her government continued to exercise important Land powers in the administration of police, education, and justice, and controlled sizable state-owned forests, mines, and public works. In the capable hands of Braun and Severing, traditionally autocratic Prussia became a stronghold of republicanism. The forcible ousting of this Social Democratic ministry by Franz von Papen in 1932 ruptured one of the last dikes against the flood of Nazism.[4]

In both the Prussian and the Reich cabinets the SPD was hampered in carrying out the specifically socialist parts of its program by the opposition of its bourgeois coalition partners. It remained the obvious task of the party to win the absolute popular majority necessary for the final achievement of socialism. Requisite to this perspective of the road ahead was, of course, the maintenance of democratic government. The defense of the Republic against its domestic enemies therefore, always stood highest on the list of the SPD's political objectives. The Heidelberg Program of 1925 declared: "The democratic republic is the most favorable basis for the struggle of the working class for liberation, and thereby for the realization of socialism. Therefore the Social Democratic Party guards the Republic and seeks to perfect it."[5] Since its inception in 1863 the SPD had advocated political democracy. The establishment of the Weimar constitution in 1919 marked the third and most profound step in the Social Demo-

4. For the role of the SPD in Prussia see Earl R. Beck, *The Death of the Prussian Republic* (Tallahassee, Florida State Univ., 1959); and Hajo Holborn, "Prussia and the Weimar Republic," *Social Research, 22* (1956), 331–42.

5. From the Heidelberg Program, printed in *Protokoll des sozialdemokratischen Parteitages, 1925, in Heidelberg* (Berlin, Dietz, 1925), p. 7 (hereafter cited as *Prot. [year]*).

crats' transformation from opposition party to government party. In or out of office, the SPD was determined to protect the Republic, while at the same time pursuing, through the democratic process, its major socialist aims.

Foremost among these aims traditionally was the socialization of the means of production. This demand occupied a prominent place in both Weimar programs of the party. Yet the movement away from socialization so evident in the Bonn SPD was already beginning in the period of our concern. During the November Revolution, party leaders displayed remarkably little enthusiasm for the transfer of industry to public ownership, despite the unparalleled opportunity furnished them by the sudden acquisition of sovereign power. This attitude was due in part to unfavorable times. Social Democratic spokesmen, arguing against immediate socialization, pointed to the exhausted condition of the German economy and the need to restore production quickly without costly "experiments"; they also expressed fear that the Allies might seize nationalized property as reparations. But some of their arguments questioned the wisdom of socialization as such, quite apart from temporal considerations. Government ownership would pose the danger of bureaucracy and over-regulation, while workers' control of management raised the threat of anarchy and Bolshevism. Some Social Democratic leaders, it seems clear, were already abandoning the traditional goal of socialization.[6]

The abandonment was by no means universal or immediate. The SPD secured in the Weimar Constitution a provision sanctioning the legal nationalization of private property with compensation. A government socialization commission led by the Social Democrat Rudolf Wissell was appointed, and on its recommendation the party introduced legislation in

6. Berlau, *Social Democratic Party*, pp. 265–84.

1919 to socialize certain "mature" industries—coal, potash, electric power. Only the last was ever actually transferred to public ownership.

When the Great Depression broke in 1930, the party's arguments for socialization ought to have regained their cogency, but Social Democratic leaders were still reluctant to press the issue. Indeed, as we will see, they pursued an almost laissez-faire economic policy in the depression: socialization, if desirable at all, was a dream for the distant future when the nation stood solidly behind the party's banners. The declining enthusiasm for this traditional socialist demand in the Weimar period presaged its almost complete abandonment by the Bonn SPD in recent years.

Other parts of the party's traditional economic and social program were more amenable to compromise and piecemeal legislation. They did not attack the capitalist system head on and therefore met easier success. The constitution itself had registered many such gains in its social and economic clauses, as noted above. The right of collective bargaining and the eight-hour day were substantial trade-union victories. In 1923 an Old Age Pension Act was passed and in 1927 a comprehensive Unemployment Insurance Act. The party programs urged still other reforms in the social and economic spheres: protection of the right to organize, elimination of child labor, annual paid vacations, more steeply progressive income and inheritance taxes, elimination of all student tuition fees, and so forth.[7] In or out of office, the Social Democrats worked painstakingly, if unimaginatively, for the gradual democratization of the social structure. In the long run, they hoped, Germany would merge, without any decisive struggle for power, almost without realizing it, into the long-sought socialist commonwealth.

7. Heidelberg Program, *Prot. 1925*, pp. 7–10.

Between 1924 and 1928, its electoral strength reduced to 26 per cent, the SPD was formally in opposition to the Reich government, yet even during these years the party loyally supported the government's foreign policy—i.e. the foreign policy of Gustav Stresemann. Like virtually all Germans, the Social Democrats had been dismayed by the harsh provisions of the Versailles Treaty, but they quickly realized that the only hope for revision, particularly of the economic sections, lay in a policy of acceptance and attempted compliance. When the Allies saw that Germany, despite sincere efforts, could not possibly fulfill the terms of the treaty, they would willingly lighten the crushing burden. Thus the Social Democrats were early and consistent advocates of the pro-Western "policy of fulfillment" that came to be identified with Gustav Stresemann. They supported the Dawes Plan (1924), the Locarno Pact (1925), German entry into the League of Nations (1926), the Kellogg–Briand Pact (1928), and the Young Plan (1929). Without this substantial support from the SPD, Stresemann's success would have been extremely doubtful.

The traditional internationalism of German Social Democracy revealed itself during the Weimar years in several other policies. The party participated actively in the revived Socialist International. It advocated the creation of an economic union of all European states. It not only supported German entry into the League of Nations, but also the strengthening of that organization by the establishment of courts to which all member nations would be required to submit their disputes for binding arbitration.[8]

These policies did not imply a total rejection of nationalism. Warm patriotic sentiments and the spirited defense of legitimate national interests did not, in the Social Democratic

8. Ibid., p. 10.

36

view, contradict the party's international orientation.[9] The SPD never renounced its wartime support of the Imperial government, and its denunciations of the Treaty of Versailles were strongly nationalist in tone. When the French occupied the Ruhr in 1923, the party initially backed the bitter national campaign of passive resistance. There was a profound difference, however, between the "liberal" nationalism of Social Democracy and the "integral" nationalism of the Right. This difference can best be discerned in the area of military policy, which touches on both foreign and domestic affairs.

The SPD renounced war as a means of policy. Alone among the government parties the SPD did not demand revision of the military clauses of Versailles so as to expand the 100,000-man army. Rather it urged other nations to disarm, following Germany's example. A 1929 pronouncement on military policy included the following unique passage:

> To the German Republic has fallen the historic mission of leading the way to international disarmament. She cannot fulfill this mission if she violates her armament limitations (even though these were forcibly and unilaterally imposed) and if, by trying to evade or violate them, she gives other powers a reason or an excuse to renounce international disarmament agreements and build up even stronger armaments.[10]

Thus the Social Democrats sought to restore Germany's position in the world not by military revival but through an equalizing universal disarmament.

With such an underlying view, the SPD naturally opposed

9. For the attitude of the SPD toward questions of foreign policy, see Reimund Klinkhammer, *Die Aussenpolitik der Sozialdemokratischen Partei Deutschlands in der Zeit der Weimarer Republik* (Freiburg, 1955); on nationalism, see Hermann Heidegger, *Die deutsche Sozialdemokratie und der nationale Staat, 1870 bis 1920* (Göttingen, 1956).

10. From "Guidelines on Military Policy," printed in *Prot. 1929*, pp. 288–89.

Germany's secret rearmament. In spite of legal persecution, Social Democratic leaders publicly exposed the evasions and violations of the arms limitation in which even Stresemann had a hand. And for these exposures the SPD earned the undying hatred of right-wing nationalists and Reichswehr leaders. If the SPD was responsible in 1918–19 for giving German militarism a new lease on life, it sincerely endeavored in the years following to restrict that lease as tightly as possible.[11]

The Social Democrats returned to power after the elections of 1928 and had the political misfortune of being in office when the Great Depression struck. Far from waiting in Marxist anticipation of the crisis, they were caught totally off guard. By the late 1920s most party leaders accepted, either tacitly or positively, Bernstein's views on the diminishing importance of the business cycle. They looked forward confidently to a stable and expanding economy. In this vein one Social Democratic intellectual, Emil Lederer, wrote: "The theory of 'general overproduction' is only an apparition scared up by empty speculation. It is neither theoretically tenable, nor proved by experience. Are we not producing at a fabulous tempo?"[12] These lines appeared in August 1929, two months before the American stock market crash!

The unavoidable fact of depression put the Social Democrats in a perplexing dilemma, classically delineated by the trade-union leader, Fritz Tarnow, in 1931:

Are we sitting at the sickbed of capitalism, not only . . . as doctors who want to cure the patient, but also as cheerful heirs who cannot wait for the end and would like to

11. See G. A. Caspar, "Die deutsche Sozialdemokratie und die Entstehung der Reichswehr (1918/1921)," *Wehrwissenschaftliche Rundschau,* 8 (1958), 194–207; and Harold J. Gordon, *The Reichswehr and the German Republic 1919–1926* (Princeton, 1957), pp. 372–95.

12. "Die Umschichtung des Proletariats," *Die neue Rundschau, 40* (1929), 147.

hasten it with poison? Our entire situation is expressed in this image. We are condemned, I think, to be doctors who seriously desire a cure, and yet we also maintain the feeling that we are heirs who wish to receive the entire legacy of the capitalist system today rather than tomorrow. This double role, doctor and heir, is a damned difficult task.[13]

As "heirs" the Social Democrats seemingly should have done nothing to overcome this crisis of capitalism, but rather have used it to win support for a socialist alternative. As "doctors" they seemingly should have undertaken a massive anticyclical program of deficit public spending to expand mass purchasing power and stimulate business revival. Because they were taken by surprise and torn by the alternatives, the Social Democrats pursued neither policy with any consistency.

As a government party and a working-class party facing mass unemployment, the SPD could not entirely renounce immediate measures of relief and revival. As Tarnow put it, "If we know of a medicine that, if it will not cure the patient, will at least stop his death rattles so that the masses again have something to eat, then we must give him the medicine and for the moment ignore the fact that we are also heirs and await his rapid demise." Yet the Marxist heritage of the party discouraged any tampering with the "natural" development of the economy. The memory of 1923 also militated against an inflationary program. Consequently the Social Democrats sought on the one hand to cut government spending, balance the budget, and maintain the gold value of the mark, while at the same time they resisted any cuts in unemployment benefits that would adversely affect their own supporters. Such a program would have satisfied neither Marx nor Keynes.[14]

13. *Prot. 1931*, pp. 45–46.
14. See especially Adolf Sturmthal, *The Tragedy of European Labor, 1918–1939* (New York, 1943), pp. 83–97, 129–43.

Unwillingness to cut unemployment benefits caused the Social Democrats to fall out with their coalition partners. The Müller cabinet resigned early in 1930. It proved to be the last parliamentary government of the Weimar Republic, for the ensuing Reichstag elections so increased the strength of the Nazis and Communists that no stable majority could be found. The new chancellor, Heinrich Brüning, ruled by decree, using the emergency powers of Article 48 in a kind of constitutional dictatorship. For the Social Democrats, fear of a Nazi victory now overrode all other political considerations. During the next two years, they reluctantly "tolerated" the Brüning dictatorship as a lesser evil, declining to vote no confidence lest Brüning's fall bring Hitler's ascent. The toleration policy was fraught with difficulties: the SPD had neither the authority of a party in power nor the electoral advantages of genuine opposition. It continued to lose votes and in 1932 was eclipsed when the Nazi Party (NSDAP) replaced it as the largest in the Reichstag.[15]

Social Democratic opposition to Nazism proceeded from a bottomless ideological chasm that separated the two mass movements. The former stood for political democracy; the latter for totalitarian dictatorship. The former was identified with international reconciliation and disarmament; the latter with nationalist irredentism and military revival. The SPD had always struggled against the anti-Semitism that formed the essential cement of Nazi ideology. The one party drew its support primarily from the working class; the other from

15. For the SPD during the rise and establishment of Nazism, see the previously cited works of Anderson and Landauer, together with Lewis J. Edinger, *German Exile Politics* (Berkeley and Los Angeles, 1956); and most importantly, Erich Matthias, "Der Untergang der alten Sozialdemokratie 1933," *Vierteljahrshefte für Zeitgeschichte, 4* (1956), 179–226, 250–85, which the author has expanded in his contribution to Erich Matthias and Rudolf Morsey, eds., *Das Ende der Parteien, 1933* (Düsseldorf, 1960).

the petty bourgeoisie. If both spoke in favor of "socialism," the SPD understood by that term the extension of democracy to the social and economic realm—the creation of a classless society. The Nazis genuinely abhorred such a vision and meant by "socialism" a structured society in which the selfish interest of the individual would be subordinated to the overriding interest of the *Volk,* as embodied in an authoritarian state. In all its major philosophical assumptions, Social Democracy was an offspring of the Enlightenment, while Nazi ideology grew out of German Romanticism.

In their struggle against Hitler the Social Democrats were restricted by their very adherence to democracy and the forms of legality. When Franz von Papen ousted the constitutional government of Braun and Severing in Prussia, the SPD responded by taking the case to the courts. When Hitler legally became chancellor, the Social Democrats urged their followers to remain calm and stand ready to resist the first unconstitutional act of the new government. But Hitler, always one jump ahead of his opponents, introduced legislation into the Reichstag which would legally grant him dictatorial powers (the Enabling Act). The Social Democratic deputies voted against it, but it passed despite their opposition. Since the Reichstag had voluntarily abdicated its power, any rising against the Hitler dictatorship would constitute rebellion. The Weimar Republic was not destroyed by force; it committed suicide.

Despite their belief in legality and their revulsion against violence, the Social Democrats did on a few occasions consider extraparliamentary resistance, but the prospects for such action were not good. A general strike under conditions of mass unemployment bore no great chance of success and, further, would almost certainly dissolve into civil war. In such an armed conflict, the forces behind Social Democracy, while numerically large, would be militarily unprepared, and

41

they would face a magnificently trained and equipped Reichswehr, backed up by Hitler's storm troopers and the Stahlhelm (literally: Steel Helmets; a paramilitary organization associated with the Nationalist Party, DNVP). Though the war would be long and bloody it appeared to the SPD leaders that they would lose. Consequently they decided against resistance, even when Hitler dissolved the trade unions and then the party itself late in the spring of 1933.

If Social Democratic opposition to Nazism ultimately proved ineffective, it remained the most consistent and untarnished opposition offered by any of the major Weimar parties. The Nationalists, by entering a coalition with the NSDAP, had first made Hitler's chancellorship possible. The Center had negotiated (unsuccessfully) to enter the same coalition. Both the Center and the liberal parties had voted for the Enabling Act, leaving the SPD alone in its negative vote. Even the Communist Party was tainted by its earlier collaboration with the Nazis in such ventures as the Prussian plebiscite of 1931 and the Berlin transport workers' strike of 1932.

The only compromises marring Social Democratic opposition to Nazism came after the destruction of democratic government when, in the final days, some party leaders committed lesser acts of appeasement in a last desperate effort to save their organization from extinction. In the twelve years that followed, remarkably few publicly known Social Democrats went over to the Nazis or worked for them in official capacities. On the other hand, large numbers of Social Democrats—known and unknown—distinguished themselves in the underground resistance to the Hitler tyranny.

The SPD did not save German democracy. One may argue that the party made mistakes that substantially weakened the Republic, left it defenseless, or even crippled it from the outset. But one must also recognize that, without the Social

Democrats, the Republic would not have been created in the
first place, nor would it have survived even fourteen years
without their constant support.

In the broadest sense, German Social Democracy lacked
the vitality to stop Hitler, and the reasons for this lack lay
to a large extent within the party itself. It is to these internal
conditions that we must now return.

The Statutes of 1919 and 1924

The first postwar SPD congress was held at Weimar in June
1919, while the National Assembly was in temporary recess.
The radically changed conditions of political life clearly
dictated a revision of the 1912 statute. An organization
commission, appointed by the party council, drew up a proposal which was accepted without significant amendment by
the congress.[16] The reforms of this statute modernized the
SPD apparatus to fit the needs of Weimar politics.

First, the basic unit of the party was changed from the
electoral district organization (Wahlkreisverein), founded on
the old imperial constituencies, to an electoral region organization (Bezirksverband), based on the new electoral regions
of the Republic. Proportional representation required much
larger electoral divisions than the constituency system. Instead of nearly 400 districts there were now only 35 regions.[17] With certain exceptions the old Social Democratic
Land and regional organizations were adapted to fit the
Weimar electoral divisions and, in this shape, became the
new regional units. They inherited en bloc most of the func-

16. *Prot. 1919,* pp. 18, 344–45.
17. The National Assembly had been elected under a provisional electoral law, and the new regions had not yet been permanently drawn up in
June 1919. Consequently the final delineation of the Social Democratic
regional organizations had to be left up to the executive.

tions of the former district organizations: they had the final word in the selection of Reichstag candidates, ran the campaigns, and served as the party's basic administrative units for finances, congress elections, etc.[18] The prewar Land and regional organizations, as such, were dissolved in consonance with the centralizing features of the Weimar Constitution. But where a Land had two or more regional organizations they were permitted to meet together, should any pressing state issue arise.[19]

It was, of course, necessary to subdivide the thirty-two new units, and here again the Weimar Constitution supplied the framework. Article 17 provided for equal, universal suffrage as the basis for municipal government, which gave the signal for the full-scale entry of Social Democracy into local politics. By 1920, 36,951 SPD representatives sat in city and municipal assemblies.[20] In view of this situation, the old local organizations (Ortsvereine), abandoned back in the Wilhelmian period, were re-established, this time not to deal with national party policy but to handle municipal affairs. Between the local and regional levels, subregional units (Unterbezirksverbände), usually identical with the former district organizations, were left as a bond between the old system and the new. They retained the power to initiate the nomination of Reichstag candidates.[21]

In terms of the power structure within the party, the significance of these new arrangements stems from the greatly increased distance which now separated the leadership from the rank and file. The new centers of party authority, the regional organizations, were far too large for direct democracy. Their affairs were handled by regional executives and

18. Ibid., pp. 319–21.
19. Ibid., p. 517.
20. *Prot. 1920*, Appendix, p. 39.
21. *Prot. 1919*, pp. 321–22.

congresses. The only units small enough for rank and file participation, the locals, had no national function; delegates to the party congress were now elected by the regional congresses.[22] Henceforth national congresses were twice-removed from ordinary members. That the latter understood and resented this diminution of their influence is demonstrated by the continuous demands to restore the direct election of delegates.[23] Thus the remodeling of the SPD organization in 1919 incidentally abetted the decline of intraparty democracy.

The new statute is also noteworthy in what it omitted. The November Revolution had not been carried out by the SPD or any other party, or by the trade unions, but by brand-new organizations—the soldiers' and workers' councils—created especially for that purpose. Significantly, the 1919 organization commission rejected any scheme for rearranging the party structure to fit these organizational forms that had sprung up from below during the Revolution. On the contrary, the SPD leadership showed continual hostility to the council movement and was instrumental in having it converted into a harmless appendage of the trade-union apparatus.[24] With regard to party organization the Revolution meant nothing more than a change in the mechanics of electioneering.

The new statute also made several additions to the authority of the executive. First of all the sentence defining the

22. These elections were still carried out under a system of representation that favored small regions over large ones (ibid., p. 518). But, since small regions no longer necessarily meant rural regions, the system lost its advantage for the conservative party leadership and was dropped in 1924 when complete equality of representation was finally introduced (*Prot. 1924*, p. 7).

23. See, for example, *Prot. 1921*, p. 336, and *Prot. 1924*, p. 142.

24. See Berlau, *Social Democratic Party*, pp. 261–65.

function of that body was harmonized with contemporary practice. The old prescription, "the party executive manages the business of the party," was revised to read, "the leadership of the party rests upon (obliegt) the party executive." The income of the central treasury was raised, despite grumbling, by increasing the percentage of dues it received from 20 per cent to 25 per cent, and by imposing a 20 per cent tax on the net profits of all "party undertakings of a business nature." Perhaps more important, the executive was declared "owner of all existing funds *and other property.*"[25] (Emphasis added.) It thereby acquired nominal ownership of all party property, including the press. According to Fritz Bieligk, this move constituted a retroactive "legalization" of the seizure of *Vorwärts* during the war and a basis for possible future seizures.[26] Yet it was casually explained by the official spokesman, König, as being introduced "out of practical experience in this area and on legal advice."[27] No doubt the "practical experience" of the leadership was superior to that of the delegates who let such a carte blanche measure slip through virtually unnoticed.

In 1919 the entire structure of the SPD organization was altered—ignoring the revolutionary council movement—to fit the electioneering demands of the Weimar political system, an alteration which incidentally encouraged the decline of intraparty democracy. At the same time the trend toward the centralization of power in the hands of the executive continued uninterrupted.

When the Independents came back to the fold at Nurem-

25. *Prot. 1919*, pp. 517, 519.
26. "Die Entwicklung der sozialdemokratischen Organisation in Deutschland," *Die Organisation im Klassenkampf* (Berlin, n.d. [1931]), pp. 73–74.
27. *Prot. 1919*, p. 327.

berg in 1922, a commission representing both parties was appointed to work out a new statute for the united organization. This commission presented its draft proposal at the Berlin congress of 1924. According to Lipinski, the official spokesman, the proposal was based on "the old statutes of Social Democracy and the Independent Party, from which the best was selected and supplemented through experience and deliberation."[28] But in fact, not a single feature of the USPD's more democratic organization was incorporated into the draft proposal. The 1924 statute turned out to be little more than a rehash of the 1919 statute, seasoned with some new leadership prerogatives.

Because of the inflation no party congress could be held in 1923. In light of this, the new statute gave the council authority, by a three-quarters majority vote, to suspend the convening of a congress for one year, "if important reasons present themselves."[29] Apparently such reasons often appeared, for no congresses met in 1926, 1928, 1930, and 1932. After 1925 it became customary to hold congresses biennially, which of course automatically doubled the terms of officers elected by that body and lessened their actual accountability to the party membership.

Also during the inflation the executive had to be given emergency power to adjust the percentages of dues it received, according to the fluctuations of the currency. But in 1924 this emergency power became a permanent one. Henceforth the executive, in conjunction with the council, was to determine its own proportion of the party income without any check whatsoever from below.[30] *Ce n'est que le provisoire qui dûre!*

28. *Prot. 1924*, p. 141.
29. Ibid., p. 7.
30. Ibid., p. 6.

The executive likewise acquired certain influence in the selection of parliamentary candidates:

> The party executive . . . has the right to take part, in an advisory capacity, in all meetings of all party institutions, and to advise in the nomination and recall of candidates for the Landtage and the Reichstag.
>
> The party executive has the right to resolve disputes, if requested by the organizations concerned, arising out of the selection of Reichstag candidates.[31]

Moreover it was to be the executive, together with the party council, which chose candidates to run on the Reich election list—i.e. the candidates elected by leftover ballots from the thirty-five regions. This enabled the party high command to appoint from six to nine members of the Reichstag fraction.[32]

Finally, a new prerogative was given the executive in expulsion cases. The procedure for expelling delinquent members had evolved over a period of decades. Arbitration courts at the lower levels judged accused persons according to criteria laid down in the statute, which also guaranteed the right of appeal all the way up to the party congress. The 1924 statute, however, added the following:

> Further, no one can belong to the party who is a member of another political party or supports it financially, or works for it *or against the Social Democratic Party. In such cases the executive can pronounce immediate expulsion.*[33] [Emphasis added.]

No court hearings. No appeals. Persons expelled in this fashion could only apply to the next congress for readmission into the party. The introduction of this measure provoked

31. Ibid., p. 8.
32. Ibid., p. 6.
33. Ibid., p. 10.

the sole floor fight of the session, as Left Social Democrats pointed to its sweeping criteria and the possibility of its being used against any dissenters. Lipinski assured them it was inserted only to fight Communist infiltration, and in the end the provision passed easily.[34] As matters turned out, the fears of the Left Social Democrats were justified: in 1931 the executive employed this special expulsion power to effect the separation of the whole left-wing grouping that was to become the Socialist Workers' Party.[35]

The reforms of 1924, then, had nothing to do with the merger of the USPD but rather added a crown to the long accumulation of executive prerogatives. This body now held power of near-dictatorial proportions within the party. Other changes in the statute were undertaken in 1925 and 1929; they affected only minor details, however, and need not concern us here. For our purposes, the great reforms of 1919, supplemented by those of 1924, established the SPD organization in the shape it was to retain until the advent of Hitler. The principles of Lassallean organization had overborne those of Eisenach.

The State within a State

By the period that concerns us, German Social Democracy had grown into a truly gigantic and amazingly complicated political organism. It will be worth while, at this point, to step back and survey the full extent of this leviathan, which claimed the loyalty of about 1 million members and from 6 to 11 million voters (20 to 38 per cent of the electorate), and which sent from 100 to 163 deputies to the Reichstag.

34. Ibid., pp. 148–52.
35. *Jahrbuch der deutschen Sozialdemokratie, 1931* (Berlin, Dietz, 1932), p. 107. Hereafter cited as *Jahrbuch* [*year*]. For an account of these happenings, see below, pp. 232–33.

At the apex of the organizational pyramid were the central institutions of party leadership: the executive, the Reichstag fraction, the party council, the control commission, and the congress. Underneath these lay the 33 regional organizations, each with its own congress and executive. Then came some 400 subregional units, and beneath them roughly 8,500 locals. Each local was further subdivided into agitation groups, to organize the comrades of individual street sections, factories, and the like. Yet this impressive structure constituted only the organization for regular party members, alongside of which stood a network of special groups. The Social Democratic youth movement consisted of a series of organizations for different age levels: the Nest Falcons (6 to 10), the Young Falcons (10 to 12), the Red Falcons (12 to 14), the Socialist Workers' Youth (14 to 20), and the Young Socialists (18 to 25), the last being for young members of the adult party. Women comrades, while belonging to the regular organization, had committees of their own, ran special programs and other activities, and held a national women's conference whenever the party congress met. Finally, there were special leagues for Social Democratic lawyers, teachers, and other professional groups, including even an association for party functionaries. All these organizations, of course, had their own pyramids of leadership.

The SPD presented its views to the public chiefly by means of the printed word, and over the years the party had constructed an elaborate publishing apparatus. This included *Vorwärts,* its official daily newspaper and (in 1927) 187 other dailies, reaching a total of 1,188,401 regular subscribers.[36] The party also put out *Die Gesellschaft,* a monthly theoretical organ; *Der Wahre Jacob,* a humor magazine; and a variety of special periodicals for youth, women, teachers,

36. *Jahrbuch 1927,* p. 223.

civil servants, and so on. The Dietz-Verlag in Berlin published the party's books, pamphlets, and leaflets. In 1929 alone over 60 million pieces of literature were distributed.[37] The SPD had its own international press service to gather news independent of "bourgeois" sources. In later years the new medium of the film was also exploited to spread the Social Democratic gospel.

In addition to press and film, the party made contact with the general public through an intricate network of ancillary organizations. These may be grouped into three categories: (1) welfare institutions attending to such diverse needs as nursery care, adoption, unemployment and health services, travelers' aid, old age care, etc.—literally a cradle-to-grave program; (2) educational facilities for children and adults, both part time and full time, covering every conceivable subject, together with organized vacation trips and even a Party School for the training of future SPD officials; (3) sport and hobby groups embracing everything from the Workers' Cycle Club and the Workers' Photography Club to the Workers' Mandolin Club![38]

Special mention must be given the republican paramilitary defense organization, the Reichsbanner Schwarz-Rot-Gold. Officially this group was supported by all the "Weimar" parties (Social Democrats, Democrats, Center) as well as by the Free Trade Unions and other prorepublican organizations. It was founded in February 1924—shortly after the Hitler Putsch in Munich—by the Social Democratic leader, Friedrich Otto Hörsing, "for defense against possible attacks by political enemies on the Constitution or on the Republic

37. *Jahrbuch 1929*, p. 170.
38. An annual review of the entire party apparatus can be found in the reports of the executive to the congress, e.g. in *Jahrbuch 1927*, pp. 171–241. Also see Bieligk, *Organisation im Klassenkampf*, pp. 62–65.

itself."[39] Despite its official multiparty character, the organization was led, manned, and financed predominantly by the SPD and Free Trade Unions. With 3.5 million members, it far outweighed Hitler's storm troopers (who never expanded beyond half a million prior to 1933), and was the largest private paramilitary force in the world. It was, of course, weaponless, and its usability in an emergency hinged upon the procurement of arms.[40]

The financing of these diverse organizations was founded primarily on members' contributions. In 1927 the regional organizations of the regular party boasted a total income of 7.7 million marks, of which 4.6 million derived from ordinary dues. The regions turned over a quarter of their income to the executive which, with money from other sources, had a budget of 2.5 million marks.[41] Some institutions, such as the press, supported themselves; such "party enterprises" did a volume of business worth 75 million marks in 1928, and showed a net profit of 1.8 million.[42] Most of the ancillary groups depended on extra contributions from their supporters. The organizations gathered together in the Reich Council for Socialist Education possessed a budget of 1.25 million marks in 1929.[43] The amount of money passing through the whole organization in a year cannot even be guessed at.

The first task of the party machine was to win elections, and campaign expenses ranged from 0.88 million marks for the presidential contest of 1925 to 2.6 million for the 1928

39. Friedrich Otto Hörsing, "Das Reichsbanner Schwarz-Rot-Gold," *Volk und Reich der Deutschen,* ed. Bernard Harms, 2 (Berlin, Reimar Hobbing, 1929), 182.

40. Ernst Posse, *Die politischen Kampfbünde Deutschlands* (Berlin, 1931), pp. 59–67; Matthias, *Ende der Parteien,* pp. 121–27.

41. *Jahrbuch 1927,* pp. 182–240.

42. *Prot. 1929,* pp. 48–49.

43. *Jahrbuch 1929,* p. 210.

Reichstag election.[44] Because of its hard core of support and continuous program of agitation, the SPD spent relatively less on these campaigns than did other parties. Thus in 1928, for example, the Social Democrats invested 0.27 mark per vote and 16,500 marks per elected candidate, as compared with 0.33 and 20,000 for the Center and 1.40 and 84,000 for right-wing parties such as the Nationalists.[45]

Weimar Social Democracy was a kind of self-contained and independent social unit. It possessed its own institutions of government, its own welfare, educational, and cultural organizations, its own mass media, its own quasi-military force, its own system of finance. Active members and their families could live virtually their entire lives without going "outside" the movement. This is what Max Weber had in mind when he spoke of the SPD as a "state within a state."

Some observers have seen totalitarian implications in this expansion of activities so far beyond what traditionally was thought appropriate to a political party. Sigmund Neumann, in describing what he calls the "party of integration," has said:

> It demands at bottom absorption of the entire person into the political organization . . . above all through its entrenchment in all areas of life. . . . The prime example of such a party organization is Social Democracy. It has been said in jest that it [the SPD] accompanies the member from cradle to grave, from the Proletarian Nursery Care (Worker's Welfare) to the Free Thinkers' Cremation Club.[46]

It can be argued that, by politicizing activities which prima facie are nonpolitical (welfare, cultural pursuits, sports, hobbies) and by encouraging members to live as much as pos-

44. Ibid., p. 173.
45. Richard Lewinsohn, *Das Geld in der Politik* (Berlin, 1931), p. 72.
46. *Die deutschen Parteien, Wesen und Wandel nach dem Kriege* (Berlin, Junker and Dunnhaupt, 1932), p. 109.

sible "within" the party, the SPD attempted to acquire a totalitarian grasp over its members.

Most writers, however, distinguish the Social Democrats in this respect from completely totalitarian parties. Neumann himself later differentiated "parties of democratic integration" from "parties of total integration," including socialist and Catholic parties among the former, and communist and fascist among the latter.[47] Maurice Duverger suggests a principle of discrimination: while both types of movements endeavor to create a separate life for their followers, parties of total integration are based on a doctrine that requires "an absolute pledging of the whole human being, which admits of no distinction between public and private life, but claims the same right to direct the latter as the former."[48] Social Democracy still recognized the domain of private life. Unlike the Communist Party, for example, it made no religious requirement for membership; Protestants and Catholics belonged to the party along with freethinkers. This extended even to the leadership, where ten practicing Protestants sat in the 1930 Reichstag, as well as seven practicing Catholics and two practicing Jews.[49] The Nazi Party, however, also permitted religious diversity among its followers. Ultimately the distinction suggested by Neumann and Duverger may be more quantitative than qualitative, but it is not necessarily less important for that reason.

Also one must recognize the complexities of motivation. It would be overly simple to see in the development of Social

47. Sigmund Neumann, ed. *Modern Political Parties* (Chicago, Univ. of Chicago Press, 1956), pp. 403–05.

48. *Political Parties, Their Organization and Activity in the Modern State*, trans. Barbara and Robert North (London, 1954), pp. 2, 116–20; also see Seymour M. Lipset, *Political Man, The Social Bases of Politics* (New York, Doubleday, 1960), pp. 85–87.

49. *Kürschners Volkshandbuch Deutscher Reichstag, 1930* (Berlin, n.d.), p. 13.

Democratic ancillary organizations a deliberate design to acquire a totalitarian grasp over the party followers. Two other considerations must be taken into account. The growth of these organizations before the war reflected in part the alienation of German workers from existing society, and a similar alienation explains why Catholic Centrists also developed an elaborate ancillary apparatus. The organizations of both parties provided services and experiences for their members that were otherwise unavailable to them or, if available, were provided in an alien or hostile atmosphere. The bourgeois parties did not need such auxiliaries precisely because they were "bourgeois."

A second and obvious motive is recognized by Duverger, who explains:

> Certain parties which are not really totalitarian parties also try to multiply their ancillary organizations. The development of these is a good way of attracting members or of keeping them: a man who is bored at the branch meetings of the party will enjoy its Sports Club; a man who will not attend meetings will be quite willing to listen to the few words spoken by the leaders at a fair or a rural fête. The ancillary activities of the party can be a means of retaining lukewarm members, as well as a means of strengthening the loyalty of the faithful.[50]

These considerations were most likely uppermost in the minds of the Social Democrats themselves.

Quite apart from the question of ancillary activities, there were of course many differences between the SPD and the totalitarian parties, foremost of which was its unequivocal commitment to political democracy. The party also allowed room within the fold for differences of opinion and did not demand unquestioning acceptance of every aspect of its

50. *Political Parties*, p. 118.

ideology. The party organization, if quite oligarchic in practice, still rested on democratic principles that were not entirely forgotten. Moreover, the party was not selective in the recruitment of members and did not expect those admitted to devote all their waking hours to the service of the cause. Judged as a whole, there can be no doubt that the SPD was a party of democratic, as opposed to total, integration.[51]

The Party Bureaucracy

Now that we have seen something of the extent of the Social Democratic organizational complex, we can appreciate how great the task of running it was. Victor Adler once wrote that the greatest danger for socialism would arise out of its own bureaucratization.

Administration of the giant party naturally required a legion of paid officials and functionaries. In 1929 SPD administrative expenses amounted to 3.2 million marks, or more than was spent on the election campaign of the previous year.[52] Estimates of the size of the party bureaucracy range from a conservative, Social Democratic figure of 10,000 to a highly imaginative Communist one of 300,000. Apart from politically inspired exaggerations, the sum arrived at depends on who is counted. The author of the first figure, Carl Mierendorff, scored only "influential and productive offices of consequence."[53] But reckoning in all the officers and functionaries of the ancillary organizations, Alexander Schifrin,

---

51. On the general distinction between democratic and totalitarian parties, see the discussions of Neumann, *Modern Political Parties,* pp. 400–05, and Duverger, *Political Parties,* pp. 116–32.

52. *Jahrbuch 1929,* pp. 172, 268.

53. "Wieviel 'Bonzen' gibt es?" *Neue Blätter für den Sozialismus,* 2 (1931), 142–43.

a moderate Left Social Democrat, emerged with a census of 70,000 to 80,000.[54] Still others would include every SPD representative at all levels of government, a group totaling 39,983 in 1926.[55] Party businesses employed 7,397 workers and sales personnel in 1929.[56] Not everyone who owed his livelihood to the socialist movement, however, should be considered a part of the bureaucracy proper. Perhaps most reasonable as the number of "officials and leading functionaries" is Schifrin's estimate of 20,000 to 30,000.[57]

A great deal has been written about the effects of bureaucratization on the SPD. Even before the war, Robert Michels in his classic study pointed to the encouragement it gave to oligarchical tendencies within the movement. A paid official was usually not subject to annual elections; moreover, as a full-time professional he could naturally influence party policy more than ordinary members. Increased specialization bestowed on him the status of an expert:

> He would incline more and more to regard everyone as an "incompetent," an "outsider," and "unprofessional," who might wish to judge questions from some higher outlook than the purely technical; he would incline to deny the good sense and even the socialism of all who might desire to fight upon another ground and by other means than those familiar to him within his narrow sphere as a specialist.[58]

Over the years the bureaucrats gathered more and more power in their hands. Of the party secretaries in particular,

54. "Parteiapparat und Parteidemokratie," *Die Gesellschaft,* 7 (1) (1930), 513.

55. *Jahrbuch 1926,* p. 21.

56. *Prot. 1929,* p. 49.

57. *Die Gesellschaft,* 7 (1), 513.

58. *Political Parties,* trans. Eden and Cedar Paul (Glencoe, Ill., Free Press, 1915), p. 188.

Julius Leber has written: "Their influence was boundless; their accountability, on the other hand, was small. As a strict and jealous hierarchy they defended their position and power to the last. No one rose to the top who had not come from their ranks or at least shown himself worthy of their benediction."[59]

With the waxing authority of the bureaucracy, the role of ordinary members in party life became smaller. Indeed, SPD officials as a rule were distrustful of a politically active rank and file. The November Revolution had taken place not under their direction but in spite of it. Their one experiment in mass action, the general strike against the Kapp Putsch, seemed to justify every apprehension: in several areas the officials lost control and ultimately had to suppress the strike by force.[60] "Ever since the days when a general strike was called to defeat the Kapp Putsch in 1920," wrote Otto Kirchheimer, "both the SPD and the unions have shied away from mobilizing the active support of their followers."[61] Concentration of authority in the hands of experts, and a passive and obedient rank and file—such was the bureaucrats' recipe for a well-ordered socialist movement.

Besides contributing to the decline of intraparty democracy, the bureaucracy exerted a conservative political influence on the movement. Michels described the function of the apparatus as a "class-raising machine": it attracted the most intelligent, ambitious, potentially dissatisfied workers into the organization, securing for them white-collar status and a steady income visibly above the average of their comrades. In this way such persons acquired a stake in the movement as an end in itself. No longer need the victory of socialism have

59. *Ein Mann geht seinen Weg* (Berlin, Mosaik, 1952), p. 195.
60. See Carl Severing, *1919/1920 im Wetter und Watterwinkel* (Bielefeld, 1927); also discussion of Kapp Putsch below, pp. 181–85.
61. "West German Trade Unions," *World Politics, 8* (1955–56), 486.

such urgency for them; their personal social revolution had already taken place.[62]

Important though this may be, Carl Schorske has argued that salaries and prestige do not suffice to explain the conservatism of the SPD bureaucracy. Lenin too built up an organization of professionals without noticeably lessening their revolutionary zeal. More decisive were the circumstances under which, and the purposes for which, the bureaucracy came into existence. Created during a long period of social stability and economic expansion, it was hired to run election campaigns, handle finances, disseminate the press, and do everything possible to attract new members and new voters. It was not expected to mount the barricades or overturn existing society, but only to work within it for the attainment of a socialist majority.[63] Oriented toward winning over half-convinced and marginal voters, the functionaries wanted a moderate, easy-to-sell program appealing to the widest possible audience. They resented criticism of this tactic and opposed any thought of changing it, even when the social stability and economic prosperity upon which it rested ceased to exist.

The conservatism of the bureaucracy expressed itself in another way. Having labored painstakingly for years to build up an electoral machine with a yearly income of several million marks, and capital assets worth millions more, the officials were loath to approve any undertaking that might destroy the edifice or endanger its continued operation.[64] In moments when decisive action might involve considerable

62. "Die deutsche Sozialdemokratie, Parteimitgliederschaft und soziale Zusammensetzung," *Archiv für Sozialwissenschaft und Sozialpolitik*, 23 (1906), 527 and passim.

63. Carl E. Schorske, *German Social Democracy, 1905–1917* (Cambridge, Mass., 1955), p. 127.

64. Michels, *Political Parties*, pp. 365–76.

risk, they threw their weight against such action. It is generally acknowledged that one of the two or three most important reasons for the August Fourth decision was the fear that refusal to approve war credits would bring in its wake a police dissolution of the party and destruction of the apparatus.[65] Again in the events surrounding Hitler's seizure of power, the pressure of functionaries was exerted against the adoption of any radical—and therefore risky—countermeasures.[66] Fear for the organization made the bureaucracy timid and compromising in tight situations.

Finally, a third effect of the party's bureaucratization needs mention, a depoliticizing effect, resulting from the increased emphasis on administrative detail. A section of the 1928 executive report read as follows:

> With still greater pride . . . can we report that already on the 22nd of January, 1929—after only 22 days!—all the financial accounts from the 33 regions and their 8916 locals were on hand. . . .
>
> This is a paragon accomplishment for the Social Democratic functionaries, which gives evidence of their glowing idealism for our cause.[67]

That speedy financial reports are taken as evidence of "glowing idealism" for the socialist cause is a sad indication of the depoliticizing influence of the party bureaucracy. The Left Social Democrat, Kurt Laumann, observed in 1931 that "work within the organization shows more and more a transfer from political activity to purely administrative work."[68]

With this shift, the allegiance of the paid officials to the party tended to lose any kind of political character. For them

65. Anderson, *Hammer or Anvil*, p. 20; Schorske, *Social Democracy*, pp. 287–89.
66. Matthias, *Vierteljahrshefte für Zeitgeschichte, 4*, 281 and passim.
67. *Jahrbuch 1928*, p. 130.
68. "Organisation und Apparat," *Organisation im Klassenkampf*, p. 133.

the business of electioneering was an end in itself. Whether or not one agreed with the election program had only secondary importance:

> When we stand before our opponents, before the indifferent, we must support the party with our full energy, even where it goes against our grain. The Nationalists during the last war constantly repeated: "My country, right or wrong!" Before the general public we must also say: "Right or wrong —always for the party!"[69]

So spoke Konrad Brosswitz, long-time secretary for the Hessen–Nassau organization. Corollary to such sentiments was the bureaucrat's attitude toward his job, which he regarded as a kind of civil-service position that ought to be secure from (internal) partisan politics. When Karl Bethke, a conservative party secretary in Saxony, was forced out of his office by the leftist membership during the Saxon Conflict,[70] he complained bitterly on the ground that he was "one of the oldest party secretaries" and "had a large family."[71] It made no difference that his political viewpoints were contrary to those of the membership. Bethke obviously regarded himself as a "neutral" administrator hired to do the paper work of the unit. He refused to recognize that, in the nature of things, the party secretaries were important political spokesmen and policy makers for their organizations.

The various auxiliary institutions of the SPD also tended to depoliticize party life in general because it added so many nonpolitical concerns. The functionary who ran the Workers' Photography Club clearly spent far more time in photographic pursuits than in propagating socialism. And the more time used in such activities, the less remained for real politi-

69. *Prot. 1927*, p. 71.
70. See below, pp. 210–21.
71. *Prot. 1925*, p. 124.

cal discussion and education. Bieligk reported that "there are numerous locals in which no topical political lecture is given for many months at a time, and still fewer political discussions take place."[72] These lines were written in 1931, hardly a serene year! The preoccupation with administration and ancillary aids tended to obscure the original purpose of the party as an instrument for political action.

Thus, the giant apparatus created by the SPD to capture votes did not fail to influence its creator: it encouraged the trend toward oligarchy, it steered the movement into more conservative waters, and it bureaucratized and depoliticized party life. It was, perhaps, the most salient feature of Weimar Social Democracy.

72. *Organisation im Klassenkampf,* p. 66.

3. Central Party Institutions: The Leadership

Although the Social Democratic bureaucracy affected every area of party life, it was not, as such, the responsible policy-making body. To determine policy was the job of the central party institutions: the executive, the control commission, the party council, the congress, and the Reichstag fraction.

The Party Executive

Among the institutions of the Weimar Social Democractic Party the executive manifestly ranked first in power and influence. The expansion of its authority characterized the entire Wilhelmian era and continued uninterrupted in the republican period. We have already seen how the formal prerogatives of this body in matters of finance, property rights, expulsions, and the nomination of Reichstag candidates were broadened by the statutory reforms of 1919 and 1924. It will prove fruitful now to probe the sub rosa influence of the executive in party affairs and examine the mode of its election and the background and character of its membership.

The executive exerted a control in party affairs even beyond the generous prescriptions of the statute by means of its paid secretaries and its grasp on the Social Democratic press. As mentioned above, a 1904 resolution permitted the executive to select and hire secretaries nominated by the organizations concerned. As salaried employees, the secretaries were not subject to annual election and owed primary loyalty to the executive that paid them. About sixty such persons were maintained by the central treasury during the Weimar period. Bieligk described the result:

> The party executive, from its own funds, hired two secretaries in each regional organization. These regional secretaries acquired thereby an immediate dependence upon the executive. All the more since the executive demanded a decisive voice in their appointment. The party members of a region were not allowed to elect the secretary, who in their opinion should represent their political views; rather they had to let themselves be humbugged by a political agent of the executive. This helps explain why—with few exceptions —the regional secretaries have stood on the side of the executive in all political decisions within the party.[1]

These full-time professionals, as we have already seen, accumulated enormous influence in their organizations. "Where the elected party leaders do not consist of very strong men, the secretary will speak the most important word in the resolution of all questions."[2] The secretaries performed yeoman service in keeping the majority of the regional organizations in line with executive wishes.

The Social Democratic press issued an increasingly standardized party line. The editorial board of each paper was

1. "Die Entwicklung der sozialdemokratischen Organisation in Deutschland," *Die Organisation im Klassenkampf* (Berlin, n.d. [1931]), p. 75.
2. Ernst Eckstein, "Wie soll die Organisation aussehen," ibid., p. 160.

chosen formally by a press commission representing the organization concerned, while the executive retained the right "to control the ideological position" (prinzipielle Haltung). In practice the executive had never utilized this right (no machinery existed for its exercise) but ensured conformity in the bulk of the press by other devices.[3] In 1916 it illegally seized the property of *Vorwärts* and delegated one of its own members to supervise the editorial policy of the party's central organ. Henceforth *Vorwärts* was safely under executive control, much to the vexation of the radical Berlin organization which continually demanded a separate organ.[4] In 1919 the executive acquired nominal ownership of all party property, and in 1925 it created Konzentration A.G., an umbrella organization designed to coordinate the business activities of all SPD undertakings.[5] By means of the financial controls thus obtained, the executive managed to unseat a number of editors hostile to the reformist tactic.[6]

The sole source of national and international news for most of the small provincial newspapers was the Social Democratic Press Service, an enterprise that put forth the official line both in news stories and in "canned" editorials. In the Saxon Conflict, to be discussed below, the position of the leftists was unknown to most party comrades for the simple reason that the Press Service distributed only the right-wing version of the dispute.[7] In former times the Social Democratic press had served as the vehicle for vigorous intraparty debates, as during the great Revisionist controversy. But increasingly the leadership thought it illogical and dan-

3. Ludwig Kantorowicz, *Die sozialdemokratische Presse Deutschlands* (Tübingen, 1922), pp. 71–72, 93.

4. See, e.g., *Prot. 1927,* pp. 65–67, 86–89.

5. *Prot. 1925,* pp. 110–11.

6. In Halle and Bochum, for example (ibid., pp. 72–74; Bieligk, *Organisation im Klassenkampf,* pp. 70, 76).

7. Ibid., pp. 70–77.

gerous to permit criticism of official policies in party organs.[8]
The Left Social Democrat, Kurt Rosenfeld, complained to
the 1927 congress:

> *Vorwärts* excludes on principle any discussion of party
> policies, and the Social Democratic Press Service likewise
> reveals its "official" character at all times. I was recently at
> the French party congress and read there an article by Com-
> rade Blum in *Populaire*. In it he requested the advocates of
> a viewpoint contrary to his own to express themselves . . .
> in the central organ of the party. I would like to see the day
> when something like that happens in *Vorwärts*.[9]

While denied access to the central organ, Left Social Democrats did manage to retain control over a few provincial
newspapers, as well as at least one nationally distributed
periodical. Here they could still present their views to the
public. The bulk of the party press, however, became in the
Weimar period merely an instrument for publicizing and
justifying the policies of the SPD leadership.[10]

In view of the crucial weight held by the executive within
the party, one might expect elections to it to be hotly contested among the ideological factions and interest groups in
the SPD. This was not the case. Just twice in the entire
Weimar period do the records show that any of the higher
posts (chairmen, treasurers, secretaries) were seriously challenged.[11] In fact, only one nomination was usually made for

8. *Prot. 1927*, speeches of Wels, pp. 32–33, and Stampfer, pp. 86–88.
9. Ibid., p. 62.
10. See Kurt Koszyk, *Zwischen Kaiserreich und Diktatur, Die sozialdemokratische Presse von 1914 bis 1933* (Heidelberg, Quelle und Meyer,
1958), for an excellent discussion of the entire press question.
11. The facts and statistics in this and the next paragraphs which relate
to the executive membership all come from the congress minutes in *Prot.*:
1919, pp. 354, 405; *1920*, 186, 258; *1921*, 256, 268, 311; *1922*, 97, 192;
1924, 138, 199; *1925*, 225, 267; *1927*, 162, 225; *1929*, 172, 232; *1931*, 189,
242.

each of these positions, and the slate compiled from these single nominations, it seems clear, was drawn up by the leaders themselves. In 1924 the party council, without any statutory prerogative in this regard, took the liberty of nominating such an "official" slate. In other years one of the lesser delegates would read out the approved names, although no one else was ever permitted to make nominations verbally from the floor. The official list invariably included all the incumbents still living and able to accept office. When replacements became necessary new names appeared on the list, names which must have been selected in the back rooms, for there never occurred any discussion of nominees on the open floor. No statutory restriction prevented the addition of more names to the ballot, but only for the lesser positions, the associates, did this happen (with the two exceptions mentioned above). And only once did a candidate not on the official list ever *win* one of these posts. Normally such contenders ran over one hundred votes behind the lowest winning candidate.

Since any delegate could make nominations, and the voting took place by secret ballot, it is difficult to explain why there was so little competition for these all-important offices. Part of the answer lies in the composition of the party congress, as we shall see. No doubt the popularity of the incumbent leaders and the appeal of their practical experience likewise played a role. Yet all these reasons can scarcely explain the fantastic degree of unanimity displayed year after year in executive elections. An additional factor, a psychological one, must be taken into account: most Social Democrats felt a powerful loyalty to their leaders, quite independent of politics.

The conception of such a nonpolitical loyalty reveals itself lucidly in a speech of Otto Wels at the 1929 congress, when he was inveighing the delegates to re-elect the executive. Rank-and-file feeling against the leadership was extremely strong at this congress because the SPD-led government had recently approved construction of a new pocket battleship in violation of the party's election promises. Wels said:

> Comrades! We know that the possibility exists of expressing through the election of the party executive a vote of confidence [in Müller and Hilferding, who were cabinet ministers as well as executive members]. The custom of past years when unanimous elections took place has not yet reestablished itself in the party. We believe however that it must be the duty of the Social Democratic party congress to act politically; I can imagine that a few comrades will not view it as sufficient to resolve differences objectively through votes on resolutions, but will deliver still another judgment on the activity of our ministers by means of an adverse vote [in the election of the executive]. . . . Our political enemies would create material out of that [etc.].[12]

Apart from the cruder aspects of this speech, one point shines through: Wels treated as commonplace the idea that opposition to the leaders' policies should not be turned into opposition to the leaders as such. To vote against resolutions should suffice for any loyal opponent, but to vote against the leaders was downright treasonous! And these sentiments seem to have been accepted by the congress at large. While over a third of the delegates had just rejected the military policy of the leadership, only one delegate had the presumption to write in a vote against the chairmen of the executive who carried it out.

Why would a member endorse the leadership of someone whose ideas and policies he opposed? The answer quite likely

12. *Prot. 1929*, p. 172.

lies in the early history of Social Democracy, when persecution reinforced strong personal bonds. As Michels has said:

> The failure to re-elect a comrade who has assisted in the birth of the party, who has suffered with it many adversities, and has rendered it a thousand services, would be regarded as an act of cruelty and as an action to be condemned.[13]

Whatever its genesis, this phenomenon was very much in evidence throughout the Weimar years and even into the period of the Bonn Republic. Writing in 1954, Richard Petry noted a "strong and personal feeling of comradeship: tried and true comrades are not set aside simply because one disagrees with them."[14] Such a strange, almost feudal, allegiance to the person rather than to the political policy he represents, goes a long way toward explaining the remarkable stability of the Social Democratic leadership.

For a faction to run a candidate against the official slate was a sign of extreme hostility and portended a schism. Only twice in the period between 1905 and 1933 was the chairmanship challenged. The leftist opposition had backed Robert Dissmann in 1913 at the last congress before the wartime split. And Max Seydewitz ran in 1931, shortly before the second expulsion of the radical wing. He received only fifty-four votes. Left Social Democrats tried for the lesser "associate" offices more or less continuously, but never with any success. They also asked repeatedly for a system of proportional representation on the executive, such as in the French Socialist Party, to assure different ideological tendencies within the movement a fair voice in the leadership. These were dismissed as mad requests.

13. *Political Parties*, trans. Eden and Cedar Paul (Glencoe, Ill., 1915), p. 101.
14. "Die SPD und der Sozialismus," *Frankfurter Hefte*, 9 (1954), 665.

The helplessness of an opposition-minded member before these steam-roller elections is poignantly expressed in the following resolution, introduced—but of course not accepted —at the 1920 congress:

> At all elections, including the executive election, only one-third of the incumbents may be re-elected, two-thirds being new members so that opportunity may be given other party comrades to develop their abilities in this regard; we need a great deal of vigor, but the gates to such a development are closed because the same comrades are always the only ones put up as candidates and given a chance. Those elected lose their contact with the party comrades, and confidence above all suffers from this.[15]

Elections to the executive, while formally democratic, amounted in practice to a disguised system of co-option, where the leaders held their offices indefinitely and hand picked their own successors.[16]

Such being the electoral realities, it is not surprising to find that the Weimar executive leadership constituted a very narrow group. In 1919 the executive included twelve persons; by 1933 the number had grown to twenty, but in the entire period only thirty-one people ever served on that body. Membership tended to carry lifetime tenure. In the British Labour Party, of twenty-three people on the executive committee in 1924, only ten remained by 1928.[17] The corresponding figures for the SPD are seventeen out of nineteen

---

15. *Prot. 1920,* p. 279.

16. Apparently prewar elections were equally perfunctory; according to Michels, ballots bearing the names of the "official" nominees were distributed, and if a comrade wanted to vote for someone else he had to erase one of the printed names and write in his choice (*Political Parties,* p. 99).

17. Alexander Schifrin, "Parteiapparat und Parteidemokratie," *Die Gesellschaft, 7* (1) (1930), 526.

—the other two had died! During the whole Weimar period eleven persons left the executive: eight died in office, two resigned to accept ministerial posts, and only one was defeated in an election.[18] The thirty-one members served an average of eleven years each, the longest being old Wilhelm Pfannkuch who could boast thirty years in office before his death in 1923. Eduard Bernstein seems to have been right when he wrote that "a leader who conscientiously carries out his duties is more secure in the labour movement than is a minister in the Prussian kingdom founded on the grace of God."[19]

Predictably enough under these circumstances, the top posts were filled by older men. The average age of the thirty-one Weimar executive members in 1925 was 52; six were over 60; only four under 40. This marked tendency toward superannuation in the leadership did not find an effective counterbalance in the rise of fresh new faces. To reach the top in Social Democracy, given the practical results of the nomination system, one had to please the old leaders. And they were not pleased by startling new ideas or spirited young enthusiasm: "Only those were let in [the party elite] who offered security that they would keep discipline faithfully and honestly, and who would push neither those above nor those below. Good intellectual mediocrity and drilled-in routine commanded the field, and the power of the leaders insured that the road to the top opened only through this gate."[20]

18. This was Franz Künstler, a former USPD leader who was brought into the executive by the 1922 merger and who became the head of the Left Social Democratic Berlin organization. Although on the "official" slate he was defeated in 1924 by a rising trade-union official, Emil Stahl. The circumstances remain obscure; perhaps the leadership really backed Stahl and endorsed Künstler formally only to placate the ex-Independents. In any event it was a unique happening.

19. Quoted in Michels, *Political Parties,* p. 106, n. 4.

20. Julius Leber, *Ein Mann geht seinen Weg* (Berlin, 1952), p. 195.

71

Leber's description may be tested by a glance at the five replacements who entered the executive after 1923.[21] Emil Stahl, 45 years old when chosen, had already served for seventeen years as a trade-union official. Johann Vogel, 46, had been SPD regional secretary in Franken for nineteen years. Max Westphal, 32, had risen from the youth movement and had been active as a youth organizer. Carl Litke, 34, possessed nine years' experience administering the party's hospitalization insurance program. Rudolf Breitscheid, 47, had been a principal figure in the USPD and was only in 1931 restored to grace in the directorate of the old party. Thus, of the five replacements, three had come from long bureaucratic careers in the party or trade union apparatus. Only Breitscheid had a first-rate political intelligence, and only Westphal can really be counted as "young blood."

For a closer look at the background and mentality of an average executive member, one could find no better subject than Otto Wels himself, co-chairman of the SPD and boss of the party machine. Wels was born in Berlin in 1873, the son of lower-class parents. After a public school education he was apprenticed to the trade of paper hanging and joined the socialist movement at the age of 14. At this time the party was still underground, and Wels sympathized with its most radical spokesmen. His youthful radicalism, however, gradually wore away as he advanced into the socialist bureaucracy. In 1906 he became a paid official for the paper hangers' union. The following year he shifted to the party apparatus as secretary for the new provincial organization of Brandenburg, which became a model of bustling efficiency under his capable management. In the great controversies

21. Excluding Friedrich Stampfer, who formally joined the executive in 1925 but had previously sat in its meetings as editor of *Vorwärts*. Biographical data in this paragraph come from Cuno Horkenbach, *Das deutsche Reich von 1918 bis heute, 1918–1930* (Berlin, 1930), pp. 631–774.

of prewar Social Democracy, Wels loyally delivered the block of votes under his control to whichever side was supported by the executive.[22] His administrative and organizing abilities soon drew the notice of Bebel, who secured him a place on the party executive in 1913.

Through the years of war and schism Wels sided with the Majority Socialist position. He rose to national prominence during the Revolution as commandant of Berlin, earning the hatred of the radicals by the role of his troops in the December 6 shootings and by his tragicomic rigidity regarding the palace keys, which precipitated the sailors' insurrection of December 23. This latter incident ended Wels' short military career, but a new position was found for him—replacing Ebert as co-chairman of the SPD executive in charge of the party apparatus, a post he then held until 1933. Not noted for extraordinary intelligence or vision, Wels was nonetheless a tough and capable administrator. Kurt von Reibnitz has described him as follows: "Not a man of the world or a person of great intellect or countenance, neither a pliant yes-man, he is a self-made man with a raw voice, a robust powerfully-built Berliner who gladly empties a stein of beer and is not ashamed of his rough dialect."[23] Wels was a perfect stereotype of a party boss.

A few statistics will bear out the similarity of Wel's background to that of his colleagues on the party executive. Of the twenty-seven members for whom biographical information is available, eighteen began their working lives in proletarian or artisan occupations. Only six had attended a university; four held degrees. Previous to their election five had served in the trade-union apparatus, thirteen in the party

22. Carl E. Schorske, *German Social Democracy, 1905–1917* (Cambridge, Mass., 1955), pp. 141, 221, 280.
23. *Im Dreieck Schleicher–Hitler–Hindenburg* (Dresden, Reissner, 1933), p. 46.

bureaucracy, and fifteen in the Social Democratic press (allowing for a little overlapping owing to changes of occupation). Only fourteen of the number had been, in their pre-executive careers, primarily concerned with national politics.[24]

Of the executive in general, Reibnitz has said: "Instead of a real leader Social Democracy has a directorate of industrious, dutiful old officials."[25] Without setting up any rigid arrangements of cause and effect, it may be asserted that the attitudes and actions of the executive members were powerfully influenced by their career backgrounds and the circumstances under which they held office. To begin with, the very stability of their positions gave them a feeling of independence vis-à-vis the rank and file and something like contempt for criticism from below. As "organization men" of long standing, they made honest and capable administrators but tended to lose sight of the purpose for which the apparatus was created. So highly did they prize the organization that, where risks to it were involved, their actions betrayed a distinct timidity, a timidity which certainly did not help them during the struggle against Hitler. Their long apprenticeship in the tedious work of party administration imbued the executive members with a keen appreciation of the "practical" —they prided themselves on being hard-boiled realists—but left them open to the accusation of unimaginativeness and political myopia. They could envisage no other means of struggle than the ceaseless electioneering to which they had dedicated the organization. What illusions these men had stemmed from the faith in economic progress and the "inevitability of gradualism" upon which the reformist ideology rested. They knew exactly what to do in the orderly, pros-

24. Compiled from biographical data in Horkenbach, *Das deutsche Reich, 1918–1930*, pp. 631–774.
25. *Dreieck*, p. 45.

perous Germany of Wilhelm II but were quite out of their clement in the turmoil and crises of the Weimar Republic. And no one among them possessed that spark of charisma that can transform an able official into a magnetic popular leader.

The noted historian of socialism, Gustav Mayer, has left in his posthumous memoirs a pithy evaluation of the Weimar SPD leadership:

> I admit that there was scarcely a single figure in the entire leadership cadre of the SPD who, measured by a strict standard, aroused within me any profound ethical respect and admiration. Petty bourgeois pedantry was combined in many of them with egotism and ambitious placehunting.
>
> The individual policies that Hermann Müller, Scheidemann, Ebert, and so forth, attempted to carry out were often correct, certainly more so than what the demagogic cliques on the right proposed, but the smallness of their moral and intellectual frame made them completely unfruitful.
>
> These new statesmen appeared to me to be more or less all little people who saw themselves placed before great tasks which could only have been tackled by unusual personalities and by means of unusual methods.[26]

Such was the directorate that led German Social Democracy between the eras of Bebel and Schumacher.

The Party Congress

A great deal of the independence enjoyed by the SPD executive stemmed from the lack of effective checks on its authority. Theoretically it was overseen by the control commission,

---

26. *Erinnerungen* (Munich, 1949), pp. 308–09, quoted in translation by Koppel S. Pinson, *Modern Germany* (New York, Macmillan, 1954), pp. 415–16.

the council, and of course the party congress to which it was responsible. The ineffectiveness of the first two institutions can be quickly shown; the power, limitations, and political composition of the congress will need more discussion.

In the election of the control commission there were the same procedures as in the case of the executive, and with the same consequences: narrow range of membership, lifetime tenure, and superannuation.[27] Since its emasculation in 1912, the only functions left to this body were the review of central party finances and the power to judge cases involving complaints against the executive or between party organizations. None of these cases required political decisions and none, according to its reports, was ever decided against the executive. Indeed, so useless did the control commission appear to its own members that in 1928 they suggested the institution be abolished. But the executive, seemingly embarrassed, persuaded them that its continued existence constituted a "necessity for the party."[28]

The party council, composed of a delegate from each regional organization plus some women representatives, was supposed to keep the executive in contact with grass-roots sentiment, and to advise it on all important political issues, together with matters of party business. Its resolutions, however, were not binding, and it met regularly only four times a year. Never did its published reports cite anything but full agreement with the executive. A typical report stated that, in the past year, "the opinion of the party council has always been in accord with the political actions of the executive and the Reichstag fraction."[29] Such harmonious relations become more understandable when one learns that "the great majority of party council members are regional secretaries

27. Same sources as above, p. 66, n. 11.
28. *Jahrbuch 1928*, pp. 202–03.
29. *Prot. 1924*, p. 30.

hired by the executive."[30] Thus the executive was advised chiefly by persons on its own payroll!

The party congress, according to the statute, formed "the supreme representative institution of the party." The executive and control commission were elected by it and were responsible to it, as was the Reichstag fraction. The congress "enacted" the party program and had authority to pass resolutions "on all questions affecting party life."[31] The parallel to a national legislature breaks down, however, when one considers that the congress met only five days a year or in the later period five days every other year. At best it could set forth the broad outlines of a policy and then elect leaders to carry it out. But in actuality the congress never exercised even this much power: its electoral duties, as we have seen, were perfunctory, and its "legislative" authority boiled down to the choice of ratifying or not ratifying resolutions presented to it by the leadership. The relatively passive role played by this body stemmed partly from the influence the executive held in its functioning, partly from the way it was constituted.

As first co-chairman of the congress, elected by the familiar single-nomination system, there appeared year after year the omnipresent Otto Wels[32] (a rather awkward circumstance considering that, as co-chairman of the executive, he was supposed to be submitting his past year's actions for congress approval). In the chair Wels put to good use the myriad small procedural powers attendant upon that office in order to guide the flow of party business. Moreover, the executive, together with the party council, set the agenda of the congress and appointed spokesmen for each topic to

30. Bieligk, *Organisation im Klassenkampf*, p. 76.
31. *Prot. 1919*, p. 519.
32. Two exceptions were 1919 and 1920 when Paul Loebe and Hermann Müller, respectively, acted as first co-chairman.

present the "official" case to the delegates.[33] After the discussion the spokesman had the privilege of summing up and making a plea for a favorable vote. In prewar years, where an important and controversial issue had to be decided by the congress, two spokesmen were customarily appointed, one for each side. But in the Weimar period the practice of double reports was opposed by the executive and fell into disuse. All these arrangements no doubt made for the smooth and efficient expedition of party business but hardly left the congress "supreme" in anything but name.

In elections to the congress, certain practices tended to overrepresent the conservative elements in the party. Delegates in the Weimar period were no longer elected directly by the membership but rather by regional congresses, gatherings which consisted mainly of party bureaucrats and functionaries from the local level.[34] And delegates had no obligation, in any event, to vote according to instructions; indeed, the agenda of the national congress was not published until shortly before its convocation, so they could not be instructed on specific issues at all.[35] In addition to elected delegates, the members of the executive, the control commission, the party council, and one-fifth of the Reichstag fraction participated in congresses, voting on all questions except those concerning their own activities. This added about 100 votes, the great majority of which the executive could count on in any dispute. By examining the voting record of the congress we can discover the actual political composition of that body.

Roll-call votes were taken only rarely when an extremely controversial issue had to be resolved. Such an issue occupied the 1929 Magdeburg congress, which met a few months after

33. *Prot. 1919*, p. 520.
34. Kurt Laumann, "Organisation und Apparat," *Organisation im Klassenkampf*, p. 137.
35. Ibid., p. 139; *Prot. 1924*, p. 144.

the Müller government had approved the construction of Pocket Battleship A. The entire military question arose in a stormy debate during which the Left Social Democrats were able to gain wide support for their opposition to the party leadership. Roll-call votes were taken on three resolutions dealing with this question: I, a resolution supported by the executive to table several leftist-sponsored proposals against the construction of Pocket Battleship A, against the military budget, and against further participation in the Great Coalition; II, a resolution, opposed by the executive, to delay the fixing of any military policy until the next congress (this was a leftist attempt to gain more time); III, a resolution to accept the executive's proposed policy statement called "Guidelines on Military Policy." The over-all results of the three contests appear in Table 1 (to simplify matters all votes for the side supported by the executive have been labeled "positive votes," those against, "negative votes").[36]

TABLE 1. *Distribution of Vote on Three Resolutions of the 1929 Congress*

Resolution	Total Votes	Positive Votes	Percentage	Negative Votes	Percentage
I	393	254	64.6	139	35.4
II	391	225	57.5	166	42.5
III	389	242	62.2	147	37.8
Total	1,173	721	61.4	452	38.6

There were no wide variations from one vote to the next. The stable conservative majority hovered around three-fifths of the total, averaging out at 61.4 per cent. Now if we add

36. Calculated from *Prot. 1929*, pp. 269–72.

together the votes from all three contests and treat them as a whole, we can ease further analysis. Of the 1,173 votes cast, 285 belonged to members of central party institutions and 888 belonged to elected delegates. Separating the ballots in this way, we can see in Table 2 whether the voting habits of the broad party leadership differed from those of rank-and-file delegates.[37]

TABLE 2. *Distribution of 1929 Vote According to Type of Delegate*

Type of Delegate	Number Present	Total Votes	Positive Votes	Per-centage	Negative Votes	Per-centage
Ex Officio						
Executive	19	54	50	92.6	4	7.4
Control com.	7	16	12	75.0	4	25.0
Council	44	132	93	70.5	39	29.5
Fraction	30	83	62	74.7	21	25.3
Total	100	285	217	76.1	68	23.9
Elected	297	888	504	56.8	384	43.2

It is apparent that the representatives of party institutions stood far more solidly behind the executive than did elected delegates. With the latter, the winning and losing sides were separated by only 13.6 percentage points; with the former, by 52.2 percentage points. The negative votes in the executive came from Konrad Ludwig, who opposed the majority in votes on II and III but made it clear during the debate that he did so for reasons of his own which differed from those of the radicals. Marie Juchacz voted the same way, apparently

37. This table and later figures are derived by comparing the voting results (ibid.) with the list of delegates and their position in the congress, to be found ibid., pp. 298–306.

out of antimilitarist conviction. The radicals had one friend
on the control commission, Lore Agnes, who supported them
in all three votes; the other negative ballot was cast—in-
explicably—by Paul Loebe in the vote on I. The party council showed the least unanimity, but it is significant that all
the adverse votes here came from members who represented
regions under radical control. The Reichstag group, com-
prising one-fifth of the total Social Democratic fraction,
likewise split in the main according to the region represented.
In general, then, the broad party leadership stood to the right
of the elected delegates; usually the radicals could get their
men into the national leadership only where they controlled
an entire regional organization.

Where were these centers of leftist strength? Above all,
in Saxony. The four regions of Saxony (Dresden, Leipzig,
Chemnitz, Zwickau), together with the Prussian province of
Saxony (Halle), formed the vital core of Left Social Democracy. Then Thuringia, Greater Berlin, and Pomerania (because of the port of Stettin) were solidly radical. Not
unanimous but still possessing left majorities were Breslau,
Lower Rhine, Hessen–Offenbach, and Baden. If we consider
these radical regions as a single unit, we find an 11.6:88.4
division against the official military policy. Conversely, the
rest of Germany, the conservative area, delivered an 87.9
per cent majority to the executive. Radical power lay in the
heart of industrial Germany where the SPD found its greatest
following.

To turn to the distribution of the vote by sex, at first
there appears to be no significant variation: the 50 women
at the congress were divided almost exactly as were the 347
men. By probing somewhat more deeply, however, we discover a remarkable discrepancy. Elected women delegates
gave considerably more support to the executive (62.2 per
cent) than did their male counterparts (56.1 per cent). But

—and here is the surprising feature—women in party institutions favored the left (42.6 per cent) far more heavily than did the corresponding males (19.5 per cent). Thus, while less than one-fifth of the men leaders of the SPD opposed its official military policy, over two-fifths of the women leaders did. Apparently, Left Social Democrats of the female sex encountered fewer obstacles than men in rising through the party hierarchy. Probably the conservative leadership felt less threatened by women, who were bound to remain a permanent minority in the organization and who never held chairmanships or other crucial posts.

In its general political composition the party congress of 1929 may be divided into four groups: (1) the representatives of party institutions, about 78 of whom were in the executive camp; (2) the convinced radicals, numbering approximately 128; (3) the convinced conservatives; and (4) the lesser members of the party bureaucracy, who automatically voted for the executive position—those whom Schorske has rightly dubbed the "back-benchers of Social Democracy."[38] This group of lesser functionaries, present at the congress because of the election practices described above, had essentially unpolitical jobs in the party and, having no independent views, never spoke in the debate but always delivered their votes to the side indicated by the executive. It is of course impossible to distinguish their votes from those of the convinced conservatives, yet in a roundabout manner we can speculate as to their strength. If we let the 34 radicals who spoke at the congress represent the approximately 128 radical delegates present, then the 26 conservative speakers, using the same ratio, would represent 96 convinced conservatives, leaving 72 as a rough estimate for the number of back-benchers.[39] In broad figures then, the executive could reckon on a stable

38. *Social Democracy,* p. 139.
39. Calculated from the list of speakers, *Prot. 1929,* p. 308.

majority of 78 institution members, 96 convinced conservatives, and 72 back-benchers to defeat the 150 radical delegates.

The votes of the back-bench yes-men and the ex officio delegates were essential to conservative predominance. The representatives of party institutions by themselves could always be counted on to turn a close decision into a safe majority. In the vote on II, for example, if 8 elected delegates had shifted their votes to the left, the radicals would have possessed a majority of the rank-and-file representation. But the 70 positive votes from party institutions would easily have saved the day for the executive. The radicals recognized their disadvantage in this matter and continually pressed for the disfranchisement of the ex officio delegates, pointing out that in the congresses of the Free Trade Unions such persons did not vote.[40]

Had this disfranchisement been carried out, and had the practices that permitted the election of automatic yes-men been stopped, the division in the party congress between right and left would have been quite different. Under such circumstances it is quite conceivable that the Left Social Democrats would have gained control of the party. At the 1929 congress, for example, the 128 elected radical delegates would have had a solid majority over the 96 convinced conservatives! It must be emphasized, however, that the latter figure is a hypothetical calculation and that this congress represented the high-water mark of Left Social Democratic popularity. In any event, no such organizational reforms were considered and, while the congress was not impotent like the control commission nor a rubber stamp like the party council, it remained in the last analysis safely in the hands of the executive.

40. For example, ibid., p. 73.

The Reichstag Fraction

The Social Democratic Reichstag fraction, alone among party institutions, had no statutory definition. Except for the ruling that it submit reports to the party congress and that one-fifth its number be represented there, the statute made no prescriptions. The relationship of the fraction to other party institutions and to the party as a whole were matters of tradition.

This tradition differed profoundly from that of the older parties, where there remained the liberal conception of the free and independent parliamentarian, responsible only to his conscience and bound to his constituents only by his desire to be re-elected. As explained above, the SPD did not originate in parliament but as a socialist agitation group which took part in elections as one of several activities. The policies of the party, including its general parliamentary policies, were made at the annual congresses by delegates elected by the entire mass membership. Social Democratic deputies, therefore, were neither policy makers nor free agents but were expected to act as a disciplined body carrying out the program and resolutions of the party congress. Refusal of the Reichstag fraction to abide by congress instructions could theoretically lead to its expulsion en masse from the party, although such a proceeding understandably never took place.[41]

In the early years when the primary aim of participating in elections was only to gauge the strength of the movement, the Social Democrats who were elected actually had little to

41. The closest thing to such a mass expulsion in the Weimar period took place in 1926 when 23 Social Democratic members of the Saxon Landtag were expelled from the party for refusal to carry out the instructions of the Land congress.

do in the Reichstag. (Some comrades thought they should not even attend.) With the party's policy of "pure opposition," their parliamentary duties were perfectly described in the slogan: "Diesem System keinen Mann und keinen Groschen!"[42] But as decades passed the fraction members took more and more interest in bringing about practical reforms and became, in the process, skilled parliamentarians. With these changes, their influence over the day-to-day political policies of the party naturally grew. For, although bound by the program and congress resolutions, they possessed a certain leeway: where the congress had not specified a policy they were free to set their own, where the resolutions were vague they could interpret, and where the specification was exact but seemed out of date they could disregard it and present the next congress with a fait accompli. As the Revisionist, Ludwig Frank, said: "It would go ill with the party if it lacked men with sufficient courage to ignore congress resolutions when these are altogether impracticable."[43]

By the Weimar period the Reichstag fraction was no longer merely the instrument of a higher power, but constituted an integral part of the political leadership of the SPD. The party's position on each piece of legislation was ultimately determined in its caucuses. Paul Loebe, leading Social Democratic parliamentarian and president of the Reichstag, declared: "The fraction, like the executive, is an executive organ of the party."[44] In this form, however, Loebe's definition is misleading, for the fraction and the executive never were clearly separate bodies. All the prominent mem-

42. "To this system not one man and not one penny!"
43. Quoted in Michels, *Political Parties,* p. 161. The view of the fraction's evolution given in this paragraph comes from Boris Goldenberg, *Beiträge zur Soziologie der deutschen Vorkriegssozialdemokratie* (Heidelberg, 1932), pp. 38–39. Also see Bieligk, *Die Organisation im Klassenkampf,* pp. 76–77.
44. *Prot. 1929,* p. 155.

bers of the executive (in 1928, fourteen out of nineteen) sat in the Reichstag, and the political co-chairman of the executive, Hermann Müller, also chaired the caucuses of the fraction.[45] Moreover, four members of the control commission and thirteen members of the party council could be found in the 1928 fraction together with twenty-eight trade-union officials—the Social Democratic leadership was an interlocking directorate.

Internally, the fraction was organized into eighteen standing committees and an executive. Members of the committees (which paralleled the legislative committees of the whole Reichstag) had the task of discussing new bills within their special provinces and recommending a position to the entire fraction. They also counseled the fraction on which members to send to the interparty legislative committees. The executive presided over all caucuses and represented the fraction in meetings with other parties and with the cabinet. It grew steadily from seven in 1915 to twenty in 1930.[46] Hermann Müller, as already noted, was chairman. A new executive was selected after every Reichstag election, but the familiar pattern of nomination recurred here as well: "The old fraction executive simply informed the new fraction that it had concerned itself with the question of electing a new executive, and if there were no objections, the old executive could be reelected en bloc." So wrote Leber about the 1930 elections, where not a single member of the "new" body was under fifty years old.[47]

45. Until his death in 1931. Horkenbach, *Das deutsche Reich, 1918–1930*, p. 718.
46. Wilhelm Dittmann, "Wie kommt ein Reichsgesetz zustande?" *Jahrbuch, 1929*, pp. 452–53; Walther Lambach, *Die Herrschaft der Fünfhundert* (Berlin and Hamburg, 1926), pp. 16–17; Karl Liebknecht, *Klassenkampf gegen den Krieg* (Berlin Vereinigung Intern. Verlags-Anstalten, n.d.), p. 42; Leber, *Mann*, p. 236.
47. Ibid.

The selection of Social Democratic candidates for Reichstag elections remained one of the few relatively decentralized decision-making processes in the party. Before the war candidates had been chosen by the membership of the electoral district organizations, and these bodies, called subregional organizations in the Weimar period, still made the initial selections. The all-important power of arranging the candidates in a priority list, however, was given to the regional leadership, while the regional congresses had to deliver final approval. The exact prescription of the party statute read as follows: "Proposals for candidates for the Landtag and the Reichstag are made by the subregional organization, arranged in a list by the regional executive, and confirmed by the regional congress." The national executive worked out the Reich list (from which six to nine candidates were elected with leftover ballots) in conjunction with the party council, and also had the right to give advice in the regional selections and to decide, if asked, in cases of dispute.[48] How much use the executive made of these latter privileges is difficult to determine directly. It probably had a voice in placing two conservative executive members on the slate of the radical Berlin organization. And the reports of the control commission show one instance of executive intervention to secure a more favorable position on the list for a Leipzig conservative.[49] But aside from occasional pressure the executive seems not to have encroached upon the normal procedure, which meant that right-wing regional organizations put up conservative candidates and left-wing organizations put up radical ones. The thirty-man fraction delegation sent to the 1929 congress split 74.7–25.3 on the military question, showing that the left, while underrepresented, was nonetheless able to get a substantial number of its spokesmen

48. *Prot. 1924*, pp. 6, 8.
49. *Jahrbuch, 1928*, pp. 201–03.

87

into parliament. Here the principles of Eisenach remained largely in force.

Once in the Reichstag, however, Left Social Democrats must have felt extremely frustrated. A single speaker normally was appointed for each formal debate to present the official position of the SPD and, of course, by a party tradition that dated back to 1876, the fraction had to vote as a unit on the Reichstag floor, once a policy had been decided upon in caucus. This tradition was modified somewhat in 1915, as a concession to the antiwar opposition. A deputy whose conscience absolutely forbade him to vote with the rest of the fraction might absent himself from the session. But he could not vote against the party, or even abstain, on the Reichstag floor.[50] Occasionally, on especially critical votes, the fraction even denied its members the privilege of staying away, as in the acceptance of the Treaty of Versailles.[51] Thus the policies of the executive were guaranteed the unanimous parliamentary support of the Reichstag fraction.

It occasionally happened that dissident deputies openly violated fraction discipline, although this always constituted a serious step. The party leadership reacted to these violations in different ways, depending on the gravity of the situation. It might choose to ignore the matter, preferring silence to an open faction fight; it might bring the violators before the next congress for formal censure; or, in the most threatening cases such as the antiwar opposition of 1916–17, it might cause the expulsion of the offenders from the fraction and ultimately from the party itself.[52]

Since biographical sketches are available for Reichstag deputies, the Social Democratic fraction can also be studied

50. Eugen Prager, *Geschichte der USPD* (Berlin, 1921), p. 54.
51. Eckstein, *Organisation im Klassenkampf,* p. 163.
52. Examples of each response can be found below, on pp. 214, 231, and 193 respectively.

from a sociological angle. The results for selected years over a period of several decades will present an invaluable social portrait of the broad SPD leadership and its historical evolution.

The first eye-catching feature of such an analysis is the gradual aging of the fraction. The party leadership was not replacing itself in the younger generation, partly because of war losses in this age group but mainly because of losses to the left, as illustrated by Table 3.[53]

TABLE 3. *Age Distribution of Socialist and Communist Reichstag Fraction Members*

Age	1912 SPD	1919 SPD	1928 SPD	1928 KPD	1930 SPD	1930 KPD
20–30	1	1	1	2	0	8
30–40	10	19	23	33	20	47
40–50	51	71	49	17	49	20
50–60	30	59	56	1	51	1
60–70	13	14	21	0	22	0
Over 70	5	1	2	1	1	1
Total	110	165	152	54	143	77
Percentage						
Under 50	56	55	48	96	48	97
Over 50	44	45	52	4	52	3

53. The figures for 1912 and 1919 are tabulated from manuscript data graciously lent to me by Professor John L. Snell, who has presented a sociological survey of the 1912 fraction in "German Socialists in the Last Imperial Reichstag, 1912–1918," International Institute for Social History, *Bulletin,* 7 (1952), 196–205. Data for 1928 come from the *Reichstags-Handbuch, IV. Wahlperiode, 1928* (Berlin, 1928), p. 473; for 1930, from *Kürschners Volkshandbuch Deutscher Reichstag, 1930* (Berlin, n.d.), p. 10. Also see Theo Haubach, "Die Generationenfrage und der Sozialismus," *Soziologische Studien,* dedicated to Alfred Weber (Potsdam, Protte, 1930), p. 111 and passim.

What happened to the young men who "normally" would have been rising in Social Democracy? The answer leaps out in striking proportions—they were in the Communist Party! It is symbolic that the oldest deputy in the 1928 Reichstag was the octogenarian Social Democrat, Wilhelm Bock, who could remember the Eisenach congress he attended in 1869; the youngest was Konrad Blenckle, 27, a rising product of the Communist youth movement.[54]

Promising young workers and intellectuals of the uprooted Weimar generation were not usually attracted by the prosaic reformism of the SPD. Even those who did not stand to the left of the party leadership politically were bound to feel restless in the adult-controlled youth section, discouraged by the long apprenticeship awaiting them in the lower echelons of the apparatus, dismayed by the methods of advancement. The gifted young Social Democratic intellectual, Julius Leber—one of the "Young Turks" to be discussed below—wrote in retrospect of his Reichstag experience:

> The slightest advancement in the fraction was possible only with the help of the existing leaders. Whoever did not have this help either remained a nameless ballot porter or was treated with the deathly formality of an outsider. Every novice had to seek this help, his connection to the top, and thereby strengthened in his own way the gentle dominion of the hierarchy. Over the years there did arise out of the group several self-willed figures who, under certain circumstances, might have been able to give Social Democratic policies a different look. But they never appeared as a unified force. In actuality there was no younger generation.[55]

It should be mentioned that after 1930 the SPD made special efforts to advance its younger leaders, and new faces

54. *Reichstags-Handbuch, 1928,* p. 473.
55. *Mann,* p. 237.

began to appear in the Reichstag fraction.[56] This development came too late, however, to alter the fateful course set by the older generation, or to reverse the process of ossification that was settling on the movement.

Sixteen Social Democratic women deputies made up 11 per cent of the 1930 fraction (women comprised about 20 per cent of the total party membership). There were only thirty-nine women in the Reichstag at that time, and the SPD together with the KPD claimed twenty-eight, or 72 per cent of them.[57]

An analysis of the social composition of the fraction will throw light on the much-disputed question of the party's *Verbürgerlichung*.[58] First we may ask: Did an increasing proportion of leading Social Democrats come from bourgeois backgrounds? Table 4 shows the occupations in which the fraction members began their working lives.[59] Between 1903 and 1912 the percentage of middle-class leaders grew considerably, but the figure for 1930 is almost identical with that for 1912, showing no evidence of further Verbürger-

56. *Prot. 1931*, pp. 190–231, 294–95; Haubach, *Soziologische Studien*, pp. 112–13. The youth question is further discussed below, pp. 106–11.

57. *Kürschners Volkshandbuch, 1930*, p. 12.

58. *Verbürgerlichung* (*embourgeoisment* in French) is a word for which no widely accepted English equivalent exists. Literally it means "bourgeois-ification," that is, the process of making bourgeois. Originally it referred to the tendency of the working class to adopt or imitate a middle-class or lower middle-class style of life. The word is used here with reference to the SPD in a somewhat broader sense that will be discussed fully in chapter 4. (The term derives from the verb, *verbürgerlichen*, and its past participle is *verbürgerlicht*, or "bourgeois-ified.")

59. Data for 1903 come from Robert Michels, "Die deutsche Sozialdemokratie: Parteimitgliederschaft und soziale Zusammensetzung," *Archiv für Sozialwissenschaft und Sozialpolitik*, 23 (1906), 527; 1912, Snell, MS.; 1919, *Handbuch der verfassunggebenden Deutschen Nationalversammlung* (Berlin, 1919), passim; 1930, *Kürschners Volkshandbuch, 1930*, passim. Because of borderline cases and possible errors due to scanty information, this table must be taken only as a close approximation.

TABLE 4. *Original Occupational Status of Reichstag Fraction Members*

Occupational Status	1903	1912	1919	1930
Middle class				
Intellectuals	13	28	21	29
White collar	0	9	16	20
Working class				
Artisans, Skilled wkrs.	68	59	107	79
Unskilled wkrs.		2	14	11
Percentage				
Middle class	16	34	23	35
Working class	84	66	77	65

lichung, in this sense, during the Weimar period. Other indicators reinforce the same conclusion: 22 per cent of the 1912 SPD fraction had attended universities; 21 per cent of the 1930 fraction had done so. Those holding doctor's degrees made up 11 per cent of the earlier fraction, 9 per cent of the latter.[60]

One can also discern from Table 4 the remarkable degree to which the SPD drew its leadership from two social groups: intellectuals and skilled workers. The surprising lack of former unskilled workers in this group, combined with their scarcity in the membership at large (as we will observe in the next chapter), gives some credence to the idea that the Social Democratic movement was dominated by the "labor aristocracy," the most skilled and best-paid stratum of the working class.

Another important sense of the term, Verbürgerlichung, is implied in the question: How many SPD leaders exchanged

60. Snell, *Bulletin, 7,* 200; *Kürschners Volkshandbuch, 1930,* p. 17.

their proletarian occupations for bourgeois occupations during the course of their lives? Table 5 reveals the occupations listed by fraction members at the time of their election to the Reichstag.[61]

TABLE 5. *Current Occupations of*
Reichstag Fraction Members

Occupation	1903	1912	1919	1930
Party Secretaries	} 35 {	13	22	25
Trade-union officials		20	54	31
Other officials		7	18	26
Editors and writers	} 17 {	40	33	31
Other professions		7	6	9
Self-employed	29	22	15	3
Workers	0	1	9	3
Housewives	0	0	7	7

At no time in the period under scrutiny did actual workers make up more than a small proportion of the fraction. Almost all the originally proletarian leaders had advanced into white-collar occupations before they entered the Reichstag. The Verbürgerlichung of the fraction, in this sense, was virtually complete, and stood in sharp contrast to the Communist fraction. Thus in 1930, for example, 58 per cent of the KPD deputies (if we may believe their own testimony) were workers, as compared with 2 per cent of the SPD deputies.[62] The broader implications of the practically total Verbürgerlichung of the Social Democratic Reichstag fraction will be discussed in the next chapter.

61. Data for 1903 come from Michels, *Archiv für S. und S., 23,* 551–52; 1912 and 1919, Snell, MS.; 1930 *Kürschners Volkshandbuch, 1930,* p. 21 and passim. Here again, because of ambiguities and double occupations, the table must be accepted only as an approximation.
62. Ibid.

Table 5 also reveals a striking trend toward political professionalism. Deputies included in the first four occupational categories (party secretaries, trade-union officials, other officials,[63] editors and writers) almost all depended on the socialist movement in one way or another for their livelihood. And their number swelled from 64 per cent in 1903 to 73 per cent in 1912, to 77 per cent in 1919, to 84 per cent by 1930. Within the group, moreover, the share of officials (Beamten) grew most rapidly, reaching 61 per cent by 1930. Thus the paid bureaucrats of the movement came to dominate the party's Reichstag deputation.

Using all this sociological information, we might now attempt to construct the model of an SPD leader. Born of working-class parents, he would enter a skilled trade after an elementary formal education, but superior ability would soon open a door for him into the party or trade-union bureaucracy where the drudgery of administrative work would gradually erode away whatever idealistic radicalism or independent thinking he might have exhibited in his youth. As his practical experience grew he would advance slowly through the hierarchy. His income and white-collar status would increasingly separate him from the proletarian world out of which he came. By his late forties he would reach the level of national leadership and would hold a seat in the Reichstag as well as one or more prominent offices in the party or trade-union apparatus. Here, with an ossifying set of political conceptions, he would be secure for the rest of his life. In the broad Social Democratic leadership, then, we find the career of Otto Wels many times multiplied.

---

63. This category includes officials of the ancillary organizations as well as government officials, almost all of whom held "political" posts (ministers, mayors, etc.). Thus virtually all derived their living from the socialist movement in one way or another.

The bureaucratic deformation discussed in the last chapter and the oligarchic characteristics analyzed in this chapter were not unique to Social Democracy, but can be seen to a greater or lesser degree in other German parties and, indeed, in all modern political parties, as Michels so early recognized. The exact form and degree of these influences appear to vary according to the character of the party and according to the electoral system under which it operates.

The other German parties, for example, had never been internally democratic, but their prewar organizations had remained far less bureaucratic and centralized than the SPD. In 1918–19 all these parties were organizationally revamped to harmonize with the democratic spirit of the new Republic. Even the right-wing Nationalist Party established yearly congresses and made other concessions to the idea of popular-membership sovereignty.[64] In appearance, then, and ironically, the bourgeois parties were becoming internally more democratic at a time when the SPD was becoming less so. But appearances should not mask the underlying reality: the bourgeois parties, despite their statutory democratization, succumbed no less than the SPD to the encroachments of the bureaucracies they had created to run their election campaigns. Local autonomy and the independence of the parliamentarians were both eaten away by the central bureaucratic authority, while any close ties between leaders and followers were loosened or dissolved by the intrusion of the impersonal vote-getting apparatus. In the Weimar years the bourgeois parties acquired most of the bureaucratic attributes of Social Democracy without really losing their oligarchic traits.[65]

64. Werner Liebe, *Die Deutschnationale Volkspartei, 1918–1924* (Düsseldorf, 1956), pp. 34–39.

65. Karl Dietrich Bracher, *Die Auflösung der Weimarer Republik* (2d ed. Stuttgart and Düsseldorf, 1957), pp. 77–83. Detailed studies of the bourgeois party organizations in the Weimar period remain to be undertaken.

The list system of proportional representation used in the Weimar Republic, though often unjustly maligned, undoubtedly did much to encourage these bureaucratic and oligarchic tendencies. Large electoral districts necessarily diminished the possibility of close personal contact between the Reichstag deputy and his constituents. And since the selection (and ranking) of candidates was largely transferred from the local district to the regional level, a disproportionate influence was placed in the hands of regional bureaucrats who generally found favorable spots for themselves on the parties' lists. Such functionaries, many of them virtually unknown to the general public, tended to replace the old-style parliamentarians, as bitterly observed by Julius Leber:

> The list system simply excludes all those self-willed personalities who do not want to resign their fate to the party bureaucracy. In place of several hundred popularly elected and trusted men, there enters the rule of the organization and the secretariat. . . . The regime of the party bureaucrats —no matter where they come from—in the long run encourages a general mediocrity. It lacks the free competition of struggling personalities: men of strong character quickly fall into conflict with the all-powerful cliques and interest groups and become lonely outsiders.[66]

Certainly, speaking ability and personal charisma became all but superfluous in a system that compelled the voter to cast his ballot for a party list rather than an individual. The organization became the backbone of every campaign, making party affiliation an absolute necessity for all candidates. Their dependence upon the party machine was reflected in tighter fraction discipline and subordination to the central leadership. In these various ways, proportional representa-

66. *Mann,* p. 222.

tion gave encouragement to bureaucratic and oligarchic tendencies in all the Weimar parties.[67]

It would be a mistake, however, to suggest that these tendencies derive exclusively from proportional representation and would not exist without it. They stem also from the general requirements of electioneering in an era of mass democracy, where vast impersonal organizations necessarily eliminate the club-like quality of political life that existed among the enfranchised elites of nineteenth-century Europe. Michels had already documented the bureaucratic and oligarchic trends, with examples from many European countries, before the era of proportional representation. They were certainly apparent in German Social Democracy before 1914, and we have noted that the bourgeois parties also began the construction of bureaucratically run mass organizations prior to the war. Moreover, many of the same tendencies can be seen in countries that never introduced proportional representation. Ostrogorski was aware of their influence in Great Britain when he wrote his classic study in 1902,[68] and the recent work of Robert McKenzie confirms their continued existence. Analysis of British politics, he writes, shows "ample evidence of the working of what Michels calls the 'technical' and 'psychological' factors which tend to ensure the emergence of, and the retention of power by, a small group of leaders in each party." McKenzie notes the scant chances of candidates not supported by a party machine, the ever tighter discipline enforced by the party whips, and at least in the Labour Party the influence of the national organization in choosing candidates. The trend is clearly recogniz-

67. The most exhaustive analysis of the effects of proportional representation on German politics is still F. A. Hermens' bitterly critical *Democracy or Anarchy? A Study of Proportional Representation* (Notre Dame, Univ. of Notre Dame, 1941), pp. 214–300.

68. *Democracy and the Organization of Political Parties* (London, 1902).

able, although not so far advanced as in Germany. The author emphasizes that the parliamentary parties have not become mere servants or spokesmen of their mass organizations. "The 'law of oligarchy,' " he writes, "is certainly not an 'iron' law."[69]

The German Social Democrats developed, to be sure, under utterly different conditions, but in a sense one may apply McKenzie's conclusion to them as well. Although the SPD was probably the most bureaucratic of the Weimar parties, it was not necessarily the most oligarchic. The admittedly strong deformations of the party structure appear even stronger precisely because of its democratic organizational heritage—a heritage entirely lacking to the bourgeois parties. The principles of Eisenach, as we have seen, had not been entirely discarded by the SPD, and one might guess that, in spite of everything, it remained the least undemocratic of the major Weimar parties.[70]

69. *British Political Parties* (New York, St. Martin's, 1955), p. 587 and passim.

70. This must remain a guess until the appearance of detailed organizational studies of the other parties. Even then such judgments will undoubtedly remain controversial.

4. Party Members and Voters

Moving down the organizational pyramid, we direct our attention to the party membership, and beneath that to the Social Democratic vote. Concern with the social roots of the party's support leads to an examination of how and why the Social Democrats sought to transform themselves from a Klassenpartei (class party) into a Volkspartei (people's party, or party for all people).

Party Members

A sociological investigation of the Social Democratic membership is hampered by the lack of such complete statistical information as existed for the central party leadership. Nonetheless, we can treat such questions as gross membership fluctuation, social composition, and age distribution, the last of which leads to a consideration of the youth movement.

Gross membership figures in Table 6 disclose the relative decline of party strength in the later Weimar period after its success in the initial years.[1] The uninterrupted expansion of

1. These figures come from the annual executive reports in the *Protokolle* and, after 1925, the *Jahrbücher,* except for the last figure, which comes from Erich Matthias, "Die Sozialdemokratische Partei Deutschlands," *Das Ende der Parteien, 1933,* ed. Erich Matthias and Rudolf Morsey (Düsseldorf, 1960), p. 119, n. 2.

TABLE 6. *SPD Membership in the Weimar Period*

Date	Membership
April 1, 1914	1,085,905
April 1, 1918	249,411
1919	1,012,299
1920	1,180,208
1921	1,221,059
1922	1,174,106
1923	1,261,072
1924	940,078
1925	844,495
Jan. 1, 1926	806,268
1927	823,520
1928	867,671
1929	937,381
1930	1,021,777
1931	1,037,384
1932	1,008,953
Sept. 30, 1932	971,499

the Wilhelmian period had culminated in the much advertised million-member party of 1914. Then the war temporarily but drastically decimated SPD ranks, as the 1918 figure indicates. The revolution quickly restored prewar strength and stimulated further growth to a new height in 1921. But then losses to the Communist Party, the economic crisis, and other factors contributed to a five-year decline, in which the influx of 206,000 returning Independents (included in the 1923 figure) is scarcely noticeable. With the general economic recovery, membership swelled once more, though it never again equaled even the prewar figure. After 1931 another decline began to set in just before the demise of the Republic.

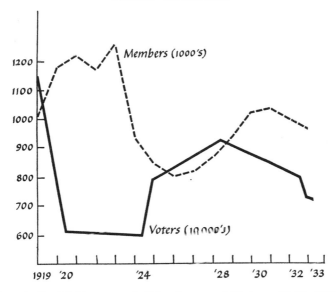

FIG. 1. Social Democratic Members and Voters, 1919–1933.

A comparison of the curve formed by membership fluctuation with a similar curve for voting strength (see Figure 1) shows a greater stability for members than for voters. The apex and nadir of the first curve are separated by 34 per cent of the peak figure, by 48 per cent for the second curve. This membership stability can be shown in another way: a 1930 SPD survey revealed that 21 per cent of the members had been in the party more than fifteen years; 27 per cent more than ten years; 53 per cent more than five years. Thus a quarter of the 1930 membership had been paying dues during the entire Weimar period, a fifth since before the war. Only 8 per cent were members of a single year's standing.[2] The SPD probably possessed the highest degree of membership stability of any of the Weimar parties, and contrasted particularly with the Communist Party which probably pos-

2. *Jahrbuch 1930*, pp. 194–95.

101

sessed the lowest. Of the 180,000 dues-paying Communists at the end of 1930, only 20.5 per cent had more than a year's standing; 143,000 had entered the party during the year, but 95,000 had left it.[3]

From a comparison of the two curves one may also perceive that the rise and fall of membership seemed to follow the rise and fall of votes, but with about a two-year delay. Note that the first peak of voting strength was 1919, of membership 1921; the low points were 1924 and 1926 respectively; and the second summits, 1928 and 1931. It is difficult to explain this delayed reaction. Probably success at the polls stimulated membership recruitment. Probably, too, there remained a greater loyalty among members in periods of decline. Thus in 1920 when almost half the Social Democratic voters had deserted to the Independents, the membership figure continued to climb. And in 1930 when the party suffered heavy voting losses to the KPD, membership held steady for the time being. Voters evidently responded more quickly to external circumstances than did members. In any event this lag caused the member:voter ratio to fluctuate considerably—1:5 in 1921, 1:10 in 1928. The latter figure comes closer to the Weimar norm and represents the best member : voter ratio of any of the German parties.[4]

In our examination of the social origins of Social Democratic parliamentary leaders, we discovered that in 1930, 35 per cent began their working lives in occupations above the proletarian level; of these, 21 per cent were bourgeois intellectuals. It would be interesting to contrast this distribution with that of the membership at large. Fortunately for our purposes, the party conducted an excellent survey of over

3. Siegfried Bahne, "Die Kommunistische Partei Deutschlands," *Ende der Parteien,* p. 661.

4. Sigmund Neumann, *Die deutschen Parteien, Wesen und Wandel nach dem Kriege* (Berlin, 1932), p. 123.

100,000 members in 1930, the results of which appear in Table 7.[5]

TABLE 7. *Occupational Breakdown of the 1930 SPD Membership*

Occupation	Percentage of Total Sample
I. Intellectuals	
Free professions	0.6
Teachers	0.9
II. Petty bourgeois	
Civil servants	3.1
Salaried employees	10.0
Self employed	4.2
III. Workers	
Skilled and semiskilled workers	53.0
Unskilled workers	5.4
Agricultural workers	1.1
IV. Other	
Housewives	17.1
Pensioners	4.6
Total	100.0

As might be expected, intellectuals formed a far greater portion of the leadership than of the rank and file. If one reckons the housewives (the bulk of whom must have been married to workers) in with category III, then the party membership was about three-quarters proletarian, about one-quarter nonproletarian. Women made up a quarter of the total sample and were distributed among themselves as follows: 0.4 per cent intellectuals, 8.1 per cent petty bourgeois, 17.8 per cent workers, 67.1 per cent housewives, and 6.6 per cent pensioners.

5. *Jahrbuch 1930*, p. 194.

103

Now in order to introduce a historical perspective, it will be necessary to exclude these women members from further consideration. Michels' study of the Leipzig and Frankfurt organizations in 1904 and 1905 was undertaken at a time when women were not permitted to belong to political parties. For comparative purposes Table 8 also includes a survey of Bremen, Hamburg, and Hannover members made in 1925 and 1926 (likewise excluding women).[6] The striking feature

TABLE 8. *Social Composition of the SPD Membership, 1905–1930, by Percentage*

Occupation	1905–06	1925–26	1930
I. Intellectuals	0.4	2.3	1.9
II. Petty bourgeois	6.4	17.2	21.2
III. Workers	93.2	80.5	76.9

of these statistics, insofar as they may be taken as typical, is the historical growth of the nonproletarian element in the membership. During the Weimar period the SPD became a "respectable" party. Sizable numbers of intellectuals were attracted to Social Democracy, especially after the decline of the Democrats, because of its role as the principal defender of the Republic.[7] Then the efforts of both the party and trade unions to organize among the lower middle classes substantially increased their weight in the membership. Category II would include some elements from the old middle class (peasants, independent craftsmen, shopkeepers) but chiefly

6. Robert Michels, "Die deutsche Sozialdemokratie, Parteimitgliederschaft und soziale Zusammensetzung," *Archiv für Sozialwissenschaft und Sozialpolitik, 23* (1906), 504–09; *Jahrbuch 1926*, p. 23; *Jahrbuch 1930*, p. 194.
7. S. Neumann, *Parteien*, p. 29.

elements from the new middle class (white-collar employees, civil servants), as may be discerned from Table 7.

The bulk of the rank and file remained wage workers. Within this category we may differentiate industrial from agricultural workers, and skilled from unskilled workers. With regard to the latter distinction, an analysis of the 1905 Munich membership revealed that 4,500 of the 5,000 working-class members were skilled—i.e. 90 per cent. In Marburg, a much smaller town, 94 per cent were in the skilled division.[8] The 1930 party survey revealed that 91.8 per cent of the male industrial workers fell into the skilled and semi-skilled category. Agricultural laborers never constituted an important element (only 1.8 per cent of all male workers in 1930.) There appears to be a great deal of truth in the Communist assertion that the SPD represented only the "labor aristocracy." It is impossible to tell, of course, what proportion of the party's *voting* strength came from unskilled labor, but of course, only *members* had any voice in party affairs. In general one may agree with the Social Democratic official who described the SPD as the party of those workers "who have more than just their chains to lose."[9]

On the other hand, our very limited statistical knowledge of the KPD does not reveal so sharp a contrast as might be expected. Among the 97,383 industrial workers who belonged to the Communist Party in 1927, 58.6 per cent were skilled.[10] While this percentage probably decreased in the subsequent depression years, it suggests that both socialist parties recruited disproportionately large numbers of skilled workers to membership. This very likely reflects a higher level of political understanding and commitment among

8. Harry Marks, "The Sources of Reformism in the Social Democratic Party of Germany, 1890–1914," *Journal of Modern History*, 9 (1939), 353.
9. Quoted in S. Neumann, *Parteien*, p. 29.
10. Bahne, *Ende der Parteien*, p. 660.

skilled workers, regardless of party affiliation. The Social Democratic figures must be understood within such a context.

Lack of data prohibits any analysis of the age distribution of the membership over a long period of time. We do have two studies done in the Weimar period, one of the Hannover and Bremen organizations in 1926, one of the 1930 sample mentioned above. The results are shown in Table 9.[11] The SPD was a party of middle-aged men and women. Over half its members had seen their fortieth birthday, while by 1930 the portion over 60 exceeded the portion under 25. For contrast—and a politically important contrast—one may note that 31.8 per cent of the KPD's 1927 membership was under 30 years old, compared to 17.3 per cent (1926) or 18.1 per cent (1930) for the SPD; 64.5 per cent of the Communist group were under 40 years old, but only 42.6 per cent (1926) or 44.6 per cent (1930) of the Social Democrats were under 40.[12] The party's chief youth organization, the Socialist Workers' Youth (14 to 20 years old), numbered 54,898 members in 1931, a ratio of 1:20 of regular party members. Juxtaposed, the Communist youth organization, while smaller in absolute terms (between 37,000 and 43,000 in 1931), achieved a ratio of 1:5.[13] Clearly Social Democracy was not reproducing itself adequately in the new generation. Bieligk wrote in 1931: "Whoever is active as a speaker

11. *Jahrbuch 1926*, p. 24; *Jahrbuch 1930*, p. 195.

12. Bahne, *Ende der Parteien*, p. 660. In absolute numbers, of course, the Communist membership was much smaller than the Social Democratic, so there is some justice in Ollenhauer's 1931 defense: "We have in the Party 80,000 members under 25 years old, and if we add in those between 20 [sic] and 35, then the Party has no fewer than 320,000 members under 35. . . . Thus we have more young people than the entire Communist Party has members." (*Prot. 1931*, p. 197.) The really crucial question, however, was not absolute numbers but replacement in the younger generation, and here the SPD, as indicated by the statistics above, was far outstripped by the KPD.

13. Bahne, *Ende der Parteien*, pp. 661, 666.

TABLE 9. *Age Distribution of the*
SPD Membership, by Percentage

Age	1926	1930
Under 25	7.7	7.8
25–30	9.6	10.3
30–40	25.3	26.5
40–50	30.4	27.3
50–60	20.2	19.6
Over 60	6.8	8.5
Total	100.0	100.0

in the various regions will confirm that there have been party meetings of thirty or more comrades in which no one under 25 was to be found, and only a few under 35. In the last year this has improved somewhat."[14]

The failure of the SPD to attract the younger generation stemmed in great part from external conditions. Young people just reaching maturity in the Weimar period could remember little of Wilhelmian Germany, could little appreciate the real accomplishments of the party in the Revolution. They had grown up in a time of war and social unrest; traditional values were collapsing; inflation and unemployment robbed them of a chance for a secure future. Under such circumstances the practical and prosaic reformism of Social Democratic politics could scarcely appeal to them. Indeed, the entire rationalistic structure of SPD ideology seemed out of harmony with the dominant mood of German youth. Far more in tune was the antirationalist nationalism of the Nazis, or the "barricade-romanticism" of the Communist Party.[15]

14. "Die Entwicklung der sozialdemokratischen Organisation in Deutschland," *Die Organisation im Klassenkampf* (Berlin, n.d. [1931]), p. 61.

15. Ibid., pp. 60–62; S. Neumann, *Parteien,* p. 32.

But if the times were unfavorable, the party elders did not help matters. Never sympathetic toward youthful exuberances, they did not even create a youth section until 1908 when independently organized socialist youth groups threatened to grow up outside the party household. At that time the leadership took care to see that the newly created movement was controlled by adults and safely steered away from political activity into "educational" work.[16] The young comrades chafed under this paternal regime, and in the revolutionary period they bolted in large numbers to the Independents and Communists.[17] These desertions, combined with other effects of the war—notably the draft—nearly extinguished the party youth movement. Its strength fell from 100,000 in 1913 to 36,643 in 1919.[18]

Reorganized after the Revolution as the Socialist Workers' Youth (SAJ) the group obtained somewhat more autonomy. But its governing body still accorded executive-appointed adults equal representation with youth leaders; the former were instructed to permit self-determination "as far as possible."[19] Like its predecessor, the SAJ was organized for the education of its members and not for political activity. Heinrich Schulz was the adult director, and Erich Ollenhauer and Max Westphal were the most prominent youth leaders. The group only once (in 1924) regained its prewar strength. For most of the Weimar period it could retain only 50,000 to 60,000 members.[20] Its composition must have been over-

16. Carl E. Schorske, *German Social Democracy, 1905–1917* (Cambridge, Mass., 1955), pp. 97–108, contains an excellent account of this early history.

17. Theo Haubach, "Die Generationenfrage und der Sozialismus," *Soziologische Studien,* dedicated to Alfred Weber (Potsdam, 1930), p. 111.

18. Schorske, *Social Democracy,* p. 271; *Prot. 1919,* p. 24.

19. Ibid., pp. 110–11.

20. Determined from the annual executive reports in the *Protokolle* and the *Jahrbücher.*

whelmingly working class: a special student organization numbered less than 2,000 in 1930.[21]

The SAJ included youths from 14 to 20 years old, but those over 18 were permitted to join the regular party. In 1920 a group of such young party members—from 18 to 25 —demanded and received sanction to hold special meetings and to organize themselves separately, but within the party, as the Young Socialists.[22] The movement began as a vague intellectual current of romantic, ethically based socialism, but in 1925 a radical Marxist segment, the "Hannover" wing, gained control, and the organization moved into the Left Social Democratic camp.[23] This proved too much for the conservative SPD leadership: in 1927 they tied the Young Socialists closely to the party educational committees, putting them under strict adult supervision. The radical mood among the youth, however, could not be quelled. Even a second reorganization in 1930 failed to produce the desired conformity.[24]

There obviously existed a gap and a conflict between the older and younger generations in the Weimar SPD. Theo Haubach has pinpointed the fundamental antagonism:

> The youth frequently saw the party of the grown-ups as flabby and tired, as over-cautious, as lacking will and conviction; on the other hand, the elders who had built and developed the party with unspeakable personal sacrifice felt bitterly that their work was endangered by these youthful muddle-heads.[25]

21. *Jahrbuch 1929*, p. 216.
22. *Prot. 1920*, pp. 318–19.
23. Bruno Neumann, "Wandlungen des Jungsozialismus," *Die Gesellschaft*, 3 (2) (1926), 516–17; *Prot. 1925*, p. 109; *Prot. 1927*, pp. 35–36, 85–86.
24. *Jahrbuch 1927*, pp. 220–21; *Jahrbuch 1930*, pp. 278–79.
25. *Soziologische Studien*, p. 110.

Besides the heavy hand of adult control and the conflict between generations, one of the most discouraging features of party life for promising young people was the long apprenticeship required before positions of leadership could be attained. Rapid advancement was possible in the KPD and the NSDAP, but Social Democracy had become too settled a movement. It appeared that before young comrades could be trusted with responsible posts, all signs of radicalism and independent thinking had to be worn away by the monotony of petty administrative work. Not until the 1930 election were the party elders shocked into a realization of their failure in the whole youth question. Ollenhauer was hastily scheduled to speak to the 1931 congress, where a new youth program was rushed through, one designed to encourage a more rapid absorption of young members into the hierarchy of the apparatus.[26] This crash program had some success; we have already noted that a few new faces appeared in the Reichstag fraction in the last years of the Republic. In 1931, Carl Litke was taken into the executive at the age of 34, and the executive shake-up of April 1933 brought in Ollenhauer at 32, Erich Rinner at 31, and Paul Hertz at 45.[27] But, of course, two months later the party was dissolved.

TABLE 10. *Membership of the Socialist Workers' Youth*

Date	Membership
Jan. 1, 1927	56,239
1928	55,342
1929	53,373
1930	55,958
1931	54,898
1932	50,465

26. *Prot. 1931*, pp. 190–231, 294–95.
27. Lewis J. Edinger, *German Exile Politics* (Berkeley and Los Angeles, 1956), p. 24.

110

While some younger people were absorbed into the hierarchy, the 1931 program produced no permanent improvement in the general recruitment of youth. Thus the figures for SAJ membership fluctuate as shown in Table 10.[28] The recovery of 1930–31 had exhausted itself by the beginning of the next year. The Ollenhauer program had come too late; in this period, radicalized working-class youths were not looking for a call to the bureaus but for a call to the barricades.

The Social Democratic Vote

Beyond the circle of SPD party members lay a circle, about ten times larger, of Social Democratic voters. To complete the sociological survey the characteristics of this broader group must now be described, insofar as that is possible.

First let us examine the pattern formed by the fluctuations of SPD voting strength in the entire Weimar period. Table 11 indicates this strength both in absolute figures and in percentages of the total vote, together with the number of deputies returned in each of the Reichstag elections, beginning with the National Assembly contest of January 19, 1919.[29]

A sense of stagnation emerges from these figures. After half a century of almost continuous, apparently inexorable expansion, the movement ceased to grow. Already in 1913, according to Schorske, many signs of stagnation were manifest.[30] In this light the National Assembly election must be counted as a mere temporary enthusiasm of the revolutionary period. After 1919 the party was never able to attain even its prewar peak of 34.7 per cent. Of course, the loss of the radical wing accounts partially for the electoral disappoint-

28. Taken from the annual executive reports in the *Jahrbücher*.
29. Koppel S. Pinson, *Modern Germany* (New York, 1954), pp. 574–75.
30. *Social Democracy*, pp. 267–69.

TABLE 11. *The Social Democratic Vote in Reichstag Elections 1919–1933*

Election	Vote	Percentage	Deputies
1919	11,509,100	37.9	163
1920	6,104,400	21.7	102
May 1924	6,008,900	20.5	100
Dec. 1924	7,881,000	26.0	131
1928	9,153,000	29.8	153
1930	8,577,700	24.5	143
July 1932	7,959,700	21.6	133
Nov. 1932	7,248,000	20.4	121
1933	7,181,600	18.3	120

ments of the Weimar years. One must add together the figures for the SPD, the USPD, and the KPD in order to obtain a balanced perspective of the socialist movement as a whole. The combined statistics for the three Marxist parties fluctuate as shown in Table 12.[31] Here we have simply stagnation

TABLE 12. *Combined Vote of Marxist Parties in Reichstag Elections 1919–1933*

Election	Vote	Percentage	Deputies
1919	13,826,400	45.5	185
1920	11,740,700	41.6	190
May 1924	9,702,200	33.1	162
Dec. 1924	10,590,100	35.0	176
1928	12,417,800	40.4	207
1930	13,169,800	37.6	220
July 1932	13,242,300	36.2	222
Nov. 1932	13,228,200	37.3	221
1933	12,029,700	30.6	201

31. Pinson, *Modern Germany*, pp. 574–75.

at a higher level. After the Revolution, the percentage figure —the most accurate index—settled down to include slightly over one-third of the population. The inability of the German socialist movement to renew its expansion after 1919, to break through the "one-third barrier," wrought tremendous psychological damage, particularly upon the SPD. Before the war the ultimate socialist victory seemed assured; each election brought fresh proof of the Marxist doctrine of inevitability. But Weimar elections served only to confute that doctrine, and Social Democracy appeared doomed to become nothing more than the permanent parliamentary lobby for organized labor.

It is also instructive to contrast the separate voting patterns of the three Marxist parties. Figure 2 shows the curve formed by the fluctuations in Social Democratic election returns during the Weimar period set against similar curves for the Independents and the Communists. Nothing illustrates more pointedly the new role of the SPD in German politics. The November Revolution was the last national crisis from which the party drew strength, as a socialist party seemingly should in crises of capitalist society. In 1919 the SPD won more votes than ever before, and outstripped the Independents by more than four to one. The very next year, however, drastically transformed this picture: continued crisis and social unrest under Social Democratic ministries, the Kapp Putsch, and other factors evoked a sharp decline in party strength. Many socialists shifted to the USPD, which now boasted 17.9 per cent of the vote, almost equaling the Majority portion. This election also brought the Communist Party onto the electoral scene with 2.1 per cent. The May 1924 contest was likewise a radical one, occurring only shortly after the great inflation and the manifold crises of 1923. Here again the SPD lost votes, falling to 20.5 per cent. A majority of those who cast ballots for the Independents in 1920 now continued their leftward journey into the KPD, which captured 12.6 per cent of the May 1924 vote. For a host of reasons the Social Democrats had been unable to utilize their revolutionary mandate to create a stable, semisocialist state,

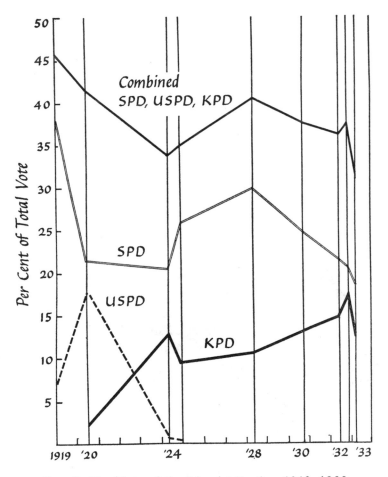

FIG. 2. The Vote of the Marxist Parties, 1919–1933.

and the subsequent five years of continuous unrest brought them nothing but defeats.

December 1924 marked electorally the return of stability under the Dawes Plan. Significantly, the Social Democratic vote now rose, as did the strength of the bourgeois parties, while the Communists and Nazis lost votes. As the country attained greater heights of prosperity in 1928, so the SPD reached a new level of popularity with 29.8 per cent, the biggest victory since 1919. To complete the pattern, one need only observe that the three depression elections of 1930 and 1932 brought a progressive diminution of Social Democratic strength, down to 20.4 per cent—almost exactly the same as the 1924 nadir. Correspondingly, the KPD forged ahead from 10.6 per cent in 1928 to 16.9 per cent in the last free election.

The new role of the SPD emerges fully from these electoral statistics. In 1919 it still functioned as a radical opposition party to which voters flocked in their disillusionment with the war and the Second Empire. But after that date Social Democracy became a *party of order*. It is interesting to note that party treasurer Friedrich Bartels explained the losses of the early Weimar period by the following reasoning: "There was the economic distress of the last years, under which broad circles of the working class had to suffer, and still suffer today. Unemployment, inflation, low wages—all furthered political indifference."[32] The Communists did not notice this strange indifference! When a socialist party explains its losses by citing unemployment, inflation, and low wages, clearly it no longer operates as a vehicle of social discontent. After the Revolution the SPD became a government party: when the Republic and the economy prospered, the SPD also prospered, but when they faltered and suffered

32. *Prot. 1925*, p. 108.

115

crises, the SPD did likewise. The Communists, and later the Nazis as well, took up Social Democracy's old calling as the party of discontent.

These conclusions require a further and somewhat paradoxical refinement. The SPD usually lost votes when it was in office, and gained votes when out of office. The disappointing 1920, May 1924, and 1930 elections were all held either during or shortly after ministries in which the Social Democrats shared power, and the losses of July 1932 occurred within the context of the toleration policy. The victories of December 1924 and of 1928, on the other hand, took place when the party was formally in opposition. Because it accepted governmental responsibility without a parliamentary majority, the SPD was never able to accomplish as much as its supporters would have liked. The Social Democratic coalition governments were bound to produce disappointingly little and lead to electoral losses. Conversely, in the two elections that took place during the five-year stable period of the Weimar Republic, the party profited from opposition to the governing coalitions. It could exploit the various advantages which the "outs" have against the "ins" in any election. But such opposition proved advantageous only so long as it occurred within a context of general stability. In crisis elections this mechanism did not work, as is indicated by the November 1932 returns when even a vigorous campaign against Papen's "cabinet of barons" failed to arrest Social Democratic decline. The party suffered, despite its formal opposition to the ruling coalition, because it was in a deeper sense a government party. It was the principal supporter of the Weimar Republic, the discredited existing order which was then experiencing its final death agonies.

The electoral decline of the SPD in the depression, set against spectacular Nazi victories, has suggested to some observers a mass transference of popular support from the one

116

party to the other. This is seen as part of a broader pattern of working-class backing for Hitler. By adding nationalism to socialism, it is argued, the Nazis were able to outbid the Marxist parties for the allegiance of the German proletariat. The attractive simplicity of this thesis is deceptive for closer statistical analysis betrays no such mass migration of socialist voters into Hitler's camp.

Table 12 (above) reveals a surprisingly constant percentage for the combined Marxist parties in the period of Nazi expansion. From the 1928 total of 40.4 per cent there is a drop of only 4.2 percentage points to the July 1932 figure of 36.2 per cent. Even this figure is deceptive, since 1928 was an unusually good year for both the Social Democrats and the Communists. If one starts from the December 1924 figure of 35 per cent, it can be argued that the Marxist parties lost only the marginal votes of 1928 and not the solid core of their support. Proceeding from still different statistical foundations, Heinrich Striefler concludes that the two socialist parties contributed only three of every one hundred votes the Nazis won between 1928 and July 1932.[33] The election of 1933 cannot, of course, be compared with the others since it took place under such a reign of terror that 30.6 per cent is more a victory than a defeat. The losses of the SPD, then, were almost entirely compensated by Communist gains. Since the KPD had no other important recruiting ground, we may assume that the great bulk of disillusioned Social Democratic voters moved into the Communist rather than the Nazi camp.

There were, of course, workers in the Nazi movement, including some who were formerly Social Democrats or Communists. What is important is that no *mass* migration oc-

33. *Deutsche Wahlen in Bildern und Zahlen* (Düsseldorf, Wende, 1946), p. 47.

curred; thousands of workers may have transferred their allegiance to the NSDAP, but not millions. The Nazis got their millions from another source. Virtually all serious analysts are agreed that the overwhelming majority of Nazi electoral support came from Protestant lower middle-class people who previously had voted for the bourgeois parties, or had not voted at all.[34] Starting in 1928 with 2.6 per cent of the total vote the NSDAP shot up to 37.4 per cent by July 1932—a net gain of 34.8 percentage points. The same period saw the decimation of the (non-Catholic) bourgeois parties: their combined net loss was 31.2 percentage points, or approximately eleven million voters![35]

The point can be made even more dramatically in graph form, using absolute figures and reckoning in the behavior of nonvoters. Figure 3 shows the gains and losses, in millions of votes, from one election to the next for (A) the Nazi Party, (B) the combined total of the non-Catholic bourgeois parties *and* nonvoters,[36] and (C) the combined total of the Marxist parties. The remarkable mirror opposites produced by lines

34. The principal statistical studies of this subject include: Striefler, *Wahlen;* James K. Pollock, "An Areal Study of the German Electorate, 1930–1933," *American Political Science Review, 38* (1944); Charles P. Loomis and J. Allen Beegle, "The Spread of German Nazism in Rural Areas," *American Sociological Review, 11* (1946); Rudolf Heberle, *From Democracy to Nazism* (Baton Rouge, 1945); Meinrad Hagman, *Der Weg ins Verhängnis* (Munich, 1946); Gunther Franz, *Die politischen Wahlen in Niedersachsen, 1867 bis 1949* (3d ed. Bremen-Horn, 1957); S. S. Nilson, "Wahlsoziologische Probleme des Nationalsozialismus," *Zeitschrift für die Gesamte Staatswissenschaft, 110* (1954), 279–311; Karl Dietrich Bracher, *Die Auflösung der Weimarer Republik* (2d ed. Stuttgart and Düsseldorf, 1957); Alfred Milatz, "Das Ende der Parteien im Spiegel der Wahlen 1930 bis 1933," *Ende der Parteien,* pp. 743–93; and Seymour M. Lipset, *Political Man, The Social Bases of Politics* (New York, 1960).

35. Pinson, *Modern Germany,* pp. 574–75.

36. Nonvoters are figured in negatively. Thus when fewer people vote, this represents a "gain" for nonvoters; when more people vote, it represents a "loss."

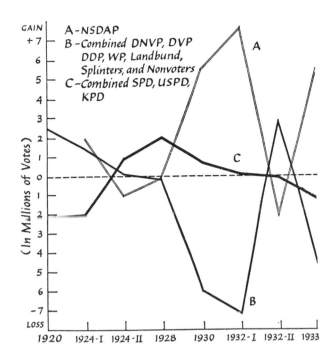

FIG. 3. The Sources of the Nazi Vote
(adapted from Heinrich Striefler, *Deutsche Wahlen in Bildern
und Zahlen* [Düsseldorf, Wende, 1946], p. 27).

A and B after 1928 give enormous cogency to the view that
the NSDAP won its support from the bourgeois parties and
from former nonvoters. As the Nazis gained strength, the
other group lost correspondingly. Even the reversal of November 1932 is faithfully reflected. The graph reveals no
such correspondence between Nazi strength and the fluctuations of the socialist parties. Quite the contrary, the Marxist
parties picked up small numbers of voters in the same elections that saw Nazi expansion, and they lost in a similar pattern (except for the special case of 1933).

Gross election returns for the entire nation cannot meet certain more subtle objections to the picture presented here. They would not reveal, for instance, a mutual exchange of votes between the KPD and the NSDAP, nor would they disclose heavy Communist losses to the Nazis if these losses were made up for by a Social Democratic influx that was in turn compensated by a heavy liberal shift into the SPD camp. A scrutiny of local and regional returns, however, does not suggest that there were any *large-scale* hidden transfers of this sort.[37]

In general, then, the Communists rather than the Nazis received the main benefit of SPD decline. It was much more natural for disillusioned Social Democrats to move one step left to a party sharing the same ideological and organizational heritage than to transfer their allegiance to a party whose entire Weltanschauung was alien to their experience.[38] This also helps explain the exceptional loyalty demonstrated by the German working class as a whole to its traditional Marxist parties at a time when millions of other voters were abandoning their former political ties to embrace Nazism.

We must turn our attention next to the geographical distribution of the Social Democratic vote. In broad outline, as might be expected, heavily industrialized regions returned more Social Democratic votes than did the rural, and Protestant areas gave more support than did the Catholic. For purposes of analysis, four electoral regions have been selected on the basis of their high degree of economic and religious homogeneity (Tables 13–16). Two regions are rural, one in a Protestant area and one in a Catholic area; the other two are urban, similarly divided. Results are given in percentage of the total vote for the socialist parties, for the most important nonsocialist contender, and for the Nazis. Four elec-

37. See especially Heberle, *Democracy to Nazism,* passim.
38. See above, pp. 40–41.

tions are included, those marking the high and low tides of Social Democratic popularity.

1. Rural Protestant: East Prussia. Here 42.2 per cent of the population found employment in agriculture, 56.9 per cent lived in communities of less than 2,000 inhabitants, and 15.6 per cent were Catholic.[39] The election results for this region are given in Table 13.[40] In 1919 the SPD made an

TABLE 13. *Regional Vote: East Prussia*

Election	KPD	USPD	SPD	DNVP	NSDAP
1919		6.2	43.5	12.8	
May 1924	11.7		15.3	38.9	8.6
1928	9.5		26.8	31.4	0.8
July 1932	12.9		19.7	9.5	47.1

excellent showing in this type of region, evidently having won over most of the rural lower classes, both agricultural laborers and small peasants. Heberle's superb analysis of Schleswig–Holstein confirms this hypothesis and further demonstrates that after 1919 the bulk of the peasantry took their votes elsewhere, in later years most notably to the Nazis.[41] But the SPD managed to establish a permanent base among the rural proletariat, which stands as a signal accomplishment of the Weimar party. One usually thinks of Social

39. These figures, and the corresponding figures for three other regions to be dealt with, come from Striefler, *Wahlen*, Appendix, Table 2.

40. The statistics for this and the next three tables come from the following sources: 1919, *Statistik des Deutschen Reiches, 291* (1), 96–97; 1924, ibid., *315*, 6–7; 1928 and 1932, Wilhelm Dittmann, *Das politische Deutschland vor Hitler* (Zürich, 1945). The figures for 1919 have been reworked to accord with the permanent electoral divisions established in the following year.

41. *Democracy to Nazism*, pp. 41–42, 94–99; Franz, *Niedersachsen*, passim.

121

Democracy as an urban movement, yet in 1920 32 per cent of its votes came from communities of less than 2,000 inhabitants, mostly in the territory east of the Elbe.[42] Rural Catholic areas, however, contributed only a small portion of this support.

2. Rural Catholic: Lower Bavaria (Table 14). Here 47.3 per cent of the population were in agriculture; 71 per cent rural; 95.9 per cent Catholic. It will be seen that the Social

TABLE 14. *Regional Vote: Lower Bavaria*

Election	KPD	USPD	SPD	BVP	NSDAP
1919		12.7	25.9	49.7	
May 1924	7.1		9.2	39.2	10.2
1928	2.2		15.3	43.7	3.5
July 1932	8.2		11.2	48	20.4

Democratic share ran about 10 percentage points lower than in East Prussia, while the Center (actually the Bavarian People's Party—BVP) polled considerably more votes than the Nationalists (DNVP) in East Prussia. Part of this may be explained by the difference in the predominant form of landholding. In Bavaria the land was tilled chiefly by small peasants, and the agricultural proletariat remained small. Nonetheless it seems true that Catholic conservatism had a greater hold on the rural masses than did its Protestant counterpart, which left Social Democracy much weaker. Also note that the Centrists' strength, unlike that of the DNVP, defied any significant encroachments by the Nazis. Let us now turn to the urban distribution.

3. Urban Protestant: Hamburg (Table 15). A scant 2.1 per cent of the population in agriculture; 1.3 per cent rural;

42. Striefler, *Wahlen,* p. 55.

TABLE 15. *Regional Vote: Hamburg*

Election	KPD	USPD	SPD	DNVP	NSDAP
1919		8.9	51.4	3	
May 1924	18.3		27.7	19.5	6
1928	16.8		36.8	12.8	2.6
July 1932	17.7		31.7	5.2	33.7

5.2 per cent Catholic. Here the SPD controlled an absolute majority in 1919, reflecting its strength among the large Hamburg working class, but including no doubt many non-proletarian votes as well. A sizable percentage of the workers, however, soon went over to the KPD, while the bourgeois parties began to win back middle-class voters. Throughout, Social Democratic strength remained about 8 percentage points above its national level, about 11 percentage points above its rural Protestant level, and approximately twice the size of the Communist vote. This represented the usual pattern for Protestant cities.

4. Urban Catholic: Cologne–Aachen (Table 16). Here 11.5 per cent of the population were in agriculture; 14.2 per cent rural; 82.7 per cent Catholic. The SPD met with more success here than in Catholic rural areas, though the gap is narrower than between the corresponding Protestant areas. Note, however, that the Social Democrats and Communists

TABLE 16. *Regional Vote: Cologne–Aachen*

Election	KPD	USPD	SPD	Z	NSDAP
1919		0.6	25.9	58.9	
May 1924	14.2		10.1	48.5	1.5
1928	10.4		18.5	42	1.1
July 1932	17.5		14.6	40.5	20.2

together formed a serious threat to Center hegemony. Their combined voting power reached 32.1 per cent by 1932. Catholic workers proved more receptive than Catholic peasants to the wooing of the Marxist parties. Johannes Schauff has reckoned that in the December 1924 election only 56 per cent of Germany's Catholics voted for the Center or the BVP; 12.1 per cent cast their ballots for the SPD and 6.5 per cent for the KPD.[43] Naturally this movement manifested itself chiefly in urban areas where industrial conditions and anticlericalism joined forces to lessen Center popularity.

It is most interesting to observe that in the two crisis elections the Communists won more backing in Cologne–Aachen than did the Social Democrats. This was no isolated phenomenon; in all the industrial regions of the Rhine and Ruhr, together with Catholic Upper Silesia, the KPD performed similar feats in the radical elections. And only two Protestant regions (Berlin and Merseburg) gave the Communists such a plurality.[44] To explain this phenomenon, several considerations suggest themselves. By coincidence German heavy industry grew up largely in Catholic areas. Traditionally, workers in mining and metallurgy showed radical preferences regardless of religion, as the returns in the Protestant region of Merseburg imply.[45]

Yet religion does appear to be involved. Cologne is primarily a commercial rather than an industrial city, yet it returned 22 per cent for the KPD and only 18.4 per cent for the SPD in July 1932.[46] Franz' statistics show the same

43. *Die deutschen Katholiken und die Zentrumspartei* (Cologne, 1928), quoted in Striefler, *Wahlen,* pp. 51–52.

44. Dittmann, *Das politische Deutschland.*

45. During the war the enormous Leunawerk, a synthetic nitrate plant, had grown up in the electoral region of Merseburg, alongside its lignite-mining and metallurgical industries; this added great strength to the radical forces.

46. Bracher, *Auflösung,* p. 649.

phenomenon on a diminutive scale even for the Catholic rural areas in the southwestern corner of Lower Saxony; these were the only areas in Lower Saxony ever to give the Communists more votes than the Social Democrats, though both parties did poorly.[47] On a national scale Schauff reckons that the KPD had the *least* Protestant electorate of any of the non-Catholic parties—69 per cent as compared with 78 per cent for the SPD.[48] It appears that Catholic workers who abandoned the party of their religion in the unstable years of the Weimar Republic found the Communists a more natural alternative than the Social Democrats. Despite vast differences, Catholicism and Communism do share certain common characteristics: both are highly authoritarian in spirit and organization; both provide their believers with an all-embracing Weltanschauung, with "correct" opinions on every conceivable subject; and both tend to be intolerant of rival world views. The high Communist vote in Catholic France and Italy lends additional weight to this interpretation.

But other complications intrude. French Protestants vote even more heavily Communist than do French Catholics.[49] Seymour Lipset points out that minority groups are often impelled leftward by a "degrading discrimination in social relations."[50] Just as Protestants are a minority in France, Catholics are a minority in Germany, albeit a much larger one. This explanation of high Communist voting can be tested by certain differences among the various Catholic areas of Germany. The Catholics of Rhineland–Westphalia and Upper Silesia clearly have more of a minority-group

---

47. *Niedersachsen,* passim.

48. *Katholiken,* quoted in Bracher, *Auflösung,* p. 91.

49. Stuart R. Schram, *Protestantism and Politics in France* (Alençon, 1954), p. 185 and passim.

50. Lipset, *Political Man,* pp. 232, 242–48.

status in Protestant Prussia than have their co-religionists in traditionally Catholic Bavaria. Significantly, urban returns in Bavaria do not show such unusually high Communist percentages. In industrial Augsburg, for example, the KPD took only 12.8 per cent of the July 1932 vote, whereas the Social Democrats captured a more impressive 26.7 per cent.[51]

A final consideration is that many Catholic workers of Upper Silesia and not a few in the Ruhr were Polish rather than German. Their double minority position—as Catholics and as members of a low-status Slavic nationality—probably pushed them to the extreme left in large numbers.

Anna Siemsen wrote in 1928 that the reasons for Social Democratic weakness and Communist strength in Rhineland –Westphalia were "so well known that they scarcely need to be enumerated." She cited the following:

> The influence of Catholicism, large foreign elements interspersed within the working class and therefore a lack of solidarity, the sudden growth of industry hand in hand with the terror of the employers as a hindrance to thorough [Social Democratic] propaganda and education, finally the catastrophes of the Ruhr occupation which have so torn and decomposed the party [SPD] that a half-way healthy and normal development will be tied up for a long time still.[52]

Whatever the reasons for the heavier Communist vote in Catholic areas, this is a highly interesting phenomenon, contrasting as it does so sharply with the voting patterns of the SPD, and it deserves far more extensive study than can be given here.

Turning next to the distribution of the vote by sex, we may touch briefly on the role of women in the SPD. The party

51. Bracher, *Auflösung*, p. 650.
52. In *Leipziger Volkszeitung*, Sept. 1928, as quoted in Kurt Koszyk, *Zwischen Kaiserreich und Diktatur, Die sozialdemokratische Presse von 1914 bis 1933* (Heidelberg, 1958), p. 190.

had not always championed women's suffrage; the Lassalleans opposed it, and only in 1891 did it become part of the official program. In 1908 women were first permitted by law to join political parties. Beginning in that year with 40,000 members (7 per cent of the total party membership), the Social Democratic women's movement grew steadily to 175,000 (16 per cent) by 1914.[53] The war gave an enormous stimulus to the feminist cause in general, and the November Revolution brought complete universal suffrage at last. In March 1919 the SPD claimed 206,354 women members, or 20 per cent of its total membership. Thereafter, the proportion of female members remained relatively constant, fluctuating slightly around the 20 per cent figure.[54]

There has been considerable debate whether the SPD, by introducing women's suffrage in 1919, actually defeated its own chances of obtaining a majority, since women tend to vote more conservatively than men. Not enough evidence exists to settle the question decisively. In the few localities where divided polls were taken, however, the results do indicate that more men than women voted for the SPD, and that the latter tended to give their ballots to the parties favored by the church (i.e. the Nationalists in Protestant regions, the Center in Catholic ones). Thus in the Catholic city of Cologne in 1919, the Social Democrats received 46.1 per cent of the male vote, but only 32.2 per cent of the female vote (together: 38.6 per cent). The Center, on the other hand, obtained 32.9 per cent of the male ballots and 47.6 per cent of the female (together: 40.8 per cent).[55] In general, the SPD got less support from women in rural areas than in ur-

53. Hans Beyer, *Die Frau in der politischen Entscheidung* (Stuttgart, 1933), pp. 56–58.
54. *Prot. 1919*, p. 54; *Jahrbuch 1929*, p. 169.
55. Max Schneider, "Die Deutsche Wählerin," *Die Gesellschaft, 4* (2) (1927), 368.

ban, and less in Catholic than in Protestant. After analyzing all the available evidence, Hans Beyer concludes that the Social Democrats by themselves probably would not have won an all-male election in 1919 but that, combined with the Independents, a clear majority would have been theirs.[56] In all likelihood, then, by carrying out its program in this regard the SPD destroyed the possibility of a purely socialist government.

The later years of the Republic brought a relative equalization in the male and female support of Social Democracy. In 1920 the available data show that of every 100 votes cast for the party, 57 came from men, 43 from women. But by May 1924 the disproportionality had dropped to 52:48, where it remained more or less constant for the rest of the Weimar period.[57] Thus it would appear that the SPD never actually gained from the introduction of women's suffrage, but that its losses were reduced as years went on. The reduction can be attributed partly to the vigorous agitation of the Social Democratic women's branch, partly to the growing respectability of the party.

The remaining method of breaking down the vote is by social class. The foregoing geographical analysis, illuminating as it is, cannot by its nature reveal which Social Democratic votes came from proletarians and which from people in higher strata. Information of this sort would be a valuable complement to the social dissections of the party leadership and membership that have been given earlier. R. Blank has estimated that already in 1903 at least 25 per cent of the SPD's electoral backing derived from nonproletarian sources. To be sure, he used a narrow definition of "proletarian" which excluded agricultural day laborers, but he argued that

56. *Frau,* pp. 61–64, 66.
57. Franz, *Niedersachsen,* pp. 28–31; Striefler, *Wahlen,* pp. 20–21; Beyer, *Frau,* pp. 65–66.

128

such laborers composed an "insignificant" portion of the total Social Democratic vote. If so, then the 25 per cent figure may be taken as an estimate of the proportion of middle-class support in 1903.[58]

The gains of the revolutionary period undoubtedly pushed this percentage upward, as many peasants in the country, and in the cities a great many petty bourgeois (white-collar employees, lesser civil servants, self-employed artisans), together with intellectuals, came over to Social Democracy. This was also the period of important gains among the rural proletariat. But then came the great exodus to the USPD and the KPD, an exodus which must have been composed principally of industrial workers, and which therefore left the party with a relatively larger proportion of middle-class support. This support likewise dwindled as peasants and many urban petty bourgeois reverted to their traditional voting habits after 1919. But the SPD retained throughout the Weimar period a substantial body of backers among the lower middle classes.[59]

Hans Neisser has estimated that 40 per cent of the party's vote in 1930 came from nonproletarian sources. Like Blank he included agricultural laborers in this category. But by reworking his data, one may break down the total Social Democratic vote of 1930 into the following components (needless to say, these figures are all estimates): 70 per cent proletarian voters, of whom 60 per cent were industrial and 10 per cent agricultural; 30 per cent petty bourgeois, including 8 per cent white-collar employees, 6 per cent civil serv-

58. "Die soziale Zusammensetzung der sozialdemokratischen Wählerschaft Deutschlands," *Archiv für Sozialwissenschaft und Sozialpolitik, 20* (1920), 513–20.

59. These trends indicated by Heberle, *Democracy to Nazism*, pp. 3, 41–42; Bieligk, *Organisation im Klassenkampf*, pp. 50–51; and Eugen Varga (ed.), *Die sozialdemokratischen Parteien* (Hamburg, 1926), p. 45.

ants and other officials, 6 per cent independent artisans and shopkeepers, 6 per cent small peasants, and 4 per cent pensioners and miscellaneous.[60] Thus the proportion of industrial workers had dropped since 1903 from 75 per cent to 60 per cent, while the proportion of petty bourgeois had risen by perhaps 5 per cent. Agricultural laborers accounted for the remainder. It must be remembered, also, that the 1930 election marked the first surge of the depression-struck middle strata to the banners of the Nazi party. If Neisser had analyzed an earlier election he probably would have found an even larger proportion of petty bourgeois votes.

Clearly, then, in the Weimar period the SPD ceased to be exclusively the class party of the industrial proletariat. That this happened was no accident but the result of a deliberate effort by the party to expand beyond its traditional sphere of influence. The principal features of this policy, and the reasons behind it follow.

From Class Party to People's Party

The various evidences of stagnation cited earlier in this chapter did not, of course, go unnoticed by the Social Democrats themselves. We have already observed their efforts to break out in the recruitment of youth and women. A further effort to smash through the one-third barrier necessitated a social expansion beyond the confines of the industrial working class into the lower middle classes. Such an effort was undertaken during the Weimar years and involved the conscious transformation of the SPD into a Volkspartei, a party for all people. It anticipated the recent and more ambitious attempt of the Bonn SPD to do the same thing.

60. Hans Neisser, "Sozialstatistische Analyse des Wahlergebnisses," *Die Arbeit*, 7 (1930), 655, 657–58.

There were several reasons for the electoral stagnation of the Weimar Social Democrats, apart from the obvious competition of the Communists, reasons which prevented even the two parties combined from winning an absolute majority. The previous, seemingly ineluctable growth of the socialist movement had taken place within a context of general population expansion. Between 1870 and 1914 Germany's population jumped from 41 to 67.8 million, but the combined effects of the First World War—war dead, lowered birth rate, territorial losses—cut back this figure to 61.8 million in 1920. Only slowly did an upturn assert itself, and by the end of the republican years Germany still had not recovered her prewar numbers (66 million in 1933). Even more fundamental as a cause of stagnation was the leveling off in the size of the industrial proletariat itself. The prewar expansion of Social Democracy was closely linked to the rapid growth of an urban working class spawned by the industrial revolution. In the Weimar period, however, a faltering rate of industrial growth combined with technological developments to reduce the need for blue-collar workers.

The relative numerical decline of this class played havoc with the traditional Marxist sociological conceptions of the SPD. In the *Communist Manifesto* Marx and Engels had depicted with a few bold strokes the changes they expected in the class structure of capitalist society:

> In proportion as the bourgeoisie, i.e., capital, is developed, in the same proportion is the proletariat, the modern working class, developed—a class of laborers, who live only so long as they find work, and who find work only so long as their labor increases capital.

> The bourgeoisie has stripped of its halo every occupation hitherto honored and looked up to with reverent awe. It has converted the physician, the lawyer, the priest, the poet, the man of science, into its paid wage-laborers.

131

The lower strata of the middle class—the small trades-people, shopkeepers, and retired tradesmen generally, the handicraftsmen and peasants—all these sink gradually into the proletariat. . . . Thus the proletariat is recruited from all classes of the population.

All previous historical movements were movements of minorities, or in the interest of minorities. The proletarian movement is the self-conscious, independent movement of the immense majority, in the interest of the immense majority.[61]

Thus Marx and Engels fully anticipated that, by the time of the workers' revolution, the "immense majority" of the population would have been proletarized, and would be in the communist camp.

The actual development of the class structure in industrial countries since 1848 has taken, of course, quite a different path. For Germany, in barest outline, one may say that, while concentration proceeded apace in some industries, others remained largely in the hands of small producers. Agriculture seemed almost totally immune to the law of concentration, and retail trade only somewhat less so. Thus a substantial independent petty bourgeoisie still existed in the Weimar period. Moreover, a "new" or "dependent" middle class, composed of white-collar workers—salespeople, clerical personnel, salaried technicians, etc.—mushroomed to remarkable dimensions in the twentieth century. This group constituted 4.4 per cent of all gainfully employed in 1895, 6.8 per cent in 1907, and 11.4 per cent in 1925. The addition of civil servants, properly included in the white-collar category, brings the 1925 total to 14.8 per cent.[62] Against

61. In *Selected Works, 1* (Moscow, Foreign Languages Publishing House, 1951), 38, 35, 39–40, 42.

62. Emil Lederer and Jakob Marschak, "Der neue Mittelstand," *Grundriss der Sozialökonomik, 9* (1) (1926), 128; Theodor Geiger, *Die soziale Schichtung des deutschen Volkes* (Stuttgart, 1932), pp. 20–21.

the refusal of the old middle class to disappear, and the expansion of the new middle class, the proletariat could not
even maintain its relative share; the proportion of industrial
and agricultural wage workers, as defined by the official occupational census, declined from 56.8 per cent in 1895, to
55.1 per cent in 1907, to 45.1 per cent in 1925.[63] Actual
factory production workers, the purest kind of Marxist
proletarians, constituted no more than 30.6 per cent of the
1925 occupational census.[64] Far from becoming the immense majority, the proletariat was actually shrinking in
relation to the total population!

Although this is an oversimplified picture, it indicates
something of the dilemma facing the German party as Marx's
social prognostications clashed more and more with reality.
Confining itself to a purely proletarian base, the SPD could
not hope to come to power by democratic means, or for that
matter make a revolution in the name of the immense majority. To win such a mandate the Social Democrats simply
had to get the backing of nonproletarian elements.

Long before the Weimar period this problem became a
focal point for intraparty controversy. An analysis of the
social trends described above formed a central part of Bernstein's revisionism.[65] He urged that the party recognize these
realities and transform itself into a people's party, adjusting
the program and tactics of Social Democracy to attract nonproletarian elements. In this he was backed by the reformist
wing of the movement, especially the southern Land organizations which had to face the peasant question directly. But
the then dominant orthodox Marxists prevented any such

63. Emil Lederer, "Die Umschichtung des Proletariats," *Die neue
Rundschau, 40* (1929), 146.
64. Geiger, *Schichtung,* pp. 20–21.
65. *Die Voraussetzungen des Sozialismus und die Aufgaben der Sozialdemokratie* (Stuttgart, 1899), Ch. 2.

large-scale transformation. They refused to water down the program and clung to the hope that economic crises would ultimately push the lower middle classes into the proletarian camp, both economically and politically.[66]

Stalemated between the reformists and the radicals, the people's-party issue remained unresolved until after the war when the expulsion of the left wing gave the reformists free rein to make whatever changes they desired. And by now there appeared a second strong incentive to woo lower middle-class voters for it was precisely among such people that the antirepublican parties found their mass base. Therefore, in the interest of safeguarding the republic and the achievements of the Revolution, the party needed to overcome petty bourgeois hostility.[67] A consequence of these twin desires to poll a majority and to safeguard the republic was the Görlitz Program of 1921, which we may take as marking the conscious metamorphosis of Social Democracy from a class party to a people's party.

The very vocabulary of the new program proclaimed this transformation. Gone were the militant Erfurt phrases asserting an "ever more bitter class struggle between bourgeoisie and proletariat." The opening lines of the new document announced: "The German Social Democratic Party is the party of the working people (des arbeitenden Volkes) in city and country. It strives to coordinate all persons who produce, either physically or mentally, and who live by the earnings of their own labor." Terms like "the struggle of the working class" gave way to "the struggle of the producing

66. Peter Gay, *The Dilemma of Democratic Socialism* (New York, 1952), pp. 190–212.

67. This was especially true among the peasantry; see Alexander Gerschenkron, *Bread and Democracy in Germany* (Berkeley and Los Angeles, 1943), p. 127.

masses."[68] It is noteworthy that in the first draft, which represented the executive's wishes in purest form, the term "class struggle" did not appear at all.[69]

The party's concern to attract middle-class voters and members was not limited to programmatic pronouncements. The Weimar period witnessed a full-scale offensive in this regard, organized on many fronts and combining the efforts of both party and trade unions. To examine this drive more closely it will be advisable to separate its urban and rural aspects.

We have already noted the phenomenal growth of the new middle class in twentieth-century Germany. Here lay a tempting field for recruitment—all the more tempting since, according to the simplest Marxist criterion of class, these people, being propertyless, really belonged to the proletariat anyway. The criterion of income seemed to point in the same direction: the lower levels of the new middle class earned no more, and sometimes less, than skilled workers. Many Social Democrats maintained that this social group was simply a part of the proletariat and would eventually join the socialist movement.[70]

Such loose categorizing, however, glosses over the real objective differences between wage workers and the new middle class, differences which, if not hard and fast, nonetheless cannot be blithely ignored. Compared with ordinary

68. Paul Weidmann, *Die Programme der Sozialdemokratischen Partei Deutschlands von Gotha bis Görlitz* (Hamburg, 1926), pp. 27–28, 75–76. Weidmann has reprinted the Gotha, Erfurt, and Görlitz programs in his dissertation.

69. *Prot. 1921,* pp. 358–66.

70. E.g. Lederer and Marschak, *Grundriss, 9* (1), passim; and Theodor Geiger, who even tries to introduce the term "new proletariat" to replace "new middle class" in his article, "Die Mittelschichten und die Sozialdemokratie," *Die Arbeit, 8* (1931), 619–35.

proletarian jobs, most salaried positions gave more security of long-term employment (implied in the very word "salaried"); most required more formal education and called for mental rather than physical exertion; most necessitated polite dress on the job (hence the characterization "white collar"); and many gave opportunity for advancement into the upper middle class. Moreover, the group had historical origins different from the proletariat; the modern office worker could count as his occupational ancestor the nonproletarian clerk, and the modern government employee derived from the highly respectable old civil servant. All these differences bestowed upon the new middle class a prestige not enjoyed by ordinary wage workers. Even those whose jobs were poorly paid and essentially unskilled could feel this prestige. Subjectively, most salaried employees simply did not think themselves proletarians, a phenomenon that Social Democrats liked to call "false consciousness" because it did not correspond to the "real" position of these people in the productive process. But to label this consciousness "false" seems arbitrary, and in any event does not lessen its strength, which explains why the SPD had to make special efforts to win white-collar votes.

A few socialist trade unions for white-collar workers had existed before the war but in 1921, shortly after the Görlitz Program came into being, the General Free Federation of Salaried Employees (AfA) was permanently established, and intensive organizing work began. The next year saw the founding of the General German Federation of Civil Servants (ADB). Both the new organizations scored some initial success: the AfA obtained 658,000 members by 1923; the ADB had some 826,000.[71] But the right-wing unions boasted still higher figures than these and, more important, their strength increased as years went on, while the two socialist

71. Lederer and Marschak, *Grundriss,* 9 (1), 134, 139.

unions declined. By 1931 the AfA had sunk to 203,000 and consisted, according to Franz Neumann, in very large measure of white-collar workers connected with the socialist movement—i.e. the employees of social insurance organizations, cooperatives, etc.[72] After some early promise the unionizing drive declined slowly into oblivion.

Besides trade-union activity, the party entered the lists directly. Its program now included economic and political demands in the interest of white-collar workers. It set up special party organizations for civil servants, teachers, lawyers, and the like. The first of these was the most ambitious and may serve as an example. In the flush of revolutionary optimism an elaborate pyramidal organization had been constructed for the purpose of agitating among civil servants. Every effort was made to show an identity of interests between government employees and the rest of the "producing masses": "The civil and economic interests of civil servants coincide in every way with those of wage and salaried workers."[73] A special weekly, *Der freie Beamte*, appeared. The Reichstag fraction worked for the passage of a modernized civil-service code and other related bills. But after an impressive beginning the movement soon lost momentum; in 1926 the annual report observed gloomily that "a great part of the civil service . . . still believes itself to be higher born, and refuses to be placed on a level with other wage and salary earners."[74] After 1926 nothing further was reported about the movement; apparently it died an early death. The short history of this organization, together with that of the white-collar unions, reveals the pattern of party efforts to win over the new middle class: great enthusiasm at first, ambitious

72. Franz Neumann, *European Trade Unionism and Politics* (New York, League for Industrial Democracy, 1936), p. 20.
73. *Prot. 1921*, p. 26.
74. *Jahrbuch 1926*, p. 41.

organization and agitation, some initial success, but then slow stagnation and decline.

The old middle class also received the solicitations of Social Democracy. Here chief concern was for the peasant; the urban petty bourgeoisie—independent artisans and shopkeepers—never attracted much special notice. The drive to recruit peasants actually antedated the white-collar movement. As early as 1895 Bavaria, Baden, Württemberg, and Hesse had adopted Land agrarian programs, and in that year the party congress fiercely debated a proposed Reich agrarian program. The Revisionists argued that the law of concentration did not apply to agriculture and that Social Democracy should champion the interests of the small peasantry. The orthodox insisted that the small holder was doomed and could not be helped.[75] The proposed program was defeated, as were all similar moves up until the Weimar period, which did not prevent rural locals and Land organizations from continuing their efforts to win over small holders.

These efforts were not entirely in vain; they bore fruit in the Revolution when the party made important gains among the peasantry. Heberle's analysis of the peasant (Geest) section of Schleswig–Holstein shows that a remarkable 33 per cent of the population there voted Social Democratic in 1919. A decline quickly set in, however, even sooner than in the case of the new middle-class supporters. Heberle's statistics for the same area in following elections reveal a drop to 14.1 per cent in May 1924, a slight recovery up to 17.5 per cent by 1928, and then an even more disastrous plunge in the depression to 9.7 per cent for July 1932.[76]

75. The Revisionist case was most thoroughly expounded by Eduard David, *Sozialismus und Landwirtschaft* (Berlin, 1903); the orthodox case by Karl Kautsky, *Die Agrarfrage* (Stuttgart, 1899). Also see Gerschenkron, *Bread and Democracy*, pp. 28–32.

76. *Democracy to Nazism*, p. 99.

Attempts to formulate an agrarian program in 1920 and 1921 did not succeed, and it was not until 1927 that the party adopted such a program. This document embodied a radical departure from traditional party views on rural questions. It can be treated here only with reference to the people's-party problem. Now in the case of the new middle class, no drastic program changes were necessary; one had to cut out the narrow class terminology and soft-pedal the blood and thunder of Marxist jargon, but the economic demands of the white-collar group were easily appended to the rest of the program. The peasant question did not lend itself to such a facile solution. Marx had been quite explicit about the fate of the peasantry: it was scheduled to disappear along with the rest of the independent petty bourgeoisie, bankrupted by presumably more efficient large-scale enterprises. Once giant capitalist farms dominated the agricultural sector, and the old peasantry worked on these farms as day laborers, the socialist position was clear. The party would demand socialization, workers' control, etc. just as in the case of industrial concerns. But until this happened nothing could be done for the condemned small holders. To aid an economically doomed class would be a profoundly reactionary move in Marxist politics.

The 1927 program marked a signal victory for Revisionist thinking on rural questions. Agriculture was permanently exempted from the law of concentration. Far from looking forward to the growth of large-scale capitalist farming, the program called for the confiscation of large estates (with compensation) and demanded that they be parceled out to small holders for intensive cultivation. Moreover, although the traditionally consumer-oriented SPD did not quite come out for protective tariffs, it demanded creation of a government monopoly to regulate grain prices and imports, a monopoly which eventually would be extended to cover other farm products.[77] With this program the party made a serious bid to overcome the peasants' hostility to socialism and the Weimar Republic, and to create a labor–peasant alliance that would sweep Social Democracy into power at last.

The price for this projected alliance was the abandonment of socialist plans for agriculture and the encouragement of private property in the form of peasant holdings, together with some sort of protection for agriculture against foreign competition. As it turned out, the price was paid without the goods ever being delivered. After very minor gains in 1928 the rural Social Democratic vote, as we have seen, went into a steady and steep nose dive. Great numbers of peasants did indeed abandon their traditional parties—not in favor of Social Democracy, however, but in favor of Nazism.[78]

All in all, the drive to recruit middle-class supporters cannot be counted an overwhelming success, although the urban movement fared somewhat better than the rural. It will be remembered that in 1903 Blank estimated 25 per cent of the SPD vote derived from nonproletarian sources. Twenty-seven years later, after extensive party agitation in this area, Neisser estimated an increase of only five percentage points for the 1930 election. In absolute numbers, Neisser's calculation amounts to 2.6 million votes, or very roughly one-fifth of the total lower middle-class vote.[79] This is not a figure to be dismissed lightly; neither was it large enough to give the SPD its long-sought majority or to alter the fate of the Weimar Republic. Apparently, in the eyes of the petty bourgeois voters, Social Democracy remained too much identified with

77. *Prot. 1927,* pp. 274, 278.

78. Gerschenkron, *Bread and Democracy,* p. 146.

79. Based on Theodor Geiger's estimates as to the total size of this social group, in "Panik im Mittelstand," *Die Arbeit,* 7 (1930), 642.

140

the working class and social egalitarianism, with "godless" Marxism and internationalism, with the treaty of Versailles and the hapless Republic.

To counteract these electoral liabilities, some right-wing Social Democrats called for the elimination of Marxism as the creed of the party. Theodor Geiger argued this, asserting that the SPD should defend national interests more vigorously, drop its antireligious attitude, encourage small entrepreneurs, and in general pare off all "nonessentials" from its ideology. Reduced to such a bare minimum, the party program could attract the most diverse elements in the population, elements which "have a common interest only in socialism, by which is meant the socialization of the means of production—nothing else. This and this alone should be the final goal of the movement."[80] Here state ownership is equated with socialism. The ideal of the classless society has apparently been relegated to the "nonessential" list.

Perhaps the question of egalitarianism lies at the core of the people's-party dilemma. To create a society of socially and economically equal, or very nearly equal, persons had always been the cardinal aim of Marxian socialism. Yet such a vision could only horrify the threatened petty bourgeoisie for they thrived on precisely those distinctions that separated them from ordinary wage workers. And the more economic developments undermined their pretensions, the more desperately they clung to them. Under such circumstances Nazism was in a far better position than Social Democracy to reap the harvest of lower middle-class discontent.[81]

---

80. *Die Arbeit, 8,* 622 and passim.

81. This point is made by Franz Neumann, *Behemoth* (New York, 1942), p. 411; and by Evelyn Anderson, *Hammer or Anvil, The Story of the German Working-Class Movement* (London, 1945), pp. 135–41.

The Question of Verbürgerlichung

We are now in a position to fit together the various aspects of the problem of Verbürgerlichung[82] that have come up in previous discussions. There appear to be two questions to answer: Was the SPD verbürgerlicht? And, if so, what effects did this have on Social Democratic politics? The reply to the first query obviously hinges on what one takes the term "verbürgerlicht" to mean. The word most frequently appears in polemical writing where it drips with moral condemnation and usually has no more precise a meaning than "conservatized." In this discussion the word will be employed in certain commonly acceptable senses and without any intended moral judgment. These senses can be made clear by drawing a few distinctions.

To begin with, we must separate the question, Verbürgerlichung of the proletariat, from the question, Verbürgerlichung of the Social Democratic Party. The former will be treated here only insofar as it affects the latter. Now, confining our attention to party leaders, members, and voters, we may distinguish "objective" Verbürgerlichung from "subjective" Verbürgerlichung. The first term denotes an alteration in the actual class composition of the movement; the second refers to changes in the ideas and tastes of individual Social Democrats and to changes in the official policies of the party.[83] With this distinction in mind let us take up first the SPD leadership and then the rank and file.

Even before the Weimar period the party leadership was completely verbürgerlicht in the objective sense. This had come about in two ways: through the influx of middle-class

---

82. On the translation of this term see above, p. 91, n. 58.
83. This division is suggested by Theodor Geiger, "Zur Kritik der Verbürgerlichung," *Die Arbeit*, 8 (1931), 535.

142

elements into positions of importance and through the social
ascent of originally proletarian leaders. We have learned in
the last chapter that the percentage of SPD Reichstag fraction members with middle-class backgrounds increased from
16 per cent in 1903, to 34 per cent in 1912, to 35 per cent by
1930. Thus in our period the proportion of such leaders had
leveled off at about one-third. But the remaining two-thirds,
who had working-class origins, could no longer be called
proletarians for they had all, almost without exception, taken
salaried white-collar positions of one sort or another. This
total objective Verbürgerlichung of the leadership was not
a new development; Michels had noticed it back in 1903.
It should be noted, however, that the older the leadership
grew, the longer the interval since any of them had been
employed as a wage worker.

Interesting as these facts are, they reveal little unless the
objective Verbürgerlichung was accompanied by acceptance
of middle-class values and tastes in matters of dress, housing,
education, etc.—in short, by the adoption of a middle-class
style of life. Such a subjective Verbürgerlichung, however,
was all but inevitable for the leaders of Social Democracy.
For, as Hans Speier has observed,

> The interest of the proletarian cause requires that function-
> aries adapt themselves to bourgeois forms and conventions.
> They yield—and to a large extent, must yield—to the spirit
> of the institutions in which they meet with their bourgeois
> opponents; this spirit however is distinctly not proletarian.
> When in 1913 the first Social Democrat entered the Reichs-
> tag presidium, Bebel asked him first of all whether he had
> formal clothes. . . . The high functionaries of different classes
> resemble one another, in the rule, far more than the classes
> they are supposed to represent.[84]

84. Hans Speier, "Verbürgerlichung des Proletariats," *Magazin der Wirtschaft,* 7 (1931), 593.

The tendency toward social assimilation into the ruling circles of the Empire had begun considerably before the war, but it received its greatest impetus during the years of Burgfrieden (the political truce during the war). At that time, for example, prominent Social Democrats made visits to the front where it had become socially possible for them to dine with commanding officers;[85] others came into contact with top government administrators because of their positions as trade-union officials aiding the war effort.[86] The November Revolution only accelerated the same trends, for the civil service, the army, the entire governmental officialdom now worked with, and under, SPD leaders. Some Social Democrats undoubtedly resisted the assimilative process but others were only too happy to accept their new status in society. No one reading the memoirs of Gustav Noske, for example, can miss the obvious delight he took in writing that a particular general "presented himself to me" or "stood at my disposal."[87] In the Weimar period formal clothes, banquets, state occasions, and the like became more or less routine in the lives of top party leaders. Their wives could attempt to keep up with the fashions; their sons could be sent to the university. The subjective Verbürgerlichung of SPD leaders reached an advanced stage in our period; they did not adopt so much petty bourgeois styles of life as those of the upper orders of society.[88]

85. See Gustav Noske, *Erlebtes aus Aufsteig und Niedergang einer Demokratie* (Offenbach/Main, 1947), p. 56.

86. Schorske gives an excellent account of these wartime changes in *Social Democracy*, pp. 291–94.

87. *Von Kiel bis Kapp* (Berlin, Verlag für Politik und Wirtschaft, 1920), p. 71 and passim.

88. There is, for example, the case of Albert Südekum, for a time Social Democratic Prussian State and Finance Minister, who somehow acquired for himself a Hohenzollern castle to live in—a case that almost tempts one to speak of feudalization! (Varga, *Die sozialdemokratischen Parteien*, pp. 58–59.)

There remains to discuss the effects of these changes on the political ideas and actions of the party leadership. It is easy enough to draw a line from Verbürgerlichung to increased conservatism. Traditionally, the bitterest complaints of the reformist wing of the party had centered on the pariah position of labor in imperial Germany, and their foremost demand had been for first-class citizenship. As Schorske put it, theirs was "a quest not for power but for *'Gleichberechtigung'* " (equal rights) and was "bound up with the desire for status and recognition within the existing order."[89] When the political and social alterations of Weimar accorded these persons a great many of the rights they desired, their deepest grievance against existing society was thereby removed. Consequently they became less enthusiastic for vigorous new offensives. Then too, social intercourse with respectable society was bound to make them feel more "responsible," more obliged to see "the other side," and less anxious in general to remold completely the society that gave them such a measure of prestige. But a note of caution seems necessary; if Verbürgerlichung can be cited as a cause of increased conservatism, the reverse is also true. Leaders who had conservative convictions to start with felt less hostility toward middle-class conventions, and hence were more easily verbürgerlicht. The pattern of causation is reciprocal, and the process of Verbürgerlichung interlocked subtly with the entire drift of the Social Democratic leadership toward more cautious politics.

Shifting now from the higher to the lower echelons of the party, we may review briefly the evidence for objective Verbürgerlichung in these quarters. The information available for the party membership indicated a substantial influx of lower middle-class elements between 1905 and 1930. Their number swelled from about 7 per cent to about 23 per cent

89. *Social Democracy*, p. 290.

145

of the total. Similar investigations for the broader circle of party voters suggested an increase from 25 per cent to 30 per cent between 1903 and 1930. Unless better statistical data become available, we must content ourselves with these approximations.

Now in the case of party members and voters who were wage workers, there can be no question of objective Verbürgerlichung. Even those whose standards of living vastly improved in the Weimar period must be counted, as long as their occupations remained clearly proletarian, among the working-class supporters of the party. All one can safely assert is that higher living standards promoted subjective Verbürgerlichung in the proletariat, a phenomenon which in our period had become too obvious to be denied any longer. As Henrik deMan stated it, "The proletariat—even the class-conscious proletariat—is succumbing more and more to the inclination to imitate, in the unpolitical areas of daily living, the bourgeois or petty bourgeois style of life."[90] Or in another place: "The proletarian masses, who instinctively feel that cultural and social supremacy is a unity, are content with attempting to imitate the bourgeoisie, which they regard as a model of culture and good manners."[91] As deMan points out, this inclination extended into the "class-conscious proletariat," i.e. the Social Democratic rank and file, and perhaps especially so since skilled and better-paid workers predominated there.

But deMan is also careful to specify the "nonpolitical areas of daily living." It would appear difficult if not impossible to establish any direct connection between such social imitation and the political behavior of the persons in-

90. "Verbürgerlichung des Proletariats?" *Neue Blätter für den Sozialismus, 1* (1930), 106.
91. *The Psychology of Socialism,* trans. Eden and Cedar Paul (London, G. Allen and Unwin, 1927), p. 257.

volved. Unlike the leaders whose subjective Verbürgerlichung was reinforced by white-collar occupational status
and close contact with the upper orders, these proletarian
imitators were still separated from a genuinely middle-class
life by their education, housing, dress, economic security,
and other realities. Were the SPD supporters who had social
pretensions more conservative than those who did not? Perhaps. But the point is not easily proved. At best one can
hazard some such general formulation as that of deMan:

> The social position of the workers makes them amenable to
> socialist sentiments; these sentiments become the primary
> motive force of attempts to improve the material and moral
> position of the working class; but such improvements as are
> effected tend to bring the workers more and more under the
> cultural influence of the bourgeois and capitalist environ-
> ment, and this counteracts the tendency towards the forma-
> tion of a socialist mentality.[92]

A great many workers appear to have lived in both worlds:
they had a petty bourgeois mentality at home but a socialist
mentality in the shop and at the polling booth.

The case of the middle-class adherents of Social Democracy is quite different. It would, of course, be logically absurd
to speak of their being verbürgerlicht—they already were
bourgeois. But their increasing numerical weight in the movement had this effect on the party as a whole. More and more
of the party's backing came from nonworking-class elements.
And the peasant, for example, who supported the SPD did
not adopt a proletarian way of life because of it. More important, he did not have to sacrifice his special class interests
because of it for the party had embraced his interests, even
at the cost of abandoning its traditional ideology. When the
SPD was deliberately remolded into a people's party, it was

92. Ibid., p. 242.

thereby verbürgerlicht in a political as well as a social sense.

This political Verbürgerlichung of official party policy must clearly be counted as another swing to the right. For the drive to win over middle-class voters necessitated, as we have seen in the last section, a soft-pedaling of the class-struggle doctrine, an abandonment of socialist plans for agriculture, a backhanded support of agricultural protection, and so on. The SPD had to appear a responsible and respectable party that a decent burgher would not be ashamed to support. Moreover, the rightward swing was self-fortifying: as more and more attention was given to the needs and predilections of the marginal, middle-class voter, more and more radicals within the party found the situation intolerable and deserted to splinter groups or the KPD. This left the party with a still greater right-wing preponderance, which alienated still more radicals, etc., etc. in an obvious circle. By its efforts to become a people's party, the SPD obtained some 2.6 million middle-class votes in 1930, but 4.6 million people voted for the Communist Party in that year. Seemingly unable to win a majority by relying exclusively on the proletariat, Social Democracy had broadened its appeal and diluted its ideology, but when the depression came these new policies appear to have gained fewer votes on the right than were lost on the left.

5. Social Democracy and the Free Trade Unions

The conservative effects of the party's Verbürgerlichung were reinforced by the influence of the Free Trade Unions. European socialist parties have generally been distinguished from bourgeois parties by, among other things, their intimate connection with the trade-union movement. Since the history of the SPD is so closely interwoven with that of the Free Trade Unions, because they were held to be but two branches (one political, one economic) of the same socialist movement, we must bring into our consideration of the internal development of Weimar Social Democracy an analysis of the relationship between these two mass organizations with particular reference to the influence the Free Trade Unions exerted in party affairs and to the growing political power of the union movement in its own right, independent of the SPD.

The Growth of Trade-Union Influence, 1868–1918

The relationship between the Social Democratic Party and the Free Trade Unions went through three stages of development before the period of our concern. In their infancy, 1868–90, the unions were dependencies of the party and were regarded merely as "recruiting grounds" for the latter. Coming of age in 1890 the unions declared their independence from the party and pursued a policy of political neutrality. Then from 1906 to 1919 the unions again tied themselves to the party, this time not as subordinates, but with a veto right over all important party decisions. Each stage represented an expansion of trade-union power in relation to the SPD.

In Germany of the mid-nineteenth century, the overriding question of national unity oriented the emerging urban proletariat more toward political than economic activity. Legal trade unionism was not even possible until 1869 when the laws against combination were repealed in the states of the North German Confederation.[1] Lassalle had taught his followers to oppose unions, whose efforts he regarded as a labor of Sisyphus since, according to the Iron Law of Wages, no permanent economic improvements for the working class could be won in capitalist society.[2]

Lassalle's successor, Jean Baptiste von Schweitzer, came to modify this intransigent position. A wave of strikes in the later sixties, the beginnings of independent trade unions, and the plans of his South German rivals to form a national union federation all combined to soften Schweitzer's orthodoxy. At the 1868 ADA congress he and Fritzsche pushed through a resolution—over strong opposition—which sanctioned the formation of unions without denying the Iron Law of Wages. It stated that "strikes are not a means for altering the basis of the capitalist method of production, but can be a means

1. Theodor Cassau, *Die Gewerkschaftsbewegung, ihre Soziologie und ihr Kampf* (Halberstadt, 1925), pp. 4–5.
2. Karl Zwing, *Geschichte der deutschen freien Gewerkschaften* (Jena, Gewerkschafts-Archiv-Bücherei, 1928), pp. 27–29.

for furthering the class consciousness of the workers, . . . and
—presupposing the proper organization—a means for elimi-
nating from present society certain oppressive social evils,
such as excessively long hours and Sunday work."[3] On this
basis a General German Trade Union Federation (Allgemeiner Deutscher Gewerkschaftsverband) was established
the same year. Because of legal restrictions the federation
had no formal ties to the ADA, but Schweitzer and Fritzsche
formed a majority on its three-man presidium, and the new
group recognized the ADA *Sozialdemokrat* as its official
organ.[4] By 1870 it claimed 20,674 members.[5] The ADA
leaders did not set up their union for its own sake but regarded it as a kind of front organization from whose ranks
the party could recruit members.

The Eisenachers' attitude toward unions reflected their
Marxian views. Marx had rejected the Iron Law of Wages;
he held trade unions to have an important role in securing
better material conditions for the proletariat. But like Lassalle he believed that the primary conflict and ultimate victory would take place in the political arena. Thus he also
regarded trade-union struggles chiefly as preparatory to the
more crucial political struggle: "Trade unions are schools for
socialism. In the unions workers are educated into socialism
because they participate daily in the class struggle."[6] Late in
1868 Bebel's organization sponsored the foundation of a
trade-union federation of its own. The two rival associations
existed side by side, along with some independent unions,
down to the unification of 1875.

At Gotha it was resolved to combine the two trade-union

---

3. Quoted in Franz Mehring, *Geschichte der deutschen Sozialdemokratie, 2* (Stuttgart, 1897), 241.
4. Ibid., *2,* 250.
5. Zwing, *Freien Gewerkschaften,* p. 40.
6. Quoted ibid., p. 31.

organizations, but the attitude toward unionism in general did not change noticeably.[7] Economic recession and police harassment delayed the formation of a united federation in the first three years after Gotha, and then the Anti-Socialist Law made any such effort impossible. Virtually all the existing unions were forced to dissolve or transform themselves into friendly societies.[8] In this early period, then, the political movement acted as big brother to the trade-union movement. The latter was regarded as a recruiting ground or preparatory school but had no great justification in and of itself.

During the eighties the government relaxed its vigil against trade unions and permitted active organizing once more. There had been no more than 50,000 organized workers in 1877, but by 1890 the Free Trade Unions could boast 227,733 members, organized in 53 national unions with 3,150 locals.[9] This rapid expansion encouraged trade unionists to set up a national federation, a move which became legally possible in 1890 with the lapse of the Anti-Socialist Law. In that year the general commission of the Free Trade Unions was created to coordinate the activity of the various craft organizations. The leaders of the general commission were virtually all Social Democrats, but they kept the new association strictly separate from the party.[10] Thus 1890 inaugurated the second period in party–union relations.

The policy of political neutrality had behind it a variety of motives. First of all, the Association Laws still forbade the creation of national organizations such as the general commission if they had political aims. By choosing the stronger, centralized mode of organization the union leaders were

---

7. Ibid., p. 47.
8. Ibid., pp. 51–52; Mehring, *Geschichte*, 2, 376–77.
9. Ibid., 2, 377; Cassau, *Gewerkschaftsbewegung*, p. 22.
10. Carl E. Schorske, *German Social Democracy, 1905–1917* (Cambridge, Mass., 1955), p. 9.

forced to renounce any formal bonds with the SPD.[11] As it happened they were quite happy to be independent of the party for the revolutionary and antireligious ideology of Social Democracy hampered their recruiting efforts. If unionizing drives were to succeed among politically "backward" and religiously devout workers, the stigma of Marxist radicalism had to be lifted from the movement.[12] Finally, the trade unionists had by now become convinced that their organizations possessed an importance in their own right, equal to that of the party. They opposed any degrading dependence on the latter and evolved the "two pillars" view of the socialist movement, wherein party and trade unions worked on an equal footing for political and economic improvements respectively.[13] Thus the trade unions left the parental home to strike out on their own.

The separation did not occur, however, without a family squabble. The more orthodox party leaders felt the move to be presumptuous and feared that the independent general commission might constitute a rival to the party.[14] Then there were the radical "localist" unions which opposed both the centralization and the neutralization of the movement. Having acquired a revolutionary zeal through earlier illegal activity, these localists held fast to the concept of militant political unionism. They refused, therefore, to recognize the general commission. But the localists were no match for the rapidly expanding centralized unions; slowly they declined in strength and drifted into anarchosyndicalist politics.[15]

---

11. Paul Merker, *Sozialdemokratie und Gewerkschaften, 1890–1920* (Berlin, Dietz, 1949), p. 22.

12. Otto Heilborn, *Die freien Gewerkschaften seit 1890* (Jena, 1907), pp. 179–80.

13. Zwing, *Freien Gewerkschaften*, p. 120.

14. Heilborn, *Gewerkschaften seit 1890*, p. 144.

15. Schorske, *Social Democracy*, pp. 9–10.

The neutrality policy had certain peculiar features. In spite of it, most union leaders remained Social Democrats, often holding top positions in the party. And the Free Trade Unions did not renounce their commitment to socialism in general, nor did they hesitate to exert what political pressure they could on legislation affecting their interests.[16] Neutrality actually accomplished two things for the unions: besides improving their organizing powers, as pointed out above, it gave them a better bargaining position with regard to party policy since they now could threaten to take their votes elsewhere.

Thus Carl Legien, head of the general commission and patriarch of German trade unionism from 1890 to 1920, addressed the 1899 trade-union congress as follows: "There is no other party in Germany except the Social Democratic Party that represents politically what we in our trade-union organizations discuss and demand. If another party appears which will also do this and which has the necessary strength, then we will be happy to deal with it."[17] While reaffirming loyalty to Social Democracy, Legien makes it clear that the support is conditional, that trade-union needs come first. The leader of the important miners' union, Otto Hué, wrote even more frankly on the subject: "Where trade-union neutrality may lead the workers politically, cannot and must not be a matter of concern for the union leader. . . . If it were true that the neutral trade union were absolutely necessary for raising the workers' position . . . but that neutrality led into antisocialist paths, then I would turn my back on Social Democracy."[18] The trade unions had come of age.

16. Richard Seidel, *Die Gewerkschaften nach dem Kriege* (Berlin, Dietz, 1925), pp. 21–22.
17. Quoted in Merker, *Sozialdemokratie*, p. 72.
18. *Neutrale oder parteiische Gewerkschaften* (Bochum, 1900), pp. 150 ff., quoted in Merker, *Sozialdemokratie*, p. 73.

154

After the economic depression of the early nineties, the unions began a rapid and steady expansion that lasted down to the war. From 223,530 members in 1893 the movement grew to 2,075,000 by 1914. This exceeded by far the rate of expansion of the SPD; in 1893 the party commanded eight times as many votes as the trade unions had members. By 1912 this ratio had dropped to less than two to one.[19] Thus Social Democratic votes came increasingly from organized workers, and the SPD increasingly had to take union demands into account. The party could no longer manage without the trade unions.

As the union movement grew it became more rooted in existing society. Besides maintaining strike funds, the organizations provided many sorts of insurance and other services for their members. Union treasuries became the repositories of great wealth; in 1905 the Free Trade Unions had an income of 25,000,000 marks—about fifty times the income of the party.[20] To manage these multitudinous activities, a bureaucracy of full-time salaried officials was created, numbering 2,867 persons by 1914.[21] Committed as they were to securing practical economic improvements within the existing order and feeling the responsibility of their growing power, the union leaders were naturally drawn to the Revisionist doctrines of Eduard Bernstein and became the bulwark of the reformist forces within the party. As long as the SPD confined itself to peaceful electioneering the trade unionists were satisfied with neutrality and the two-pillars arrangement.[22] But when, in 1905, there appeared a likelihood that the party might adopt a radical tactic, they were

---

19. Schorske, *Social Democracy,* pp. 12–13.
20. Ibid., pp. 32, 93.
21. Rudolf Schlesinger, *Central European Democracy and Its Background* (London, 1953), p. 71.
22. Schorske, *Social Democracy,* pp. 14–16.

forced to abandon neutrality and throw their weight against the leftward turn. Thus 1905 marked the beginning of the third period in party–union relations.

The radical revival of 1905 focused discussion on the general strike as a new extraparliamentary weapon in the struggle for socialism. Labor unrest in Germany, successful political strikes in other countries, and above all the use of the mass strike in Russia during the 1905 Revolution combined to stimulate radical hopes that here was a weapon to save the movement from the deadly embrace of reformism.[23] At the 1905 party congress the left-wingers and localist trade unions succeeded, with the decisive support of Bebel and the executive, in passing a resolution endorsing the mass political strike. It sanctioned the use of such a strike both defensively, against possible attacks on the suffrage or the right of combination, and offensively, "to acquire an important basic right for its [the proletariat's] liberation."[24]

The general commission bitterly opposed this resolution. In the general strike, trade-union leaders saw an abandonment of bread-and-butter unionism, a possible strengthening of the radical localist unions and, in general, a ridiculous folly that would end in the destruction of their treasuries and organizations. Shortly before the 1905 party congress, therefore, the general commission scheduled a trade-union congress, where they secured passage of a vigorous resolution condemning even the discussion of the general strike.[25] An obvious attempt to influence the impending party meeting, this move constituted a breach of political neutrality. It called into question the whole relationship between party and trade unions.

The attempt failed, however, and the radicals enjoyed a

23. Ibid., pp. 28–38.
24. *Prot. 1905*, p. 143, quoted in Schorske, *Social Democracy,* p. 43.
25. Ibid., pp. 39–42.

momentary victory. But events soon brought about a realign-
ment of forces. In some of the cities and Länder, most notably
Saxony, popular demonstrations against suffrage restrictions
late in 1905 threatened to turn the general-strike question
into an immediate reality. Bebel and the party executive,
having supported the 1905 resolution chiefly as a theoretical
concession to the left, now decided it was time to put on the
brakes lest the movement get out of hand. They refused to
consider a proposal for mass demonstrations in favor of
Prussian electoral reform. Then on February 16, 1906, they
concluded a secret agreement with the general commission
to the effect that the executive would try to prevent any
general strike but, should one nevertheless break out, the
party would assume the leadership and the financial burden,
thus permitting the unions to remain neutral.[26]

News of this agreement leaked out, causing a furor in the
radical camp. At the 1906 Mannheim party congress Kautsky
urged that the trade unions be clearly subordinated to party
discipline. But the radicals no longer had executive support.
The resolution that finally passed effected a complete volte-
face in party–union relations. It read: "In actions which
affect equally the interest of trade unions and party, the central leadership of both organizations should seek a mutual
understanding in order to achieve a unified procedure."[27]
This resolution, known as the Mannheim Agreement, gave
the unions a veto power over all important policies of the
party. It permitted, in fact, the effective predominance of
the unions. As Schorske explains:

> The party's recognition of parity in principle meant the
> recognition of control by the trade unions in practice. When-
> ever the party wished to move in a direction which threat-

26. Ibid., pp. 45–48.
27. *Prot. 1906,* pp. 131–32, quoted in Schorske, *Social Democracy,*
p. 49.

ened what Bömelburg had called the trade unions' need for peace, the unions could legally withhold their sanction, and thus act as a brake on any overt attacks on the existing order. The relationship of parity between trade unions and party was, as Luxemburg observed, like the arrangement by which a peasant woman sought to regulate her life with her spouse: "On matters of question between us, when we agree, you will decide; when we disagree, I shall decide."[28]

After fifteen years of independence the prodigal trade unions had returned to the parental roof, this time to oversee the family business!

Such was the relationship which lasted until the Revolution. While continuing to assert political neutrality during its organizing drives,[29] the general commission made full use of its new position in order to curb radical influence within the party. During the May Day controversy of 1907 and in the youth dispute of 1908,[30] the pattern of trade-union control became clear. Confronted by an unpleasant policy or radical innovation, but unable to win congress approval for its position, the general commission would act with the party executive to present the congress with a fait accompli. In the face of this double-barreled assault, the congress would settle for a compromise in which radical rhetoric hid a conservative content.[31]

The effect of this oft-repeated maneuver was to lessen the competence of the congress, as may be seen most clearly in

28. Ibid., p. 52. The official union historians, of course, do not admit such a predominance and put forth a purely legalistic case for the equality of the two branches; see for example, Zwing, *Freien Gewerkschaften*, pp. 124–25. But Selig Perlman, a strong backer of the unions, concurs with Schorske's view in his *A Theory of the Labor Movement* (New York, 1928), p. 104.

29. Seidel, *Gewerkschaften*, pp. 23–24.

30. A detailed account of these developments may be found in Schorske, *Social Democracy*, pp. 91–108.

31. Ibid., pp. 108–10.

a 1910 debate. At that time renewed agitation for Prussian suffrage reform had called forth another proposal advocating the general strike. Carl Severing, spokesman for the trade unions, declared that the congress was not competent to vote on such a resolution. Since the matter vitally affected the unions it would have to be settled by a joint meeting of general commission and party executive; their agreement might then be voted on by the following congress.[32] In this way the Mannheim Agreement severely curtailed the already waning power of the party congress. Conversely, it strengthened the hand of the executive acting in concert with the general commission.

The behavior of the unions in the war crisis of August 1914 may serve as a final illustration of the third-period relationship. The Social Democratic parliamentary caucus slated for August 3 was to decide the all-important question of voting war credits. Again the union leaders managed to present the party with a fait accompli: they scheduled a conference of the national trade-union executives for August 1. This body issued a resolution calling off all strikes in progress and suspending payment of strike funds for the duration. The funds in question were to be used instead for unemployment relief and to aid war victims.[33] Thus party leaders, meeting two days later, had to make their decision, knowing that the trade unions were already committed to the war effort and that if they should refuse credits they would split the movement.

The prewar Free Trade Unions, then, evolved from an initial position as party front organizations, through a stage of neutrality and independence from the SPD, to a final period of relative control over the party on the basis of the

32. Ibid., p. 193.
33. John L. Snell, "Socialist Unions and Socialist Patriotism in Germany, 1914–1918," *American Historical Review*, 59 (1953), 67–68.

Mannheim Agreement. In the 1860s Schweitzer regarded the unions merely as a "recruiting ground" for the party; by 1915 Carl Legien could write that he regarded the party as "the representative of the political interests of the trade unions"![34]

The End of the Mannheim Agreement

The birth of the Weimar Republic initiated a fourth period in party–union relations. The Mannheim arrangements had taken for granted the unity of the Socialist movement; when the split in the Social Democratic Party threatened to spread to the unions, it became necessary to sever the 1906 bond between the general commission and the party executive. Moreover, the Free Trade Unions began, in our period, to exert a direct influence in German politics quite independent of parties. These changes complicated the relationship between the SPD and the unions. There is no pat formula with which to characterize their interconnection. It must be analyzed in some detail.

The union leaders, as we have seen, stood solidly behind the war effort. With great alarm they viewed the beginnings of antiwar activity within the party. When Karl Liebknecht cast the first ballot against war credits in December 1914, it was Carl Legien who advanced a motion for his expulsion from the Reichstag fraction.[35] The general commission was the first to demand the resignation of the antiwar *Vorwärts* editorial staff.[36] In January 1915 Legien made an important

---

34. *Das Correspondenzblatt,* Feb. 6, 1915, p. 62.

35. Paul Umbreit, *Die deutschen Gewerkschaften im Weltkrieg* (Berlin, 1917), p. 100.

36. *Protokoll des 10. Kongresses der Gewerkschaften Deutschlands, 1919* (Berlin, ADGB, 1919), pp. 202–03. Hereafter cited as *Prot. Gewerkschaften [year].*

speech to Berlin trade-union functionaries—later circulated in pamphlet form—exhorting them to participate more actively in party life in order to counteract the growth of the opposition.[37]

As the rift developed the union leaders pressed ever more vigorously for strong action against the left. On December 29, 1915, when twenty deputies voted against war credits, Legien immediately demanded their expulsion from the fraction.[38] *Das Correspondenzblatt,* organ of the general commission, all but demanded their expulsion from the party. In a fiery proclamation the commission invoked the Mannheim Agreement, announcing that the policy of August Fourth was a "vital interest" of the unions. It thereby served notice that it would veto any party bid to oppose the war effort. Moreover, the unity of the party was brought under the aegis of Mannheim, likewise declared to be a "vital interest." On this basis the general commission virtually ordered the party executive to "subdue" the opposition as quickly as possible:

> Above all, the trade unions expect that short shrift be made of the propagandists of schism and that their influence on the further development of the party be rendered harmless. May it be perfectly clear that trade-union circles view the present crisis of the party, brought on by these unpunished breaches of discipline, as a turn of bitter seriousness which cannot leave the unions unconcerned; rather it forces them to think promptly about the protection of their own interests. May the responsible circles in the party, with equal celerity, find the strength to subdue this dangerous decomposition.[39]

The tone of this language suggests the real distribution of power within the German labor movement.

37. Umbreit, *Gewerkschaften im Weltkrieg,* p. 100.
38. Eugen Prager, *Geschichte der USPD* (Berlin, 1921), pp. 89–90.
39. *Correspondenzblatt,* Jan. 15, 1916, p. 19.

The unions apparently played no role in the formal expulsion of the Opposition from the SPD early in 1917. But when the USPD constituted itself shortly thereafter, the general commission was quick to announce that it recognized only the old party.[40] A resolution introduced at the July 1917 conference of union executives, proposing that the general commission henceforth deal with *both* parties on the basis of the Mannheim Agreement, was overwhelmingly rejected.[41] Up until the revolutionary period the union leaders pursued a policy of outright suppression with regard to the Independents, following Legien's injunction that it was "better to cut the abscess open now rather than to let it infect the entire body."[42]

But the Revolution brought about an abrupt change of tactics. The USPD at its outset attracted primarily intellectuals; only one of its original parliamentary leaders was a union functionary.[43] With the spreading war weariness of 1918, however, the new party began to acquire a mass base. It played a prominent part in the great strikes of January 1918.[44] Soon several small unions, including the shoemakers and the furriers, transferred their allegiance to the Independents. Many large industrial cities, such as Berlin, Leipzig, Dresden, Brunswick, and Stuttgart, acquired opposition locals.[45] With the coming of the Revolution, the USPD accumulated far too much support in the trade-union movement to be dealt with by simple repression. This support tended to come from newly organized unions, and from those whose membership was greatly swollen by wartime industrial

40. Snell, *American Historical Review, 59,* 72.
41. Zwing, *Freien Gewerkschaften,* p. 167.
42. Quoted in Theodor Leipart, *Carl Legien, Ein Gedenkbuch* (Berlin, ADGB, 1929), p. 135.
43. Snell, *American Historical Review, 59,* 72.
44. Prager, *USPD,* pp. 170–71.
45. Umbreit, *Gewerkschaften im Weltkrieg,* pp. 116–17.

expansion. The metal workers' union was one of the latter; its membership inflated to 1,248,338 by 1919, which made it far and away the largest union in Germany, accounting for 20 per cent of the total Free Trade Union strength.[46] In the early months of 1919 the major locals of the metal workers' union one by one replaced their old conservative functionaries with new leaders favorable to the USPD, a process that culminated in October 1919 with Robert Dissmann's election as the national chairman of the union.[47] Repression was no longer possible. If the general commission was to prevent the union movement from splitting asunder, it now had to accommodate itself to the existence of more than one socialist party.

Such an accommodation implied first and foremost an end of the Mannheim Agreement. This was accomplished by a resolution passed almost unanimously at the Nuremberg trade-union congress in July 1919. Since it defined the formal relationship of the unions to political parties for the entire Weimar period, the resolution merits full citation here:

> The tenth congress of the German trade unions declares that the unions must unite the workers, without prejudice to the political or religious convictions of the individual, for united and resolute action in defense of their economic interests.
>
> The Mannheim Agreement of 1906 with the German Social Democratic Party, which required an understanding of the two central leaderships in cases of important questions affecting the total interests of the working class, had the purpose of raising the striking power of labor through avoidance of differences between the economic and political

46. *Prot. Gewerkschaften 1919*, p. 15.
47. Fritz Opel, *Der Deutsche Metallarbeiter-Verband während des ersten Weltkrieges und der Revolution* (Hannover and Frankfurt/Main, 1957), pp. 86, 107, and passim.

movements. The political neutrality of the unions with regard to their members was not affected thereby.

But this agreement had as a prerequisite a united political representation of the interests of the German workers. This prerequisite no longer exists. The split of the Social Democratic Party endangers also the unity and solidarity of the German trade unions. The trade-union congress therefore deems it necessary to proclaim the neutrality of the unions with regard to political parties. The political differences of the workers must not weaken the striking power of their economic organizations.

The trade unions must not, however, confine themselves to representing the narrow craft interests of their members; to a much greater extent they must become the focal point of the class strivings of the proletariat, in order to help lead the struggle for socialism to victory.[48]

Thus the union leaders dissolved the Mannheim Agreement and pledged themselves to steer a neutral course in relation to political parties. But to understand this new policy, it is necessary to fathom in what sense they understood the term "neutrality."

Neutrality did not prevent the unions from taking positions on the vital political questions of the day and exerting all their influence to back up their position. Thus the General German Trade Union Federation (ADGB), as the Free Trade Union's organization was now called, played a crucial role in converting the revolutionary council movement into an appendage of the union apparatus. In the Kapp Putsch the ADGB called out and led a general strike to restore the legal government. In 1930 the refusal of the trade unions to go along with a proposed unemployment insurance scheme was one of the precipitating factors in the collapse of the last

48. *Prot. Gewerkschaften 1919*, p. 56.

parliamentary government of the Weimar Republic.[49] The Nuremberg Resolution proclaimed the aim of the ADGB, "to become the focal point of the class strivings of the proletariat, in order to help lead the struggle for socialism to victory"; this clearly indicated that the unions did not intend to eschew all political activity. Richard Seidel, official trade-union historian, explained that neutrality "does not mean a renunciation of political influence, or a renunciation of common dealings with political parties."[50]

Neutrality likewise did not prevent the ADGB from attacking certain parties and supporting others on specific issues. Indeed, this was a logical corollary to the policy described above: where the unions had taken a political stand, they naturally encouraged the parties favoring that stand and opposed the parties hostile to it. Such actions, in their eyes, did not violate the principle of neutrality.

In fact, the union leaders appealed to the principle as a justification for their fight against the USPD and the KPD within the union movement. "Dissmann and his friends," said Legien in a 1919 speech, "want to make the union organizations into a political factor, an idea which we have opposed for many years [sic!]."[51] The Communists received similar treatment. A 1924 ADGB council resolution used the following argument: "Against the resolution of the Nuremberg trade-union congress that established the neutrality of the unions with regard to political parties, the Communists are endeavoring to make the trade unions into organs of their own party policy."[52] Therefore the ADGB leaders felt justified in taking strong measures against Com-

49. These examples of trade-union intervention in German political life will receive more detailed treatment later in the chapter.
50. *Gewerkschaften*, p. 28.
51. Quoted in Leipart, *Carl Legien*, p. 135.
52. Quoted ibid.

munist influence. They regularly expelled KPD ringleaders and required of all union officials an oath not to use their posts to further the interests of any party. Violation brought automatic dismissal.[53] The unions were not neutral toward those parties that endangered their conception of union neutrality.

Finally, the neutrality principle did not prevent the ADGB from giving official support to Social Democratic candidates after 1922, or from intervening to revise the draft Heidelberg Program, or from sending representatives (after 1925) to take part in the meetings of the party council.[54] Somehow even these actions were harmonized with the Nuremberg Resolution.

Was the policy of neutrality, then, merely an elaborate hoax? Not entirely. There were two areas in which the trade unionists took neutrality seriously. First, the unions did not require their members to subscribe to any particular political or religious beliefs. This kind of neutrality, of course, was nothing new; it had been practiced by the Eisenachers in their early organizations. But the emergence of three socialist parties during the Revolution made such a policy even more necessary. The ADGB leaders did not want to force the Independents and Communists completely out of the unions, just as they did not want to alienate Catholic workers unnecessarily. Multiple unions make weak bargaining agents. In this area organizational needs dictated a neutral course.[55]

Second, the trade unionists were serious in asserting their neutrality *from* parties. They wanted to formulate union policy solely in the light of union needs and would not tolerate pressure from any party—not from the Communists,

53. Cassau, *Gewerkschaftsbewegung,* pp. 295–96; Schlesinger, *Central European Democracy,* pp. 237–41.
54. These developments will also be treated later in the chapter.
55. Seidel, *Gewerkschaften,* p. 26.

not from the Independents, not even from the SPD. Thus Leipart wrote in 1925: "The claim of the Social Democratic Party to the 'ideological leadership' of the trade unions can no more be recognized than the claim to leadership of the Communist International, which has been vainly trying for years to force its tactics and goals upon the trade unions."[56] "Independence" would describe this policy more accurately than "neutrality" for, as Seidel explained, "the purpose of neutrality is to preserve the independence of the trade-union movement from political influence."[57]

The Nuremberg Resolution, then, abrogated the formal bond between the Free Trade Unions and Social Democracy. The new policy of neutrality did not exclude the use of political pressure or party favoritism but was confined to "the political independence of the trade unions in the conduct of their struggle, and political and religious neutrality with regard to their members."[58] The ADGB leaders displayed far more zeal in preserving the independence of the unions from political influence than they did in preserving the independence of the SPD from union influence.

Trade-Union Influence in the Weimar SPD

Two organizations as closely tied by tradition and interest as the Social Democratic Party and the Free Trade Unions were bound to remain in intimate association despite the severance of formal connections. Thus the unions continued

56. Letter to Hermann Müller, Sept. 12, 1925, published by Lothar Erdmann in "Nation, Gewerkschaften und Sozialismus," *Die Arbeit, 10* (1933), 149.

57. *Gewerkschaften,* p. 24. On the whole question of neutrality, also see Richard Seidel, *Gewerkschaften und politische Parteien in Deutschland* (Berlin, 1928), pp. 63–70.

58. Walter Pahl, "Gewerkschaften und Sozialdemokratie vor 1933," *Gewerkschaftliche Monatshefte, 4* (1953), 720.

to exert a powerful influence in party affairs. In order to understand the strength and character of this influence, it is necessary to scrutinize certain features of the relationship: the comparative size of the two groups, the interlocking of their memberships and leaderships, contacts among leaders, and cases of conflict between the two organizations.

We have already observed that, even before the war, the unions had outstripped the party in size and were growing at a faster rate. In the Weimar period the ADGB was in every way the larger of the two organizations. From its 1914 membership of 2 million, the ADGB mushroomed fantastically in the favorable soil of early Weimar to 5.5 million in 1919, and 7.9 million in 1920. The inflation trimmed this figure down to 4.6 million, where it remained relatively stable for the rest of the republican period.[59] Thus, for every party member, the ADGB could count 1.9 members in 1912, 5.5 in 1919, and 4.8 in 1930. The income of the ADGB soared high above that of the party; in 1929 it reached 250 million marks, about twenty-three times the amount taken in by the SPD in the same year.[60] The trade-union press—some eighty-four weekly newspapers—reached 6 million readers, or about five times as many as the Social Democratic press.[61] When one member of a partnership is vastly more powerful than the other, its viewpoint will usually prevail in matters of contention between them.

The SPD was especially tied to the trade unions because it depended on organized labor to furnish the backbone of its electoral support. We have already noted that the ratio

59. Erich Roll, "Germany," in H. A. Marquand et al., *Organized Labor in Four Continents* (London, 1939), p. 86.
60. Ibid.
61. Gerard Braunthal, "The Politics of the German Free Trade Unions during the Weimar Period" (Ph.D. Dissertation, Columbia University, New York, N.Y., 1954), p. 198.

of Social Democratic voters to union members declined from 8:1 in 1893 to 2:1 by 1914. In the Weimar period this ratio continued to fluctuate around the low 1914 level— 2.1:1 in 1919; 0.7:1 in 1920; 1.8:1 in 1930. There were more ADGB members than SPD voters in 1920!

Of course, as the 1920 ratio conclusively demonstrates, not all trade unionists voted Social Democratic. Of 624 delegates to the 1919 ADGB congress, 179 (representing some 1.5 million members) supported the policies of the Independent Social Democrats.[62] This number declined to 138 out of 691 at the 1922 congress, while the Communists now claimed 90 delegates. KPD influence rose sharply during the inflation; according to one sympathetic source, 2.5 million unionists wore members or sympathizers of that party in 1923. But Communist trade-union policy vacillated in the following years between the tactic of boring from within and that of forming rival union organizations. By 1925 its strength in the ADGB had declined to about 400,000, or 10 per cent, and its representation at trade-union congresses never again rose above five delegates.[63]

Dealing with the Weimar period as a whole, Gerard Braunthal has estimated that 15 to 20 per cent of the Free Trade Union membership voted for parties other than the SPD. He has further calculated that 5 to 6 per cent were too young to vote and another 10 per cent did not bother with elections. This would leave approximately 65 per cent of the membership who cast their ballots for the SPD. Now, taking the 1928 election as an example, 65 per cent would equal 3,840,000 persons, or 38 per cent of the total Social Democratic turnout.[64] To this figure must be added a host

---

62. *Prot. Gewerkschaften 1919*, p. 405.
63. Ossip Flechtheim, *Die Kommunistische Partei Deutschlands in der Weimarer Republik* (Offenbach/Main, Bollwerk, 1948), pp. 82, 136.
64. Braunthal, "Free Trade Unions," p. 139.

of votes from male members' wives, most (though not all) of whom must have voted as their husbands did. It seems safe to conclude that organized workers and their wives made up a solid majority of the SPD electorate.

If the trade unions provided the most important share of the party's voting strength, they furnished a still greater portion of its membership. A report of the SPD local for Bremen stated that 80 per cent of the comrades there were trade unionists.[65] In rural areas this figure was lower. For the party as a whole Braunthal estimates two-thirds or, excluding women members, three-quarters. Looking at the question from the other direction, about 12 to 15 per cent of all Free Trade Union members were organized in the SPD, generally the more active unionists.[66] Eugen Varga has estimated that 95 per cent of the paid union officials were party members.[67] Almost all the top ADGB leaders were Social Democrats, some only nominally but most in an active capacity.[68]

For a few years after the passing of the Nuremberg Resolution the ADGB made an effort to be politically neutral. It voluntarily relinquished its traditional prerogative to select half the German delegation sent to the congress of the Socialist International.[69] It refrained from giving official support to any party in the 1920 Reichstag election.[70] But once the USPD had reunited with the main party in 1922, the unions scuttled electoral neutrality. Beginning with the December

65. *Jahresbericht 1924/25* (Ortsverein Bremen der SPD), quoted in Eugen Varga, ed., *Die Sozialdemokratischen Parteien* (Hamburg, 1926), pp. 43–44.

66. Braunthal, "Free Trade Unions," pp. 132, 138.

67. *Die Sozialdemokratischen Parteien*, p. 35.

68. Braunthal, "Free Trade Unions," p. 134.

69. *Prot. Gewerkschaften 1922*, p. 213.

70. The pre-election issue of the official union organ contains no mention of the impending contest: *Correspondenzblatt*, June 5, 1920, pp. 297–312.

1924 contest, the ADGB once again gave formal endorsement to the Social Democratic slate.[71] Theodor Leipart explained this move before the 1925 trade-union congress:

[In view of the electoral drift to the right] the trade unions have found it less and less possible to remain passive in political elections. The vital interests of the trade unions, which in this case are identical with the vital interests of all German labor, have forced the ADGB executive and council in the last few years to take a positive position toward political elections and to support Social Democratic candidates. We have made and publicly declared this decision because we were—and still remain—of the opinion that of all the political parties only the Social Democratic stands up stalwartly for the real interests of the working people.[72]

For the rest of the republican period the SPD had the open support of the Free Trade Unions.

This support, moreover, did not end with mere verbal endorsement; the unions regularly contributed substantial sums to help meet the party's burdensome campaign expenses. The amounts given were not customarily disclosed, but it is known that in the July 1932 election the SPD received 384,000 marks from the unions, or 14 per cent of the party's 2.8 million-mark campaign budget.[73] The policy of neutrality, then, affected only the Reichstag contest of 1920; otherwise electoral arrangements between the SPD and the trade unions remained quite as they had been before the war.

Shifting our attention now to the actual means by which the leadership of the ADGB influenced the policies of the party, we may first observe that the unions did not attempt, except for the Reichstag fraction, to load central party institutions with their own people. There were no trade-union

71. *Die Gewerkschafts-Zeitung,* Nov. 22, 1924, p. 459.
72. *Prot. Gewerkschaften 1925,* p. 111.
73. Braunthal, "Free Trade Unions," p. 210.

leaders on the party executive, council, or control commission (although many members of these bodies had previously been active in union affairs and still retained formal membership). Only a handful of union leaders served as delegates to party congresses: ten in 1927; nine in 1929; thirteen in 1931.[74] Two members of the fifteen-man ADGB executive attended the 1920 party congress, and the same number were present in 1921 and 1922.[75]

The unions used other avenues to influence SPD policy. One of the most important of these was the Social Democratic Reichstag fraction, where union leaders could directly affect national legislation. In 1919, fifty-one such leaders came to the National Assembly; among them were five members of the general commission, nine chairmen of national unions, six members of national union executives, twenty-three regional leaders and local officials, and eight officials of trade-union cartels.[76] These fifty-one constituted 27 per cent of the entire fraction. During the Weimar period as a whole, the proportion of union leaders in the Reichstag fraction averaged 20 per cent.[77] This figure refers, of course, only to union *leaders;* most Social Democratic deputies were *members* of a trade union. Although no exact statistics are available, Robert Goetz estimates that 83 per cent of the May 1924 fraction were union members.[78] Once in the legislature, the union leaders got themselves placed on committees strategic to trade-union interests. Thus in 1928, of twenty-eight depu-

74. Ibid., pp. 129, 147.
75. Determined by comparing names of ADGB executive members in *Prot. Gewerkschaften 1919*, p. 554, with the list of delegates at party congresses in *Prot. 1920*, pp. 407–13; *Prot. 1921*, pp. 403–09; *Prot. 1922*, pp. 116–22.
76. *Correspondenzblatt*, Feb. 22, 1919, p. 63.
77. Braunthal, "Free Trade Unions," p. 216.
78. *Les syndicats ouvriers allemands après la guerre* (Paris, 1934), p. 252.

ties on the Committee for Economic Affairs, nine were Social Democrats and six of these were union leaders. A trade unionist likewise presided over the committee. On the Committee for Social Affairs, five of the nine Social Democrats chosen were union leaders.[79] Thus the ADGB had sufficient influence to guide the legislative efforts of the fraction in matters relating to union interests.

By and large the Free Trade Unions appeared satisfied with their weight in the Reichstag fraction. When a demand was raised at the 1928 ADGB congress to ask the party for a straight one-third union representation on the fraction, Fritz Tarnow, speaking for the leadership, opposed it, explaining: "In general the unions have not been forgotten in the distribution of political mandates. . . . There are, to be sure, regions in the Reich where one has the impression that trade unionists are not wanted simply because they are trade unionists. With the responsible central party leaders, however, there exists a neighborly sort of collaboration, which gives no occasion for special demands in this regard."[80]

Nor were the unions forgotten when it came to distributing cabinet posts. In fact, the coalition governments in which the SPD participated marked high points in the political influence of the Free Trade Unions. During the Scheidemann government, for example, three of the seven Social Democratic ministers were prominent trade unionists; during the two Bauer governments, four of seven; during the first Müller government, three of six; etc. The ministries held were those crucial to trade-union interests—usually Labor, Economic Affairs, and Food.[81] Two SPD-led coalition cabinets actually had a union leader as their chancellor—Gustav Bauer. None of the trade unionists involved here occupied a position in the

---

79. Braunthal, "Free Trade Unions," p. 230.
80. *Prot. Gewerkschaften 1928*, pp. 311–12.
81. Braunthal, "Free Trade Unions," pp. 234–36.

party important enough to justify his cabinet appointment. Bauer, for instance, never held an office in the national party leadership, or even a regional secretaryship; he had been a Reichstag deputy only since 1912. What qualified him for the chancellorship was clearly his position as second co-chairman of the ADGB, Carl Legien's right-hand man. Since the majority of Bauer's Social Democratic colleagues in the cabinet were trade-union officials with no more party experience than he had, it would be more proper to term the Bauer government an ADGB-led coalition rather than an SPD-led coalition.

From their strategic posts in the government, trade-unionist ministers such as these were able to determine the day-to-day policies of the Social Democratic Party to a far greater extent than their actual positions in the party organization warranted. Thus, at the very top of the governmental hierarchy the Free Trade Unions exerted a powerful influence on SPD policy.

As a final and obvious avenue of influence one should mention the formal and informal contacts between the union and party leaderships. In response to a survey on party–union relations conducted by the International Federation of Trade Unions, the ADGB reported: "Joint discussions are held when occasion arises. There is no reciprocal representation on the respective Executives. There are however reciprocal delegations to meetings of the General Council [party council] of the Social Democratic Party and the Executive of the Centre [ADGB] (usually 1 representative in each case)."[82] Formal joint meetings of the two executives were rare, but unofficial conversations and meetings often took place.[83]

82. "Relations between Political Labour Party and Trade Union Movement in Various Countries," *The International Trade Union Movement*, 7 (1927), 127.

83. Braunthal, "Free Trade Unions," p. 145.

It is extremely difficult to assess, in the case of any specific policy of the party, the extent to which each branch of the labor movement contributed to the decision. Only where publicly known conflicts arose between them is such an assessment really possible—and disagreements rarely occurred. A great controversy, such as that over the general strike in 1905, could scarcely arise in the Weimar period. Both organizations were safely under the control of conservative leaders who saw eye to eye on fundamentals. Such harmonious collaboration, combined with the informal nature of the relationship, makes it difficult to determine the strength of trade-union influence in the SPD with any precision.

The few instances of conflict, however, are instructive; we will briefly review three of them here. When the party program commission drew up a first draft of the Heidelberg Program in 1925, Leipart objected strenuously to two of its paragraphs. In an official letter of protest to the party chairman, he wrote:

> The ninth paragraph of the introduction begins with the sentence: "The struggle of the working class against capitalist exploitation is necessarily a *political struggle.*"
>
> This formulation does not correspond with the facts. The struggle against the capitalist exploitation of the working class is in the first instance an economic struggle which must be fought by the trade unions. . . .
>
> Still more doubtful—and for the unions intolerable—is the eleventh paragraph of the introduction: *"The mission of the Social Democratic Party is to mold the struggle of the working class—the political, the trade union, and the cooperative struggle—into a conscious and united one, and to show it its necessary goal."* . . . The trade unions have in the past constantly defended themselves against any attempt by the party to prescribe the line of march or goal of the

175

unions; today, and precisely today, they insist upon an autonomous fixing of their own "necessary goal."[84] [Emphasis in original.]

In response to this blast the program writers, describing themselves as "the last to create tactical difficulties," quickly repaired the offending phrases. The ninth paragraph, though simply a verbatim repetition of a sentence in the venerable Erfurt Program, was changed to read: "The struggle of the working class against capitalist exploitation is not only an economic one, but also necessarily a political struggle"—now implying a primacy of the economic movement! The rewritten eleventh paragraph simply omitted all mention of the trade unions and cooperatives. The Heidelberg party congress then adopted the revised draft program with only two very minor amendments.[85] A mere letter from the chairman of the ADGB had effected greater changes in the program than had the entire party congress. This episode indicates how large a voice the Free Trade Unions had even in the internal concerns of the party.

Yet it must not be asserted, as the Communists have done, that the union organization completely dominated the party, that Social Democracy was nothing more than the mindless instrument of the ADGB. The party did not succumb to union pressure in certain disputes. For example, after the outbreak of the depression, the ADGB demanded that Germany halt all reparation payments; arguing from economic and nationalist grounds the trade unions urged the party to adopt the same position. But the SPD resisted this prompting and stuck to its traditional policy of fulfillment, reasoning

84. Letter to Hermann Müller, Sept. 12, 1925, in Erdmann, *Die Arbeit*, *10*, 149–50.
85. *Prot. 1925*, pp. 6, 274, 298.

that the goal of reconciliation with the Western powers should override all economic problems.[86]

A more consequential example comes from the last days of the Republic, when General Kurt von Schleicher was attempting to create a kind of labor–Nazi alliance to provide popular support for his own authoritarian rule. His ambitious scheme not only involved splitting the Strasser wing of the Nazi Party away from Hitler's leadership, but also necessitated separating the Free Trade Unions from the hostile Social Democratic Party. On November 28, 1932, he invited Theodor Leipart and other union leaders to a conference, which they attended despite vigorous party protests. Although no concrete agreement resulted, the way was left open for further conversations. And when Schleicher became chancellor a few days later, Leipart, instead of opposing the new cabinet, announced a wait-and-see policy, declaring he would not fight Schleicher until he saw "whether the deeds of the government correspond to its words."[87] At this point the party sharpened its stand on the matter. Rudolf Breitscheid, speaking for the executive in a meeting on January 6, 1933, urged Leipart not to undertake any further negotiations. According to Gustav Noske, Breitscheid even *demanded* compliance with party policy, announcing to the union leader that the SPD "refuses any collaboration with the reactionary Schleicher and expects you to take the same attitude."[88] In any event, Leipart did not meet with Schleicher again, thus making it appear that he had given in to party pressure.

86. Wilhelm Keil, *Erlebnisse eines Sozialdemokraten, 2* (Stuttgart, 1947), 428.

87. From a statement in *Alarm*, Dec. 23, 1932, as quoted by Earl Beck, *The Death of the Prussian Republic* (Tallahassee, 1959), p. 181.

88. *Erlebtes aus Aufstieg und Niedergang einer Demokratie* (Offenbach/Main, 1947), pp. 310–11.

It would be hasty, however, to jump to such a conclusion. It is not clear that Schleicher ever offered Leipart enough to constitute a serious temptation. Furthermore, by January 6, the general's attempt to split the Nazi Party had failed, the Hitler–Papen alliance had been formed, and Schleicher was clearly on the way out. Therefore Leipart may well have been ready to abandon the conversations even without party prompting. What this episode does reveal is that the Social Democratic Party was capable of following a political course independent of the trade unions, even when it led to conflict with them.

Union influence in the SPD was neither all-pervading nor insignificant. One can fairly say that, enforced by the disparate size of the two organizations, by the electoral dependence of the party on organized workers, by the presence of union leaders in the Reichstag fraction and in cabinet posts, and by the close contact of the two leaderships, the trade-union influence was usually the dominant factor in Social Democratic policy making.

What was the direction of the influence? This question can only be answered briefly here. The victory of the reformist forces within the party had been in very large measure the victory of the unions and of union ideology. "Trade-union thinking" now became, in the words of Sigmund Neumann, "the decisive influence in the attitude of the entire party."[89] Thus, the belief in the tactic of piecemeal reforms, the faith in the stability of the German economy and in steady progress toward evolving socialism, the positive attitude toward state and nation—these now became articles of faith for the party as they had previously been for the unions. The right-wing trade unionist, Walter Pahl, put it as follows: "Before 1933 the Free Trade Unions, by their renunciation of every 'ideo-

89. *Die deutschen Parteien, Wesen und Wandel nach dem Kriege* (Berlin, 1932), pp. 32–33.

178

logical corset,' contributed essentially to the deliverance of working-class socialism from the Marxist schema, and to its orientation toward concrete efforts to improve the workers' living conditions in the existing order."[90] The trade unions undoubtedly added a powerful impetus to the conservative drift of the SPD.

The Trade Unions in Politics

During the fourth stage of party–union relations we have seen that the Mannheim Agreement was abrogated and the so-called neutrality of the unions proclaimed, but that their influence in the Social Democratic Party remained much the same as before. The fourth stage exhibits another identifying characteristic. In order to achieve their political aims, the Free Trade Unions not only worked through the SPD, but were also able to intervene directly in politics, circumventing the party. Such direct influence the unions exerted through their representatives on public bodies, through pressure and lobbying, even, on one occasion, by means of a mass political strike. These actions constituted the beginnings of a movement away from the SPD toward an independent political role for the trade unions separate from all parties. Initiated during the Weimar period, this development has come to full flower in the postwar Bonn Republic, where it may be said to mark a fifth stage in the long evolution of party–union relations.[91]

To catalogue all the independent political acts of the Weimar Free Trade Unions would be neither practicable nor desirable. It must suffice to describe the development in general, offering as illustrations a few of the most conse-

90. *Gewerkschaftliche Monatshefte, 4,* 724.
91. Cf. Otto Kirchheimer, "West German Trade Unions," *World Politics, 8* (1955–56), 495–507.

quential actions, which not only illuminate the new political role of the unions but also throw more light on their relationship with the SPD. The actions selected are those taken by the unions in the Kapp Putsch (1920), in the fall of the second Müller government (1930), and during Hitler's seizure of power (1933).

One might say that the trade unions' road toward independent politics began with their decision of August 2, 1914—taken without reference to the SPD—to support the German war effort. Indeed, the war as a whole had the effect of drawing the unions into a more direct relationship with the state. The Free Trade Unions placed their organizations and funds at the disposal of the government for the purpose of administering social services to unemployed, to war victims, etc. They helped draw up and administer the Auxiliary Service Act of 1916, which brought total mobilization to the German economy. As a reward for their aid, trade-union officials received exemption from the draft.[92]

In the creation of the Weimar Republic, provision was made for a vastly increased union participation in, and influence on, state activities. Articles 157 and 159 of the new constitution guaranteed the right of association and put "the forces of labor" under the special protection of the Reich.[93] The unions were directly represented (not through the SPD) on many government agencies: the National Economic Council, the Reichsbank, the Post Office Board, the Electricity Board, the National Railroad Board, and others.[94] As Pahl has observed, "The state transferred to the Free Trade

92. Richard Seidel, *The Trade Union Movement of Germany* (Amsterdam, 1928), pp. 80–89; Snell, *American Historical Review, 59,* 71.

93. An English translation of the Weimar Constitution appears in Frederick F. Blachly and Miriam E. Oatman, *The Government and Administration of Germany* (Baltimore, 1928), pp. 642–79.

94. Braunthal, "Free Trade Unions," p. 243.

Unions a host of functions, the exercise of which simultaneously bound the latter to the state. The social power exercised by the unions became practically a public function."[95] These functions made it increasingly possible for the unions to influence governmental policy on multitudinous questions touching their interests without using the SPD as an intermediary.

Further, by political pressure and lobbying, the ADGB could often affect legislation pending before the Reichstag, or induce a cabinet minister to alter a particular policy. For example, prominent trade-union leaders assisted the Ministry of Labor in drawing up the Unemployment Insurance Law passed in 1927.[96] All in all, the political powers of the unions were so great as to lead Franz Neumann to conclude: "No important political decision was taken by the government without the trade unions. And it was very often they who turned the scale; their influence was invariably stronger than that of the Social Democratic Party."[97]

The Kapp Putsch provides not only the most significant instance of independent political action by the Free Trade Unions but an interesting case of conflict between party and unions as well. On March 13, 1920, Wolfgang Kapp and a circle of military and reactionary followers carried out a successful counterrevolutionary coup d'état in Berlin. Before fleeing the city, the Bauer cabinet then in office had encouraged the SPD to issue an appeal for a general strike, which the party executive promptly did. On the same day the ADGB executive met in emergency session, and after hearing reports from the party, decided to lead a mass political strike aimed at restoring the legal government. Representatives of the ADGB, the AfA, and later the ADB,

95. *Gewerkschaftliche Monatshefte,* 4, 723.
96. Braunthal, "Free Trade Unions," pp. 275–76.
97. *European Trade Unionism and Politics* (New York, 1936), p. 24.

formed a strike committee under the leadership of Carl Legien.[98] This action in itself constituted the most far-reaching political undertaking ever dreamt of by the unions, and a reversal of all previous union thinking. The organizations which for decades had bitterly fought any advocacy of the general strike, even as a defensive weapon, now found themselves at the head of a movement which forced the Kappists from power in less than a week. On March 17 the counter-revolutionaries fled, and the Social Democratic Reichstag fraction issued an appeal asking the strikers to return to work.[99]

It was at this point that disagreement arose. The three union organizations sponsoring the strike now refused to heed the SPD call until the government met nine sweeping demands. The most important of these were: (1) the "decisive influence" of the Free Trade Unions in the formation of a new cabinet, and in the reform of social and economic legislation; (2) immediate punishment of the Kappists; (3) dismissal of Noske; (5) purge and democratization of the civil service; (7) immediate socialization of the mining, power, and potash industries; (8) a law to expropriate landowners not producing foodstuffs for the general good; (9) dissolution of the counterrevolutionary military formations; taking over of the security police by organized labor.[100]

Had these reforms been energetically carried out they would have effected near-revolutionary changes in German government and society. Such radical demands were quite out of character for Legien and the conservative union leadership. The "decisive influence" demanded in the first point, for example, was manifestly unconstitutional. Yet the

98. *Correspondenzblatt,* Mar. 27, 1920, p. 150.
99. H. G. Daniels, *The Rise of the German Republic* (London, 1927), p. 144.
100. *Correspondenzblatt,* Mar. 27, 1920, pp. 152–53.

official organ of the ADGB defended the program in fire-eating phrases:

> [The trade unions] must intervene as a new factor in political life, with which the government and the parliament must come to terms before all decisive steps. There may be doctrinaire democrats who view such a settlement as incompatible with the constitutional rights of the people's representative bodies. To them we can only say: a parliamentarianism that hardens in external forms without caring for the vital productive powers of the people is a danger to the commonweal.[101]

Whoever has followed the politics of the Free Trade Unions can appreciate what a fantastic volte-face this represents.

Why did Carl Legien, a long-time Social Democrat, put forth these demands so embarrassing to a Social Democratic coalition government, one headed by his own second-in-command, Gustav Bauer? It certainly presents a puzzling spectacle! The answer seems to be that he was acting under extreme pressure from the left. Despite the fact that the ADGB, AfA, and ADB "assumed" the leadership of the general strike, they were not in control of the movement in several areas of the Reich—most importantly, Berlin.

When the union leaders first organized their strike committee on March 13, the Berlin trade-union commission, controlled by left-wing Independents, had refused to join. Together with leaders from the USPD and the KPD, it formed a second strike committee which demanded not simply the re-establishment of the old coalition government but the formation of a new, purely socialist government.[102] The workers of Greater Berlin accepted the authority of this committee rather than that of Legien's. Once the Kappists

101. Ibid., p. 155.
102. Ibid., p. 150; Heinz Josef Varain, *Freie Gewerkschaften, Sozialdemokratie und Staat* (Düsseldorf, 1956), p. 173.

had been dispatched, Legien was forced to take the radicals' strike aims into account: hence the first of the nine demands called for a new government rather than restoration of the old one. The other demands as well were drawn up "under the strong influence" of the radicals.[103]

Legien apparently accepted this influence because he could not get the Berlin workers back on their jobs without the cooperation of the radicals. This may be seen in the developments that followed. The three unions *and the Berlin trade-union commission* met with representatives of the government to discuss the nine points. After several hours of negotiation the three unions accepted a much watered-down version—the crucial first demand was completely emasculated—and issued a call to end the strike.[104] But the Berlin trade-union commission, together with the USPD and the KPD, refused to join the call, still demanding a socialist government. The great mass of Berlin workers stayed out, demonstrating their loyalty to the more radical leadership. Only after further negotiations and the acceptance of four additional demands did the Berlin strikers return to their jobs three days later.[105]

Legien and the leadership of the Free Trade Unions, then, did not by their own liking assume the radical position that brought them into conflict with the SPD and the Bauer government. They were driven to it by the forces of revolution which they themselves unleashed, in order to retain a semblance of control over them. Ludwig Heyde, editor of the *Soziale Praxis,* summed up the situation concisely:

> The Putsch had as its consequence a general strike, and the left-radical demagogues used the general strike as the start-

103. Braunthal, "Free Trade Unions," p. 46. Cf. Daniels, *German Republic,* p. 144, and Merker, *Sozialdemokratie,* p. 264.
104. *Correspondenzblatt,* Mar. 27, 1920, p. 153.
105. Ibid., pp. 153–54; Varain, *Freie Gewerkschaften,* p. 177.

184

ing point for an enormous propaganda campaign which found only too good a reception among the aroused, mistrustful, disappointed masses. There could be no thought of bringing the general strike to a quick conclusion unless the strikers were given, by a visible deed, a palpable guarantee that all their wishes—even those only halfway justified—would be taken into account. The political parties in no way grasped the seriousness of the situation. The trade unions either had to surrender the field to the council demagogues or themselves spring stout-heartedly into the breach.[106]

Only in this way does the strange behavior of the usually conservative, law-abiding union leadership make sense.

The Kapp Putsch nonetheless marked the undoubted pinnacle of trade-union power in German politics. The unions had called out the most massive political strike in history and had seen it to victory. They had negotiated with the *de jure* government as one power to another. They had brought about the resignation of that government, and Legien had even been offered the chancellorship in a new one.[107] Never again did the unions wield such influence in German politics.

The fall of the Great Coalition led by Hermann Müller in 1930 provides the next example of an ADGB intervention in politics which also affected party–union relations.[108] The advent of the depression had as one of its consequences a new offensive by the Right to cut burdensome state unemployment benefits. Until his death in November 1929, Stresemann was able to keep his party (DVP) behind the coalition policy of maintaining existing benefit rates.[109] But in March of the

106. In *Soziale Praxis, 29* (1920), 747. Cf. Varain, *Freie Gewerkschaften,* pp. 179–81, and Braunthal, "Free Trade Unions," p. 169.

107. Leipart, *Carl Legien,* p. 118.

108. A complete analysis of this government crisis can be found in Helga Timm, *Die deutsche Sozialpolitik und der Bruch der grossen Koalition im März 1930* (Düsseldorf, 1952).

109. S. William Halperin, *Germany Tried Democracy* (New York, 1946), p. 404.

following year, the now dominant right wing of the People's Party pressed this issue, threatening to break up the coalition and cause the collapse of the government. The Center Party proposed a compromise that called for no immediate cut, but sanctioned a possible reduction of benefits later on.[110] The SPD, which hitherto had opposed any thought of curtailment, now had to decide whether to accept the compromise or reject it and thus precipitate a government crisis.

The party was divided on the issue. Müller, Severing, and many of the conservatives in the party preferred reluctant acceptance rather than face a cabinet crisis. Minister of Labor Rudolf Wissell and the left wing of the party opposed acceptance; most Left Social Democrats by now wanted an end to the Great Coalition anyway.[111] The trade unions, because their immediate economic interests were vitally concerned, came out decisively against acceptance of the compromise. The ADGB council made scarcely veiled threats that if the party gave in, trade unionists would take their votes elsewhere in the next election.[112]

A meeting of the Reichstag fraction was called to decide the issue. As the crucial vote was about to be taken, Friedrich Stampfer tells us,

> The several trade-union leaders who were fraction members entered the room, and from their midst Hermann Müller-Lichtenberg [a member of the ADGB executive, not to be confused with Chancellor Hermann Müller-Franken] demanded the floor. . . . The speaker for the unions declared in a dictatorial tone that the compromise over unemployment insurance was completely unacceptable. Should the

110. *Schulthess' Europäischer Geschichtskalender* (Munich, Beck, 1931), *71* (1930), 91.
111. Friedrich Stampfer, *Die ersten 14 Jahren der Deutschen Republik* (Offenbach/Main, 1947), pp. 561–62.
112. *Gewerkschafts-Zeitung*, Aug. 10, 1929, p. 504.

fraction come to any other conclusion, the unions would not hesitate to make known their opposing stand as energetically as possible in the Reichstag, in the press, and in the party.[113]

Thus the warmest advocates of party discipline announced their intention to violate it should they not get their way. Actually, Müller's speech was an unnecessary tour de force; a majority of the fraction was already prepared to vote against the Center compromise. It must be remembered, as Helga Timm has pointed out, that the party had traditionally taken a strong stand on social legislation, and at the 1929 congress a sharp resolution had been passed against any reduction in unemployment benefits.[114] In any event, the balloting taken just after this address resulted in a heavy victory for the trade-union viewpoint. The government promptly collapsed.

Here again the unions followed their own political interests without reference to the SPD. They used every means available to constrain the party into acceptance of the union position: special caucuses, threats of open opposition, etc. The uncompromising stand of the ADGB on unemployment insurance helped to bring about the collapse of the last socialist-led coalition—in fact, the last parliamentary government —of the Weimar Republic.

Trade-union actions during Hitler's seizure of power in 1933 may serve as a final illustration of the unions in politics and as a conclusion to this chapter on the relationship between the SPD and the Free Trade Unions. At that time the ADGB made a complete break with the party in an attempt to save its own organization by accommodating to the Nazi regime.

113. *14 Jahre,* p. 562.
114. *Bruch der grossen Koalition,* pp. 182–85.

The depression had robbed the unions of their primary raison d'etre; the state had taken over the regulation of wage rates. Falling prices and millions of unemployed would have thwarted strike activity in any event. Desperate, the trade-union leaders cast about for some new tactic. Some of them, viewing the decline of parliamentary government, advocated severing relations with the SPD.[115] When Chancellor Kurt von Schleicher attempted to form an army–labor–Nazi alliance in 1932, ADGB leaders, as we have already observed, entered into discussions with him. Although neither of these schemes bore fruit, they served as portents of the break to follow.

On January 30, 1933, Hitler became chancellor. The trade unions joined the party in urging the workers to keep calm.[116] Party–union relations remained unimpaired until after the March 5 elections, in which the ADGB gave Social Democratic candidates its regular support.[117] But the handwriting was on the wall: the day before the election, Vice-Chancellor von Papen suggested the necessary conditions for the continued existence of the unions: "If the trade unions recognize the sign of the times and depoliticize themselves in great measure, they can become precisely at this moment a strong pillar in a new people's order."[118] ADGB leaders did not fail to get the point. On May 21 they sent a statement to the Nazi government declaring their complete independence from all political parties. In the future, it announced, the unions would not interfere in politics. Their social func-

115. See, for example, Clemens Nörpel, "Selbständige Gewerkschaften oder parteipolitische Ausschüsse," *Gewerkschafts-Zeitung,* Dec. 24, 1932, pp. 819–22; and Karl Zwing, "Um die Zukunft der Gewerkschaften," *Gewerkschaftsarchiv, 9* (1932), 241–44.
116. *Gewerkschafts-Zeitung,* Feb. 4, 1933, pp. 65–68.
117. Ibid., Feb. 15, p. 113.
118. Quoted in Erich Matthias, "Der Untergang der alten Sozialdemokratie," *Vierteljahrshefte für Zeitgeschichte, 4* (1956), 271.

tions had to be carried on "no matter what form of state
there is." The unions constituted "an indispensable part of
the social order itself, . . . in the course of their history grown
together, for natural reasons, more and more with the state
itself."[119] Thereafter the ADGB organ instructed members
not to discuss politics in their meetings.[120] Hoping by this
declaration to save the unions from dissolution, the ADGB
cut itself loose from the sinking Social Democratic Party.

Still one more step remained in the accommodation process. On April 19 the ADGB agreed to participate in the "Day
of German Labor," the Nazi substitute for May Day. The
Gewerkschafts-Zeitung called upon the membership to join
their old enemies in the impending celebration. With words
that have become famous the union organ declared: "We
certainly need not strike our colors in order to recognize that
the victory of National Socialism is our victory as well, even
though won in a struggle against a party which we used to
consider the embodiment of the idea of socialism (the SPD);
because today the socialist task is put to the whole nation."[121]
On May Day the trade unionists marched behind Nazi banners in a bizarre caricature of the traditional labor demon-
stration. Early the following morning, having served their
purpose of getting the young Hitler regime through its first
May Day without embarrassment, the trade unions were outlawed, their property seized, and their leaders arrested. Such
was the inglorious conclusion of sixty years of the Free Trade
Unionism.

The unions had come a long way in politics since their
inception as front organizations for the Social Democratic
Party. In the Weimar period we have traced two dominant
trends. One was the continued influence of the unions in the

119. *Gewerkschafts-Zeitung*, Mar. 25, 1933, p. 177.
120. Braunthal, "Free Trade Unions," p. 119.
121. April 22, 1933, p. 259.

SPD, despite protestations of neutrality, up until the advent of Hitler. The other was the increasing tendency to take direct political action without regard to the party and sometimes in opposition to it. The culmination of the latter trend was the attempt of the ADGB to accommodate itself to the Nazi regime by severing all connection with Social Democracy. This can be viewed as a regrettable act of accommodation caused by totalitarian pressure, but it also represented the natural conclusion of the tendency toward independence which we have witnessed in the whole period. And it formed a natural prelude to the unified, politically independent trade-union movement of the Bonn Republic.

6. The Rebellion against the Organization

If the trade unions exerted a conservative influence on the Social Democratic Party in the Weimar period, that influence was staunchly opposed by a less powerful but still important force within the movement—the party's left wing. No mass party is politically homogeneous, and our treatment of the internal history of the SPD would be incomplete without a consideration of the factional situation inside the movement.

By the beginning of the Weimar period the old united SPD had split into three hostile political parties, corresponding to the prewar left, right, and center. The KPD, expecting the quick economic and political collapse of the new Republic, spoke for the revolutionary opposition (although, under Russian influence, it soon became a party that was neither revolutionary nor reformist in itself but merely represented the changing interests of Soviet foreign policy).[1] The old right wing, now in control of the SPD, was committed to supporting the Weimar Republic and pursued a positive policy of social reform within that context. Somewhere between these

1. See Ruth Fischer, *Stalin and German Communism* (Cambridge, Mass., 1948); Siegfried Bahne, "Die Kommunistische Partei Deutschlands," *Das Ende der Parteien, 1933,* ed. Erich Matthias and Rudolf Morsey (Düsseldorf, 1960), pp. 655–739.

191

two poles of socialist politics lay the old center, represented in the early years by the USPD and later by what we will call Left Social Democracy. This group saw the political situation as essentially unchanged by the November Revolution: socialists were still a minority in a capitalist state. Consequently, "pure opposition" (eschewing coalitions and all governmental responsibility) should remain party policy until an electoral majority could be won.

The Communists were to remain organizationally outside and permanently alienated from the SPD. The old centrists became for the Weimar period the left wing of Social Democracy. But the existence of this large and articulate bloc created a standing organizational dilemma both for the leftists themselves and for the conservative leadership of the SPD. In the eyes of the latter the predicament appeared as follows: to leave room for the leftists within the party was to sanction their disruptive and corrosive agitation among the rank and file; but to expel them would only drive them into the eager arms of the Communists or encourage them to create still a third socialist party. For the leftists the dilemma seemed equally perplexing: there was little hope of attaining control, or even adequate minority representation, in the bureaucratically managed SPD; yet to set up a rival party involved great organizational and financial difficulties and offered little hope of winning the Social Democratic masses away from their traditional loyalties. Neither side had a permanently satisfactory solution to this predicament.

As a consequence, the history of Left Social Democracy is an account of pendular swings between the two organizational possibilities. At the beginning of the republican period this grouping expressed itself in a rival party, the USPD. A reconciliation and reunification of the two socialist parties followed in 1922. But the Saxon Conflict (1923–26) soon refocused the basic antagonism and stimulated the growth

192

of a large left minority which harassed the conservative leadership down to the end of the period. In 1931 the most militant section of this opposition split out again, founding the Socialist Workers' Party. In the fourteen years of the Weimar Republic, then, the organizational pendulum of Left Social Democracy swung from rival party to internal opposition back to rival party.

The Short History of the USPD

The Independent Social Democratic Party maintained sepa rate political existence for just over five years. To trace its history in any detail lies beyond the province of this study.[2] What is important for our purpose is the organizational and sociological relationship between the Independent Party and the SPD: how it developed from the old organization; the source of its strength; which elements it lost to the KPD and which it brought back to the Majority Party in 1922.

The formation of the USPD was accomplished in two steps, each taken as a reaction to expulsion moves on the part of the dominant leadership. In December 1915 twenty deputies violated traditional fraction discipline on the Reichstag floor by voting against the party majority on the approval of war credits. Three months later, on March 24, 1916, when an emergency appropriation came up for discussion, the Opposition no longer contented itself with negative voting but openly defended its position in formal debate. This was too much for the Majority leadership: calling a fraction caucus immediately after the Reichstag adjourned, it pushed through a resolution expelling the entire opposition group from the fraction (although not from the party, for which it lacked authority). Still retaining their party membership and,

2. See Eugen Prager, *Geschichte der USPD* (Berlin, 1921).

of course, their mandates, the opposition deputies could do little but organize a new parliamentary fraction, called the Social Democratic Working Committee (Sozialdemokratische Arbeitsgemeinschaft), with Haase, Ledebour, and Dittmann as its leaders.[3]

The second step in the creation of a new party came a year later. Early in January 1917 the Working Committee called a national conference of the Opposition to discuss the seizure of *Vorwärts* and similar violations of party legality on the part of the executive. Using this meeting as a pretext, the Majority-controlled party council expelled the entire antiwar bloc. By the very act of holding a factional caucus (Sonderkonferenz), it declared, the Oppositionists had "divided themselves from the party."[4] This move was grossly illegal: the statute did not prohibit factional caucuses, and such meetings had often been held in the past, even by the Revisionists; expulsion, moreover, could not simply be pronounced by the council but had to be undertaken by local organizations or specially appointed courts using formal trial procedures.[5] Only the most radical members of the Opposition had desired a split. But now the left centrist leaders, seeing no other course open to them, called a national con-

---

3. The group included Bernstein, Bock, Büchner, Cohn, Dittmann, Geyer, Haase, Henke, Herzfeld, Horn, Kunert, Ledebour, Schwarz (Lübeck), Stadthagen, Stolle, Vogtherr, Wurm, and Zubeil. Liebknecht had already been expelled and Rühle had left voluntarily just after him. These twenty, it should be noted, did not constitute the full strength of the parliamentary opposition. In the fraction caucus prior to the December vote, forty-three deputies—over a third of the fraction—had voted against approving credits, but only the twenty named above carried their opposition to the Reichstag floor. (Ibid., pp. 87–88, 95–96.)

4. Ibid., pp. 124–31.

5. Carl E. Schorske, *German Social Democracy, 1905–1917* (Cambridge, Mass., 1955), p. 221; on expulsion regulations see the 1912 statute reproduced in Wilhelm Schroeder, *Geschichte der sozialdemokratischen Parteiorganisation in Deutschland* (Dresden, 1912), pp. 105–06.

gress to organize a new party. On April 6, 1917, the Independent Social Democratic Party (USPD) came into being.[6]

The new organization (see chapter 1) contained the most divergent political elements, from Bernstein Revisionists to left centrists to Luxemburg Spartacists. The Revisionist group, however, was minuscule and the left centrists outnumbered the radicals at least two to one. With such a left centrist majority it is not surprising that the founding congress reaffirmed adherence to the Erfurt Program, adding only that the USPD stood in complete opposition to the existing government, specifically to the war effort and the political truce.[7]

The organizational features of the new party reflected the painful experience of the Opposition as a suppressed minority in the SPD and represented a return to the spirit of Eisenach. The congress adopted a version of the 1912 statute, amended so as to remove the worst bureaucratic and centralist abuses. Thus the new central executive (Zentralleitung) would have no authority to appoint or pay secretaries at any level, its own salaried members would have only a consultative vote, and it could not exercise any legal rights over property belonging to the party as a whole. The central executive was divided into two parts: a seven-man action committee (Aktionskomitee) composed of the Berlin leadership, and a seven-man advisory (Beirat) of provincial leaders, to be called in for the more important decisions. Women comrades were guaranteed representation in the leadership. While the composition of the executive was broadened and its powers curtailed, the party council (symbol of radical defeat in the organizational struggle of 1912) was completely eliminated.

6. Prager, *USPD*, pp. 143–44.
7. *Protokoll über die Verhandlungen des Gründungs-Parteitags der Unabhängigen Sozialdemokratischen Partei Deutschlands*, ed. Emil Eichhorn (Berlin, Seehof, 1921), p. 47. Hereafter cited as *Prot. USPD* [*year*].

These amendments embodied the left centrist desire to decentralize and debureaucratize the organization without radically altering its structure.[8]

The Spartacist minority, on the other hand, committed to Luxemburg's theory of spontaneous revolution, argued for an entirely new kind of organization without any paid employees, with only a bare minimum of central institutions, and with absolute autonomy for all local units. From the left centrist majority they succeeded in wringing two concessions: a vague guarantee of "far-reaching independence" for locals, and a provision for plebiscites of the entire membership in "all important decisions that set the position of the party for a long period."[9] In any event the Spartacists regarded the USPD only as a cover. They maintained their separate factional organization within the party and carried out only those party policies with which they were in accord—a situation that portended still another split in the German socialist movement.[10]

The USPD began under the most trying conditions, having to face not only the hostility of the old party but police persecution as well. At its creation the group counted no more than 50,000 to 60,000 members, and by the time of the Revolution this number had grown only to 100,000 (although one must remember that the Majority Party, after four years of war, had lost all but 250,000 of its million-member organization).[11] Beyond its circle of membership, however, the party enjoyed widespread support in the workers' and soldiers' councils; its spokesmen held dominant

8. Ibid., pp. 16–19, 48–49.
9. Ibid., pp. 19–23, 46, 48–49.
10. Ossip Flechtheim, *Die Kommunistische Partei Deutschlands in der Weimarer Republik* (Offenbach/Main, 1948), pp. 23–24; Prager, *USPD*, p. 188.
11. Rudolf Schlesinger, *Central European Democracy and Its Background* (London, 1953), p. 131; *Prot. USPD 1919*, p. 50.

196

power in the giant metal workers' union as well as in several smaller unions.[12] Indeed, so considerable had this popular support become that the Majority Social Democrats were forced to give the USPD equal representation in the provisional government.

We cannot deal here with the important part taken by the Independents in the first months of the Republic, but must turn instead to the substantial reshuffling of political forces within the USPD that occurred during these months. The few Revisionist intellectuals soon found their way back into the Majority Party. The Spartacists likewise departed on December 30, 1918, to establish the German Communist Party. "We have only to confirm formally," explained Liebknecht, "what for a long time we have already been in fact"[13]—namely, a separate party. The Spartacist group at this time encompassed no more than "several thousand" members, with a high proportion of intellectuals.[14] Its loss was scarcely noticeable in the now rapidly expanding USPD.

After the departure of the Revisionists and Spartacists, one might suppose the remaining left centrist Independents would have at least the advantage of ideological homogeneity. But such good fortune continually eluded them. As the only party which had opposed the war and supported the Revolution with any enthusiasm, the USPD had attracted to it most of the serious revolutionary elements in the country. Above all, this included the so-called revolutionären Obleute (revolutionary shop stewards), whose following in the factories, especially in Berlin, embraced large numbers of workers. Under the leadership of Richard Müller, Emil

12. Gerard Braunthal, "The Politics of the German Free Trade Unions during the Weimar Period" (Ph.D. Dissertation, Columbia University, New York, N.Y., 1954), p. 29.
13. Quoted in Flechtheim, *Kommunistische Partei*, p. 45.
14. Ibid., p. 47.

Barth, and Ernst Däumig, the Obleute movement pressed for full socialization of industry and government by the workers' and soldiers' councils. They remained outside the KPD only because of the putschist elements which, despite Luxemburg and Liebknecht, dominated the policy making of that party.[15] But in the view of the Independents, who were satisfied with demands of limited socialization and dual government (shared by parliament and councils), the influx of Obleute revolutionaries into their party must have seemed a doubtful blessing. And, in fact, this new dichotomy of forces in the USPD was soon to bring about a second and this time lethal schism.

Before that final catastrophe, however, the Independents were to enjoy an impressive blossoming of popularity. The radicalization of the German working class in 1919 and 1920, which lay behind the waxing strength of the USPD, had many causes: the continued economic crises, exacerbated by growing inflation; and disillusionment with the SPD, with its failure to carry out effective socialization, its hostility to the councils, its brutal repression of the left, and its reliance upon the hated Freikorps. Finally, the Kapp Putsch, and the peculiar role played by the SPD in its aftermath, pushed masses of workers into the Independent camp just in time for the 1920 Reichstag elections.

In this radical atmosphere, party membership soared from a bare 100,000 in November 1918, to 300,000 by January 1919, 750,000 in December 1919, and to a peak of 893,923 in October 1920.[16] The National Assembly election had given the Independents 2.3 million votes (7.6 per cent of the

15. Arthur Rosenberg, *A History of the German Republic, 1918–1930*, trans. Ian F. D. Murrow (London, 1936), pp. 28–33; Prager, *USPD*, pp. 191–94, 202; Fischer, *German Communism*, p. 79.

16. *Prot. USPD, März 1919*, p. 50; Prager, *USPD*, p. 207; *Prot. USPD 1920*, p. 24.

total) and 22 mandates. The Reichstag election of June 1920 elevated these figures to 4.9 million votes (17.9 per cent of the total) and 84 mandates. Simultaneously the Majority Social Democrats lost all but 5.6 million (21.7 per cent of the total) of their record 1919 poll.[17] In this great electoral victory the USPD came within a few hundred thousand votes of replacing the SPD as the major socialist party in Germany.

A regional analysis of Independent strength shows its roots in the highly industrialized areas of the Reich that constituted the oldest strongholds of the socialist movement. Conversely, rural electoral regions were scarcely affected by USPD agitation; in 1919 Mecklenburg and Koblenz–Trier returned no Independent votes at all. Even in Bavaria, where the Independent Kurt Eisner headed the Land government, the party secured a miserable 2.7 per cent of the vote.[18] The 1920 elections showed only modest gains in these largely agricultural areas. In ten predominantly industrial regions, however, the USPD captured in 1920 more than one-fifth of the vote; in seven of these it exceeded the strength of the SPD. Outstanding victories were in Berlin (USPD, 42.7 per cent; SPD, 17.5 per cent), Merseburg (USPD, 45.2 per cent; SPD, 8.8 per cent), and Leipzig (USPD, 42.1 per cent; SPD, 9.1 per cent).[19] In general, Independent voting power lay in Saxony, Thuringia, the Ruhr, and the industrial area around Berlin.

Shortly after the 1920 elections the USPD was to split in two; part of its support became Communist and part became (somewhat later) the left wing of a reunited SPD. To an important extent this division was a regional one—a fact that can be seen by comparing the 1920 USPD vote distribution with later patterns. The Communists had not taken part in

17. *Statistik des deutschen Reiches, 291* (1), 96–97; *291* (3), 2–3.
18. Ibid., *291* (1), 96–97.
19. Ibid., *291* (3), 2–3.

the National Assembly election and had received only 2.1 per cent of the 1920 vote. It was not until May 1924 that they became a real electoral force, with 12.6 per cent. Most of this voting strength must have come from former Independents. Thus, of the six regions where the 1924 KPD vote exceeded that of the SPD, three (Westfalen-Süd, Düsseldorf-Ost, Merseburg) had given the USPD over 20 per cent in the preceding election, and the other three (Oppeln, Cologne–Aachen, Düsseldorf-West) had contributed only slightly less. On the other hand, the strongholds of Left Social Democracy in the late twenties were the regions of Saxony (Dresden, Leipzig, Chemnitz–Zwickau) and Thuringia, all of which likewise had delivered more than 20 per cent to the USPD in 1920, but much less to the KPD in 1924 than to the reunited SPD.[20] Independent support in Greater Berlin seems to have separated into approximately equal halves. One can discern in this regional division between Communist and Left Social Democratic centers of power a remarkable correlation with the religious divisions of Germany. Five of the six predominantly Communist regions of 1924 were Catholic; Left Social Democrats, on the other hand, flourished only in Protestant areas. The significance of this phenomenon has been discussed in Chapter 4.[21]

We must now return to the development of the schism in the USPD during 1920. The issue that divided the left and right wings of the party into two irreconcilable camps concerned possible affiliation to the Third (Communist) International. The Russians had put forth twenty-one conditions to be met by all parties desirous of joining. To become eligible the USPD would have had to transform itself into a "democratic centralist" (i.e. Leninist) party, create a secret

20. Ibid., *291* (1), 2–3; *315, 6*–7.
21. See above, pp. 124–26.

underground organization, and adhere strictly to the policies of the Comintern. Moreover—and this was the primary Russian aim—the left centrist leaders would have to be decisively repudiated and expelled. Purged of this nonrevolutionary leadership, the Russians hoped to seduce the USPD rank and file.[22]

For the two rival forces in the Independent Party, the issue involved far more than merely an international affiliation. The whole future policy of the party lay in the balance. The Obleute wing desired a continuation of revolutionary agitation and wanted the USPD remolded into an organization capable of carrying out a revolution. The Leninist model bore the prestige of success; affiliation with the Comintern seemed a natural conclusion. In the left centrist view, the revolutionary wave had receded, and the party should prepare for a period of parliamentary opposition within the legal framework of the Republic. Subservience to Moscow and Leninist organizational techniques were abhorrent to them. And of course, acceptance of the twenty-one conditions would mean their automatic expulsion from the party they had created. On such an issue there could be no compromise.[23]

In October 1920 an extraordinary party congress met at Halle to resolve the question. It had been elected on the basis of proportional representation; the left received 144,000 votes, the right, 91,000.[24] This gave the former 220 delegates

22. The 21 conditions are reprinted in Fischer, *German Communism,* pp. 141–43.

23. Ibid., pp. 144–45; Rosenberg, *German Republic,* pp. 166–68.

24. Friedrich Stampfer, *Die ersten 14 Jahren der Deutschen Republik* (Offenbach/Main, 1947), p. 213. Since the USPD had almost 900,000 members at this time, obviously the vast majority did not take part in this polling. Had the bulk of passive members voted, Stampfer suggests, the results might have given the right wing a majority.

and the latter 158, with about 15 delegates uncommitted.[25] The bulk of the party's Reichstag fraction (61 to 21) sided with the right wing.[26] As their principal speaker the Obleute imported Gregor Zinoviev, a leading figure in the Russian Revolution and now chairman of the Comintern. In a famous four-and-a-half hour speech, Zinoviev was able to tap the broad enthusiasm for the Soviet success in order to improve the leftist majority. The crucial vote was 236 to 156 in favor of affiliation.[27]

At this point the defeated right wing made a quick tactical maneuver, catching the leftists completely off guard. Chairman Crispien simply announced that all who had voted for affiliation had, by that very act, separated themselves from the USPD. The minority then adjourned to another building to continue the congress. This coup, which had no foundation whatever in party legality, preserved for the right wing the name, property, and press of the Independent Party.[28]

The schism at Halle is often presented as a lopsided separation of the great mass of the USPD rank and file from its parliamentary leadership, as a split where "the left centrist leaders were deserted by their army."[29] While it is true that the bulk of the Reichstag fraction stood on the right, they were not without mass support. At the congress, Robert Dissmann led a bloc of some 80 trade-unionist delegates who opposed affiliation.[30] And when the 900,000-member party

25. *Sozialistische Monatshefte, 26* (2) (1920), 963.
26. Stampfer, *14 Jahre,* p. 216.
27. *Prot. USPD 1920,* pp. 144–79, 261; also see Zinoviev's own account of these events in *Zwölf Tage in Deutschland* (Hamburg, 1921).
28. Prager, *USPD,* p. 226; Zinoviev, *Zwölf Tage,* pp. 55–56.
29. Schorske, *Social Democracy,* p. 329; cf. Zinoviev, *Zwölf Tage,* pp. 11, 86.
30. Ibid., p. 19; Franz Borkenau, *World Communism* (New York, 1939), pp. 199–200.

actually divided after the congress, only 300,000 entered the KPD; about 300,000 remained in the USPD, the rest apparently leaving active politics.[31] In the electorate at large it can be demonstrated that in Saxony, at least, the great majority of Independent voters followed their party back into the Social Democratic fold in 1922, and did not turn Communist.[32] The rump Independent Party, then, consisted not only of its old left centrist leadership, but also a sizable following in the working class, a following that was later to form the core of left opposition within a reunified Social Democratic Party.

There is an ironic anticlimax to the Halle schism, which may serve to conclude this section. The Obleute wing merged with the Spartacists in December 1920 to form the United Communist Party. In one stroke the small band of intellectual Communists increased in size from 80,000 to 380,000,[33] but the leaders of the Obleute group were not unreservedly happy in their new home. While they wanted a serious revolutionary policy, they opposed irresponsible putschism. After the failure of the so-called March Action in 1921, many of these leaders, including Däumig, Hoffman, and Geyer, followed Paul Levi in breaking with the KPD. After a brief sojourn in a splinter named the Communist Working Committee, this group returned early in 1922—to the USPD! But they came back as disillusioned individuals without their mass following.[34] The dismembered Independent Party, reduced to one-third its former size, hobbled through the last year of its existence toward the reunification of Nuremberg. The first attempt to create a rival party to compete with the SPD had ended in failure.

31. Ibid.; Flechtheim, *Kommunistische Partei,* p. 70.
32. See below, p. 212.
33. Ibid., p. 235.
34. Fischer, *German Communism,* pp. 178–79.

The Nuremberg Reunification of 1922

The departure of the left wing from the USPD substantially reduced the political distance between the Independent rump and the Majority Social Democrats. Council government and socialization by this time had become more or less academic issues. The leftward sweep of German public opinion, both would agree, had not merely been halted but reversed. Only the coalition question stood in the way of accord; faithful to the policy of pure opposition, the USPD refused to participate in any government with bourgeois parties,[35] but a combination of circumstances soon brought about a certain softening even on this issue.

Maimed by the defection of most of its supporters, the USPD could no longer compete successfully in the political arena. At the Saxon Landtag election late in 1920 the party lost one-third of its votes; a similar contest in Prussia in February 1921 brought still greater reverses.[36] Membership stagnated near the 300,000 mark.[37] Perhaps most threatening of all was the financial plight of the party. In the enthusiasm of the early years the organization had been expanded too rapidly; secretaries were hired, newspapers begun, publishing houses established, and so forth. By its shrewd tactical coup at Halle the minority retained the great bulk of this apparatus, but the maneuver backfired, for now a shrunken membership had to support an increasingly top-heavy organization. Thus at the time of unification the Independents still possessed 43 daily newspapers, or one for every 6,700

35. *Sozialistische Monatshefte, 27* (2) (1921), 821.
36. Heinz Schürer, *Die politische Arbeiterbewegung Deutschlands in der Nachkriegszeit, 1918–1923* (Leipzig, 1933), p. 41.
37. *Prot. 1922,* p. 127. The 1922 *Protokoll* contains the proceedings of all three unity congresses: SPD (Augsburg), USPD (Gera), and united SPD–USPD (Nuremberg).

members, as compared to one for every 8,400 in the Majority Party.[38] With this ponderous financial burden, aggravated by the growing inflation, the USPD was close to bankruptcy and could not continue long as an independent organization.[39]

Meanwhile, in day-to-day politics, the two socialist parties drew closer together to defend themselves against their common enemies. After Halle the Independents could not but view the Communist movement as an implacable foe. In this period, USPD trade unionists such as Robert Dissmann found themselves working hand in hand with SPD unionists to preserve the solidarity of their organizations in the face of a ruthless Communist splitting campaign.[40] More ominous than the threat from the left, however, was the threat from the opposite direction. The political revival of the German right, ushered in by the Kapp Putsch, put the Independents increasingly on the defensive. To preserve the achievements of the Revolution, meager though they seemed, the USPD came into closer collaboration with the Majority Party. Late in 1920 SPD–USPD coalitions were formed in the Land governments of Saxony and Thuringia.[41] The final impetus for the reunification of the two parties proved to be the assassination of the Democratic Foreign Minister, Walter Rathenau, in June 1922.[42]

The Majority Social Democrats asked the USPD to join a coalition government for the defense of the Republic. Abandoning its policy of pure opposition the Independent

38. Calculated from figures given ibid., pp. 11, 127.
39. Fritz Bieligk, "Die Entwicklung der sozialdemokratischen Organisation in Deutschland," *Die Organisation im Klassenkampf* (Berlin, n.d. [1931]), p. 56.
40. Ibid., p. 55.
41. Schürer, *Arbeiterbewegung*, p. 42.
42. *Prot. 1922*, pp. 132–33.

central executive replied affirmatively, only to have the negotiations collapse because of opposition from the SPD's bourgeois coalition partners.[43] Shortly thereafter the Reichstag fractions of the two socialist parties came together to form a working committee (Arbeitsgemeinschaft). At their instigation a joint commission was appointed to work out the organizational and programmatic basis for a unification proposal to be presented to the approaching congresses of the two parties.[44]

At the Augsburg congress of the SPD in September 1922, sentiment was overwhelmingly in favor of unity. The Majority Party, by far the larger of the two groups, stood to lose a dangerous competitor and gain additional voting strength, without having to make any serious political compromises or sacrifice its entrenched leadership. Only the extreme right Revisionists, led by Heinrich Cunow, looked askance at the move: they feared that the rightward development of the party might be halted by fusion with the Independents. But their grumbling did not prevent the unanimous approval of the proposed merger.[45]

The USPD congress held at Gera displayed no such unanimity. Debate focused chiefly on the question of coalitions, the last real issue dividing the two parties. Three divergent points of view emerged. In favor of both unity and coalitions were the most moderate of the old centrist leaders: Crispien, Breitscheid, Dittmann, Hilferding. It was they who had committed the party to the coalition for the defense of the Republic, and they who had been instrumental in the early

43. *Sozialistische Monatshefte, 28* (2) (1922), 67.
44. Ibid.; *Prot. 1922,* pp. 133–34.
45. *Prot. 1922,* pp. 69–70; also see Heinrich Cunow, "Der Auflösungsprozess der U.S.P.," *Neue Zeit, 39* (1) (1921), 105–10, and "Zur Fusion der U.S.P. mit der K.A.G.," ibid., *40* (2) (1922), 25–28; also *Sozialistische Monatshefte, 28* (2) (1922), 1014.

unity negotiations.[46] Unalterably opposed to both coalitions and unity was a small radical minority clustered around the veteran revolutionary socialist, Georg Ledebour. This group included Rosenfeld, Kunert, and Theodor Liebknecht (brother of Karl Liebknecht). They wanted to continue the middle course between Social Democracy and Communism, feeling that the growing economic crisis would soon revitalize the USPD.[47]

The great majority of the congress, however, lay between these two camps. Robert Dissmann (with his powerful trade-union backing) and Toni Sender spoke for this group, which reluctantly favored unity but remained adamantly against coalitions. Of the 192 delegates present, 122 signed a draft resolution pledging themselves to work within the reunited party for traditional Independent policies, especially the policy against coalitions.[48]

When the unity proposal came to a vote, all but the Ledebour group responded affirmatively; the tally was 183 to 9. Ledebour announced that his faction would not enter the party of Noske but would continue to function as the USPD. At this point he lost Rosenfeld and Kunert who decided to bow to the majority will. Interestingly enough, the recently merged Communist dissidents were to be found in the majority camp.[49] With his remaining supporters Ledebour withdrew and actually did keep alive a splinter party for several years which retained the name, Independent Social Democratic Party. The group had perhaps 10,000 members, centered mainly in Berlin (secondarily in the Ruhr), and managed to attract 235,000 votes in the May 1924

46. *Prot. 1922*, pp. 131–45.

47. Ibid., pp. 145–56, 173–74.

48. Ibid., pp. 131, 157–62, 172; Toni Sender, *The Autobiography of a German Rebel* (New York, 1939), pp. 200–01.

49. *Prot. 1922*, pp. 153, 173.

election (0.8 per cent of the total).[50] The following year it suffered a further cleavage after a dispute between Ledebour and Liebknecht over the Ruhr conflict, in which the former split out with a minority of 3,000 faithful followers to establish a Socialist League (Sozialistischer Bund).[51] Both of these sects maintained a precarious existence on the margin of German politics down to 1931 when, as we will see, they entered the new Socialist Workers' Party.

Returning to the reunification proceedings, once both party congresses had accepted the draft proposal, a united congress was held in Nuremberg on September 24, 1922, to consummate the fusion. Amidst much ceremony and grand oratory the delegates solemnly voted to combine the two parties into the United Social Democratic Party (VSPD).[52]

The practical arrangements for merging the two organizations had been worked out previously by negotiation. Representation in central institutions was accorded to each group roughly on the basis of its relative strength: the SPD had brought to Nuremberg a party of 1,174,106 members, 102 Reichstag deputies, and 139 daily newspapers; the USPD had 290,762 members, 61 deputies, and 43 newspapers.[53] Depending on the measure used, the Majority Party was two to four times larger than the Independent Party. Posts on the new executive were distributed as shown in Table 17.

The new control commission included seven Social Democrats and four Independents; the Reichstag fractions had already merged. Regional and local arrangements and the uni-

50. Ibid., pp. 173, 175–78; Minna Ledebour, ed., *Georg Ledebour, Mensch und Kämpfer* (Zurich, 1954), pp. 12, 23–24; Flechtheim, *Kommunistische Partei*, p. 235; *Statistik, 315,* 7.

51. Eugen Varga, ed., *Die Sozialdemokratischen Parteien* (Hamburg, 1926), p. 32.

52. *Prot. 1922*, pp. 191–93. The term "united" was dropped about a year later.

53. Ibid., pp. 11, 127; Stampfer, *14 Jahre*, p. 301.

TABLE 17. *Distribution of Posts on
VSPD Executive, 1922*

Posts	SPD	USPD	Total
Chairmen	2	1	3
Treasurers	2	1	3
Secretaries	5	1	6
Associates	6	4	10
Vorwärts Ed.	1		1
Total	16	7	23

fication of the ancillary organizations were left up to the bodies concerned. The old 1912 party statute was to be used until a commission could draw up a new statute for presentation to the next congress. Such were the principal organizational features of the synthesis.[54]

The formal proportionality of these arrangements disguised their political content. In the all-powerful party executive, for example, six of the seven Independents admitted, including Crispien, Hilferding, and Dittmann, were right-wingers who had no significant political differences with their Majority counterparts.[55] The only genuine leftist to be accepted, Franz Künstler (as an associate), was dropped at the next congress under the peculiar circumstances outlined in chapter 3.[56] In the years that followed seven new members were to enter the ruling circle of the SPD; only one of these was a former Independent, Rudolf Breitscheid, also a right-winger. Thus, Künstler's two-year term was the only executive representation given to Left Social Democracy during the entire Weimar period.

54. *Prot. 1922*, p. 64.
55. Ibid., p. 192.
56. See above, p. 71, n. 18.

The real character of the merger also revealed itself in the new statute drawn up by the joint organization commission. The eight Social Democrats and seven Independents who made up this commission presented the fruit of their labors to the Berlin congress of 1924. Although it was supposed to fuse both the old statutes, "from which the best was drawn," the new proposal contained not a single feature of USPD organization. The democratic innovations of the Independent statute—local appointment of secretaries, no executive prerogatives over party property, membership plebiscites, etc.—were nowhere to be found. Instead, the executive acquired a battery of new powers, as described in chapter 2.[57]

Politically as well as organizationally the merger looked more like a surrender. A commission (with an SPD majority) was appointed to work out a new program for the united party, but its deliberations took three years. In the meantime an Action Program was agreed upon, and with regard to the crucial coalition question this document did not offer even a sop to the Independents. On the contrary, it stressed above all the importance of defending the Republic.[58]

Nuremberg, then, concluded the first act in the history of the left minority of Weimar Social Democracy. It also rearranged the organizational stage for the second act, in which the radical wing would play the part of suppressed minority within the old party.

Emergence of the New Left: The Saxon Conflict

Had the reunification of Nuremberg taken place in a period of relative stability, it might have effected a more permanent reconciliation between the two wings of the SPD. But scarce-

57. See above, pp. 46–49.
58. Stampfer, *14 Jahre,* pp. 299–301.

ly had the merger been completed when the party was confronted by the manifold crises of the year 1923: the French
occupation of the Ruhr, the great inflation, the reactionary
coup in Bavaria, the Hitler putsch, and so on. In January
1923 French troops moved into the Ruhr; the Cuno government replied with a campaign of passive resistance. The immediate response of the official Social Democratic leadership
was to support the government, an all-bourgeois government
of Center and Right, and aid in the resistance campaign. The
response of the former Independent leftists was to blame the
government for the crisis, protest against the resistance, and
call for negotiations with France.[59] With their fundamentally
opposed attitudes toward the state and toward the question
of coalitions, the two wings of the SPD found themselves
again at loggerheads in the first political emergency of 1923.

The left minority could do nothing about national party
policy except speak out against it. But the situation was
quite different in Saxony and in the smaller neighboring state
of Thuringia, where the left gained control of the party apparatus. Here the Social Democratic state organizations
pursued a policy in the crisis year of 1923 quite independent
of, and contrary to, the orientation of the national leadership. The protracted intraparty dispute which resulted from
these differences, known as the Saxon Conflict, will be the
subject of this section.

Saxony was a small, densely populated state in central
Germany. It contained one-thirtieth of the Reich's territory,
but one-twelfth its population. With an economy founded
primarily on the heavy industry of its great cities, Saxony
offered a natural base for the socialist movement. Here the
SPD had struck its earliest and deepest roots and had maintained, ever since 1903, the support of an absolute majority

59. Schürer, *Arbeiterbewegung*, pp. 55–56.

of the voting population.[60] Not without reason was it jokingly tagged the Red Kingdom of Saxony. The 1920 Reichstag elections gave the socialist parties in this state a combined majority of 54 per cent, distributed as follows: USPD, 25.4; SPD, 24.2; KPD, 4.4.[61] A Saxon Landtag election came in November 1922, just after the Nuremberg reunification. The socialist parties retained their majority with 52.2 per cent. The Communists captured 10.5 per cent of this turnout, the United Social Democrats, 41.7 per cent[62]—figures which show clearly that the majority of the Independent masses in Saxony did not go Communist but returned to form the left wing of the SPD.

With such a distribution of the vote, the coalition problem was bound to look different to local Saxon Social Democrats than it did to the Reich leadership. It was possible to have a purely socialist government in Saxony. The SPD did not have to compromise with bourgeois parties in order to hold governmental power. And, in fact, a kind of de facto proletarian alliance had existed since 1920; the Saxon KPD under the influence of its right-wing leader, Heinrich Brandler, had "tolerated" the SPD–USPD coalition cabinet of Johann Buck, thus enabling it to stay in power for two years as a minority government.[63] But in January 1923 the Communists toppled this cabinet in order to carry out the unitedfront policy recently instituted by the Comintern; that is, they now sought a more direct collaboration with the Social Democrats.[64] The latter were thereby forced to choose between a coalition to the left and a coalition to the right.

The SPD Landtag fraction as well as the Saxon regional

60. Walter Fabian, "Hundert Jahre sächsisches Parlament," *Die Gesellschaft, 8* (2) (1931), 378.
61. Calculated from figures given in *Statistik, 291* (3), 2–3.
62. *Schulthess' Europäischer Geschichtskalender, 63* (1922), 138.
63. *Prot. 1925,* pp. 132–33.
64. Fischer, *German Communism,* pp. 225–26.

executives favored an alliance with the Democrats. But their plans were thwarted by a rank-and-file rebellion. At a Land party congress held in the midst of the cabinet crisis, the great majority of the delegates voted in favor of a coalition with the KPD. These radical Social Democrats felt themselves far more in agreement with the moderate Saxon Communists than with the bourgeois DDP. And to make sure their resolution was put into effect they appointed a commission of nine men to carry on the actual negotiations with the KPD. At this congress the recently merged Independent leftists effectively took control of the Saxon party organization.[65]

After lengthy talks the Communists agreed to give formal support to a cabinet headed by the Left Social Democrat, Erich Zeigner, and composed exclusively of SPD members. In return they received promises of extensive social legislation and encouragement for the Proletarian Hundreds, paramilitary defense organizations to be sponsored jointly by the two parties.[66] Zeigner took office in March 1923—the workers' government had become a reality in Saxony.

These developments elicited little enthusiasm from the national leaders of the SPD who were seeking coalition partners in the opposite direction. Already in November 1921 the party had formed in Prussia an unprecedented Great Coalition which included the big-business German People's Party. In mid-1923, as the inflation and Ruhr situation grew continually more threatening, the SPD agreed to the Great Coalition at the national level, and it joined the government of Gustav Stresemann on August 13. Forty-three Left Social Democratic Reichstag deputies publicly declared their op-

65. *Prot. 1925*, pp. 121–22, 133; see Fischer, *German Communism*, pp. 223–25.

66. *Schulthess*, *64* (1923), 22, 55, 57, 70; Fischer, *German Communism*, pp. 225–26, 295.

position to this cabinet, in a breach of fraction discipline reminiscent of the intraparty struggles of the war period.[67] The contrast between Saxon coalition tactics and those of the Prussian and Reich SPD pinpoints exactly the ideological cleft within the party.

Meanwhile, a switch in the Communist party line brought events in Saxony to a climax. German and Russian Communist leaders, conferring in Moscow in September, decided that the rapidly deteriorating condition of the Weimar Republic dictated a shift from the "soft" united-front policy to the "hard" revolutionary policy. Brandler was instructed, against his own personal inclinations, to demand more influence in the Saxon government, with the aim of controlling the police and securing arms for the Proletarian Hundreds. This accomplished, Saxony would spearhead a general uprising to overthrow the Republic.[68] Zeigner and the Saxon Left Social Democrats did not, of course, know of these secret Moscow decisions. They accepted Brandler's forthcoming overtures at face value, as being motivated by the desire "to weld the working class together for defense against the fascist danger."[69] On October 10, Brandler and two other Communists sat down with four Social Democrats to form a new Saxon cabinet.

While Zeigner did not know the secret instructions of his coalition partners, he was by no means their dupe; he carefully kept them away from any influence over the police and did not permit the arming of the Proletarian Hundreds. Nor did the Communist ministers attempt to initiate any radical changes of governmental policy.[70] By accepting Brandler,

67. *Schulthess, 64,* 152–53.
68. Flechtheim, *Kommunistische Partei,* pp. 92–93.
69. Quoted in Stampfer, *14 Jahre,* p. 361; Fischer, *German Communism,* p. 332.
70. Schürer, *Arbeiterbewegung,* p. 61; Fischer, *German Communism,* p. 333.

the Saxon SPD hoped to encourage the more moderate and responsible wing of the KPD, and ultimately, if this tactic proved successful, to bring about the reunification of the German socialist movement. A united working-class front in 1923 seemed doubly necessary because of the fascist threat rising in the neighboring state of Bavaria.

But the specter of Communists in the Saxon government was sufficient to mobilize powerful counterforces. The state Reichswehr commander under the recently proclaimed state of siege, General Alfred Müller, did not trust Zeigner to keep the Proletarian Hundreds under control. On October 13 he used his military authority to dissolve these organizations. When the Hundreds refused to obey the order of dissolution, Müller obtained permission from the Social Democratic Reich President, Friedrich Ebert, to "maintain order" in Saxony. He quickly invaded the principal cities, meeting scattered resistance, and suppressed the Hundreds together with the Communist Party.[71] Then on October 27, Ebert and the Stresemann cabinet ordered Müller to depose the democratically and legally established Zeigner government and institute a temporary dictatorship by a Reich commissioner—an action that clearly violated the Weimar constitution and which seemed doubly outrageous to the Saxon Social Democrats because of the cabinet's inability or unwillingness to take similar measures against the open rebellion of the reactionary Bavarian Land government.[72]

In the midst of the Reichswehr invasion, the Saxon SPD

71. *Schulthess, 64*, 192, 200–01.

72. Ibid., *64*, 206–07; S. William Halperin, *Germany Tried Democracy* (New York, 1946), p. 275; Stampfer, *14 Jahre*, pp. 363–65. The events in the less important state of Thuringia closely followed the Saxon pattern. On Oct. 16, two Communists were brought into the left-wing Social Democratic cabinet. Early in November the Reichswehr moved in, forcing the Communists to resign. See Georg Witzmann, *Thüringen von 1918–1933* (Meisenheim/Glan, 1958), pp. 87–107.

appealed to its national leadership and to the trade unions to call out a general strike. When this appeal was denied, they realized the hopelessness of resistance and submitted to military coercion.[73] Both the party executive and the Reichstag fraction, while denying active assistance, condemned the deposition of Zeigner as "unconstitutional and illegal," and the SPD ministers resigned in protest from the Stresemann cabinet on November 2.[74] Despite this stand of the national leadership, the ouster of Zeigner enormously increased the bitterness between the two wings of the party. Blood had been shed in Saxony while Social Democratic ministers sat in the government and, although Ebert had acted as Reich president and not as a Social Democrat, he was all too easily identified with the conservative leadership of the party.[75]

These events did not end the Saxon Conflict; in fact, as an intraparty dispute it had only begun. For now the question arose: What sort of government was to replace the ill-fated Zeigner coalition? The left wing favored another attempt with the Communists, who in the meantime had reverted to a noninsurrectionary tactic. The national party executive desired a Great Coalition along Prussian lines and conferred secretly with right-wing Social Democrats in the Saxon Landtag fraction toward that end.[76] This Landtag, it will be remembered, was elected in November 1922, immediately after SPD–USPD reunification and during the period when the old Majority Social Democrats still controlled the state organization. Consequently, most of the deputies (twenty-three) were right-wingers who sided with the national leader-

73. *Prot. 1925*, p. 123; Fischer, *German Communism*, pp. 336–37.
74. *Prot. 1924*, pp. 73–74; *Prot. 1925*, p. 134.
75. Sentiment against Ebert ran extremely high: a resolution for his expulsion was introduced at the 1924 congress (*Prot. 1924*, p. 97); his old trade union apparently did expel him at this time (Schürer, *Arbeiterbewegung*, p. 57).
76. *Prot. 1925*, p. 135.

ship; a minority of seventeen spoke for the Left Social Democrats. Under these circumstances the efforts of the executive proved successful; on January 4, 1924, the fraction majority voted for a Great Coalition, to be led by their spokesman, Max Heldt. In vain the fraction minority voted no confidence.[77]

It quickly became evident, however, that this minority expressed the sentiments of the great bulk of the Saxon party membership. A Land congress, meeting in a stormy session two days later, denounced the new government in the sharpest terms. By forming a Great Coalition without congress instruction, the fraction majority had committed a "breach of party discipline." In a vote of 77 to 16 the congress demanded the resignation of the government and the dissolution of the Landtag. But when a motion of no-confidence was introduced in that assembly on January 24, the twenty-three right-wing Social Democrats ignored congress instructions and opposed it, thus saving the government.[78] The fraction majority and the Saxon party organization now stood in open conflict.

The national party congress, meeting in June 1924, applied itself to the Saxon Conflict and appointed a commission to work out a reconciliation. Before the end of the congress this commission was able to offer a compromise solution to which both sides acceded. Organizationally, the agreement clarified the hitherto ill-defined prescriptions of the statute concerning state organizations. To placate the left, the decisions of Land congresses were declared binding on Landtag fractions. But to fence in the general independence of the state units, Landtag fractions were also made responsible for their actions to the Reich congress. Moreover, the executive and party council could at any time "suspend" a Land

77. *Schulthess, 65* (1924), 4.
78. Ibid., *65,* 4, 7.

policy until the next congress, if it appeared damaging to the interests of the party as a whole. This would prevent another Zeigner-style experiment. Politically, the compromise declared a coalition with the KPD "impossible in the foreseeable future," and instructed the Saxon Landtag fraction to model its actions on the policies of the national party. But it did not actually specify a particular coalition policy (at the time the SPD was formally in opposition). In the anticipated Landtag elections, the Saxons were urged to put up candidates without reference to the now ended dispute. This compromise solution was agreed upon by both sides and ratified by a unanimous vote of the congress.[79]

The underlying causes of the Saxon Conflict, however, were not eliminated by the congress reconciliation, and soon enough each side again began sniping at the other. The leftists dismissed some local party secretaries of conservative persuasion. The Twenty-Three in turn supported certain administrative "economies" in the Saxon government which brought about the dismissal of many civil-service appointees of the Zeigner period. For this the leftist press furiously attacked Minister-President Heldt, who felt impelled to call on the party executive for help. Another Saxon Commission was promptly appointed.[80]

The Left Social Democrats by this time saw a remedy only in new elections which would dissolve the hated coalition and give them a chance to elect deputies representing rank-and-file sentiment. Conversely, the Twenty-Three correctly foresaw that new elections would ring their political death knell, and so were determined to see the Landtag sit its full term, i.e. until October 1926. The Commission devised a shrewd compromise. Meeting at Dresden with the Land congress in October 1924, it succeeded in having a resolution

79. *Prot. 1924*, pp. 63–64, 139–41.
80. *Prot. 1925*, pp. 29, 124–26.

passed which instructed the Landtag fraction to vote for immediate dissolution, but which then "recommended" that all the previous deputies be renominated.[81] In this way perhaps the right wing could retain in substance what it conceded in form.

Such hopes were quickly smashed. In many subregional units (where nominations originated) the feeling against the Twenty-Three was far too intense for any recommendation to have effect. Some of the deputies were not renominated. Viewing this as a rupture of the Dresden Agreement, the party executive then advised the Landtag fraction to vote against dissolution which the Twenty-Three were only too happy to do. But to vote against dissolution violated the specific instruction of the Land congress. The Saxon regional organizations immediately initiated expulsion proceedings. To such an impasse had the matter arrived when the next year's party congress fell due.[82]

At the Heidelberg congress in September 1925 a third Saxon Commission was appointed, which duly came up with a third compromise. The expulsion proceedings against the Twenty-Three would be dropped; the fraction majority and minority would reunite into one group. In the future the fraction would have to obey instructions given it. The Saxon organizations would not be required to put up the same candidates; on the other hand, the timing of the dissolution would be decided jointly by the fraction, regional executives, and national executive, each party having one vote. When this compromise solution was put to the congress, fifty-one of the fifty-six delegates from Saxony opposed it as inadequate, but their spokesman, Karl Böchel, declared that they would submit loyally to the majority will.[83]

81. Ibid., pp. 29, 138–39.
82. Ibid., pp. 30–31.
83. Ibid., pp. 262–65.

The Twenty-Three were now forced on the defensive, and they continually blocked any proposal for dissolution. The party executive finally began to realize that no real compromise could be made: it would have to choose between the Twenty-Three and the Saxon membership. Early in 1926 it made the crucial decision, joining with the regional executives in calling for dissolution. The Twenty-Three now defied even the supreme command of the party. They refused to commit political suicide by voting out the Landtag. The recalcitrant deputies were promptly expelled, this time with the blessing of the party executive.[84] Expulsion did not, of course, deprive these deputies of their seats or bring about the dissolution of the Landtag, but it did reconcile the Saxon leftists to the national leadership. For now the Saxon party went into opposition against the Heldt government. And while the ideological cleft remained, the leftists were content to agitate for their radical policies within the party household. They had won, after two years of bitter factional fighting, a kind of victory for Left Social Democracy.

As an epilogue to the Saxon Conflict, we may note that the expelled right-wingers set up their own press, began to build local organizations, and soon founded an Old Social Democratic Party.[85] With their crucial votes they were able to maintain the Heldt government until October 1926 when Landtag elections naturally fell due. Competing openly with the mother party, the Old Social Democrats finally had to face their electorate: they lost all but four of their twenty-three seats.[86] But it so happened that these four deputies (Heldt, Buck, Bethke, Niekisch) held the balance of power in the new Landtag. Allied with the DDP, the DVP, and

84. *Jahrbuch 1926,* pp. 10–12.
85. Ibid., pp. 12–13.
86. Cuno Horkenbach, *Das Deutsche Reich von 1918 bis heute, 1918–1930* (Berlin, 1930), p. 231.

now for the first time the reactionary DNVP, Heldt again took office in a government which was to last until 1929.[87] The Old Social Democratic Party continued in existence as a splinter group, drifting farther and farther toward right-wing nationalist politics.

With reference to the organizational dilemma posed at the beginning of this chapter, the Saxon Conflict most clearly illustrates the predicament of the conservative party leadership. Although politically and temperamentally far closer to the Twenty-Three than to the left-wing Saxon membership, the national leaders could not give unconditional backing to the former without driving the latter out of the party. With only 8 per cent of Germany's population, Saxony claimed 16 per cent of the Reich's SPD membership, much too large a segment to be alienated.[88] Ultimately the party executive had to abandon the Twenty-Three and endorse the repugnant coalition policy of the state organization in order to keep the party whole. But even this concession did not end the troubles of the executive, for after the Saxon Conflict it was confronted with a large and apparently permanent opposition within the party.

Left Social Democracy

Although the Saxon Conflict did not lead to a major split, it congealed the left opposition within the Weimar SPD. All over the Reich, radical elements in the party rallied to the defense of their Saxon comrades. Formal organization being impossible, the leftists grouped themselves around a newly established periodical put out by their intellectual spokesman, Paul Levi, called *Sozialistische Politik und Wirtschaft* (or more simply *Levi Korrespondenz*). In 1927 a more am-

87. *Jahrbuch 1926*, pp. 393–96.
88. Calculated from figures in *Prot. 1925*, p. 39.

221

bitious semimonthly, *Der Klassenkampf,* commenced publication and spoke for the group until the 1931 split.

As has been indicated before, the cardinal political difference between the left and right wings of the SPD had to do with the question of coalitions, which in turn reflected their divergent attitudes toward the Weimar Republic. The establishment of democratic institutions in Germany, according to the main current of Social Democratic thought, necessitated a reversal in the party's traditional attitude toward the state. That is to say, a democratic republic could not be regarded as a "class state"; the machinery of such a government would in itself be "neutral," a tool for carrying out whatever policies were desired by the parties in power; obviously, the SPD could influence these policies most by participating in government whenever feasible. The Left Social Democrats rejected this entire line of reasoning. In their view the advent of democratic institutions did not end the class rule of the bourgeoisie, which managed to retain its power in spite of them. Only a political ignoramus could regard the German state bureaucracy, the judiciary, and above all the Reichswehr as "neutral" instruments of government. Sharing power with bourgeois parties at best permitted only the most limited reforms; at worst it forced the party to take responsibility for oppressive measures and provide a popular cover for the reactionary forces that still held decisive state power. So long as socialists remained a minority in a capitalist country, the leftists could see no reason for changing the traditional policy of "pure opposition."[89]

This is not to say that they were completely indifferent to the form of government or that they regarded the Weimar Republic as no better than the old Empire. The Republic

---

89. See especially a series of articles by Max Adler under the title, "Über Marxistische Staatsauffassung," in *Der Klassenkampf, 1* (1927), 3–9, 39–46, 131–35; *2* (1928), 34–39, 134–39, 292–98, 622–27.

constituted "the best constitutional basis for the development of the socialist idea,"[90] and if threatened, as in the Kapp Putsch, the Left Social Democrats would come to its defense. But in the period of our present concern—the stable years from 1924 to 1930—it seemed that the possessing classes had finally accepted the Republic as a tolerable form of government. In the absence of any immediate threat, then, the party should stay in opposition:

> The task of Social Democracy in the German Republic is to represent the class interests of the proletariat against the class rule of capitalism, the struggle for social improvements and for socialism. As against this task, the struggle to maintain the Republic, with which the bourgeoisie is now satisfied, recedes in importance.
>
> The political alignments in the German Republic no longer should be formed under the words: republican versus monarchist, but socialist versus capitalist.
>
> Considering this political constellation, the tactic of Social Democracy must be: opposition not coalition.[91]

The Left Social Democrats might be defined as those who remained behind in the transformation of the SPD from a party of social protest to a government party.

On other issues the two wings differed more in degree than in principle. The leftists placed more emphasis on socialization, took a stronger stand against the Reichswehr, demanded more complete social legislation, and so forth. In foreign policy they held fast to the socialist internationalism of the prewar party, placing more confidence in international working-class organizations than in the League of Nations.[92]

90. Ibid., 2, 228.
91. From a resolution presented by Left Social Democrats to the 1927 party congress, in Prot. 1927, p. 272. Also see Siegfried Marck, Sozial-demokratie (Berlin, n.d. [1931]), pp. 29–33.
92. See the program put forth for the 1928 elections by Der Klassen-kampf, 2, 228–30.

The Left Social Democrats must not, because they stood to the left of the SPD, be taken as Communists or crypto-Communists. True, most expressed sympathy for the Soviet Union, and they desired above all else the reunification of the German working class. But they did not want this unity if it meant the adoption of violence as an offensive tactic, subservience to the policies of Moscow, or the introduction of Leninist organizational techniques. Their traditions and mentality were essentially Social Democratic and not Communist; their mentors were Bebel and Liebknecht, the pre-war Kautsky, even Rosa Luxemburg, but not Lenin, Trotsky, or Stalin; and their "workers' fatherland" was Red Vienna, not Soviet Russia.[93] In one sense the Left Social Democrats were the real conservatives of German socialism; spurning the attractions both of Weimar and of Moscow, they remained true to the classical precepts of nineteenth-century Social Democracy.[94]

On the question of party organization the left minority was strong for democratic reforms, this being a matter close to their immediate needs. Among the numerous proposals for reform, perhaps the best example is a model statute drawn up by Ernst Eckstein in 1931. In order to democratize party life, Eckstein urged: (1) that the members of all executive bodies be elected by proportional representation to insure a voice for minority tendencies within the party; (2) that the local organizations, where direct democracy was physically possible, be reconstituted as the basic units of the party; (3) that Reichstag deputies be bound to vote according to the dictates of their constituents, but not of the fraction majority;

93. Max Adler, "Die dritte Internationale und wir," ibid., *1*, 68–73; see other articles in this issue as well, on the general theme, "Unsere Stellung zu Sowjet-Russland." Likewise, Theodor Hartwig, *et al.*, *Unsere Stellung zu Sowjetrussland* (Berlin, 1931).
94. Cf. Georg Decker, "Opposition," *Die Gesellschaft*, 7 (1) (1930), 203.

(4) that only elected delegates to the party congress be permitted to vote. A second battery of reforms was aimed at the SPD bureaucracy. In Eckstein's party, "alongside the executive, which would handle just the administrative business and only need a few members, the organization would be led politically by a special council, whose election would take place on political lines." Secretaries would be hired by the branch concerned, functionaries elected on a political basis, multiple offices cut down, and so forth. The leading aims of the Left Social Democrats, organizationally, were to make party life more democratic and political and less bureaucratic.[95]

In all these ideas one can see a great deal of the old USPD. In the forefront of the new grouping, however, one does not see the faces of the old Independent leadership. Hilferding, Breitscheid, Crispien, Dittmann—the most prominent names of the USPD—were now spokesmen for the dominant wing of the party. True, most Left Social Democratic leaders were USPD veterans, but only Rosenfeld had held a high position. A few more (e.g. Dissmann and Toni Sender) belonged to the secondary leadership, but the rest had not been prominent at all. Of the twenty most important leaders of the new opposition, only five had been Independent Reichstag deputies; only six had attended the Gera party congress in 1922.[96] And, of course, the acknowledged spokesman of the group (until his death in 1930) was Paul Levi, former chairman of the Communist Party.

The twenty leaders mentioned above were, as a group, neither significantly older nor younger than their right-wing

95. Ernst Eckstein, "Wie soll die Organisation aussehen?" *Organisation im Klassenkampf,* pp. 165–79; the other contributions to this volume are likewise relevant to leftist organizational ideas; also see Marck, *Sozialdemokratie,* pp. 33–36.

96. Horkenbach, *Das Deutsche Reich, 1918–1930,* p. 403; *Prot. 1922,* pp. 175–78.

counterparts. And they belonged to several generations, from old veterans such as Heinrich Ströbel to the stormy young Saxon journalist, Max Seydewitz.[97] According to the thesis of Selig Perlman's *A Theory of the Labor Movement,* one might expect to find "visionary" intellectuals of bourgeois origin predominantly in the left wing of the SPD, while "practical" working-class leaders remained on the right.[98] No substantiation for this thesis can be found in the divisions of this period. There were at least as many intellectuals speaking for the conservative majority as for the radical minority. For example, the 1930 Reichstag fraction boasted thirteen Social Democrats holding university degrees; of these two sympathized with the Left, eleven with the Right.[99] The leaders of the SPD opposition, in short, displayed no special or unusual social background.

Nor are sociological insights extremely productive in explaining the origins of the group's mass support. The right and left wings of the SPD did not derive from an obvious class difference, as in the case of the Center Party, nor does the formula, organized vs. unorganized workers, seem acceptable.[100] If it were possible, an age analysis might prove fruitful. It is true that the Left Social Democrats for a time controlled a majority in the Young Socialists and were influential in the Socialist Workers' Youth.[101] In general, the data are too scant to warrant more than the most tentative conclusions.

On the basis of the geographical analyses of election returns made in earlier sections, however, one may make cer-

97. From biographical data in Horkenbach, *Das Deutsche Reich, 1918–1930,* pp. 632–774.
98. (New York, 1928.)
99. *Kürschners Volkshandbuch Deutscher Reichstag, 1930* (Berlin, n.d.), passim.
100. Decker, *Die Gesellschaft, 7* (1), 198–200.
101. Varga, *Die Sozialdemokratischen Parteien,* p. 64.

tain correlations. Both Communist and Left Social Democratic strength lay primarily in the centers of German heavy industry—the Ruhr, Saxony, Upper Silesia.[102] Being highly concentrated, heavy industry historically presented the strongest opposition to unionization and bargaining. These factors helped produce a leftward orientation especially among the great numbers of unskilled workers required in such undertakings: it is significant that the only large union controlled by Left Social Democrats was the metal workers' union.[103] But it further appears that within this leftward orientation, workers of Catholic origin inclined toward the KPD; those of Protestant origin, toward Left Social Democracy. At least, one finds strong Communist and relatively weak Left Social Democratic centers in the Ruhr and Silesia, whereas the latter were more powerful than the former in Saxony and most other Protestant regions.[104]

Such an analysis may help to lay bare the social roots of the SPD's left wing, but it is not a total explanation. Many other factors must have contributed: the history and tradition of the particular unit, local political conditions (e.g. the proletarian majority in Saxony), accidents of personality, and so forth. Any further treatment of this subject would have to depend on detailed regional and local studies of the party.

How strong was the Left Social Democratic grouping? Unfortunately no method exists for measuring its strength in the voting public or even in the party membership. At best one can gauge membership support by examining the political division of the congresses, bearing in mind that the leftists were likely to be underrepresented there. If we scruti-

102. See above, pp. 124, 199–200.
103. Ibid., p. 66. According to Braunthal, the Left Social Democrats were generally "more powerful and consequential" than the Communists in the Free Trade Unions ("Free Trade Unions," p. 160).
104. See above, pp. 199–200.

nize in Table 18 the votes given between 1924 and 1931 to Left Social Democrats in the elections for "associate" members of the executive (the only posts regularly contested), we can discern a pattern.[105] Throughout the period the leftists

TABLE 18. *Left Social Democratic Strength in Executive Elections*

Year	Candidate	Votes	Percentage of Total
1924	Wurm	102	28
1925	Fleissner	113	31
1927	Ströbel	123	32
1929	Levi	131	34
1931	Siemsen	92	24

could count on a substantial minority at party congresses. The bloc grew steadily from 1924 to 1929, only to suffer a heavy setback two years later in 1931.

The Magdeburg congress represents the high-water mark of Left Social Democratic strength. This meeting took place in May 1929, after Hermann Müller's Great Coalition had been in office almost a year. Thus the coalition question was bound to be debated hotly, all the more so because it was by chance tied to an explosive military issue, as explained earlier. In the elections of 1928 the SPD had opposed construction of a new pocket battleship, using as its principal election slogan, "Pocket battleship or feeding centers for children?"[106] But no sooner had the Great Coalition been formed

105. Derived from election results given in *Prot.: 1924*, 200; *1925*, 267; *1927*, 225; *1929*, 232; *1931*, 243. In each case several left-wingers ran, and I have selected neither the highest nor the lowest contender, but one in the middle who received an average vote.

106. Evelyn Anderson, *Hammer or Anvil, The Story of the German Working-Class Movement* (London, 1945), p. 123.

when the bourgeois parties demanded funds for the new vessel as a condition of their continued support. Reluctantly, to save the coalition, Müller gave in. Immediately there arose a storm of protest from the rank and file, who saw the move as a betrayal of election promises and of socialist principles. The 1929 congress convened in this rebellious spirit, and the three votes taken there concerning the military question gave the opposition its greatest support ever: 35 per cent, 42.5 per cent, 38 per cent. Counting only elected delegates, the showing was even more impressive—48 per cent in the peak vote.[107] And since even elected delegates were chosen indirectly by conventions composed chiefly of party functionaries, the following of the opposition in the actual membership was probably wider. Indeed, it is quite possible that at the apex of their popularity in 1929 the Left Social Democrats spoke for the majority of the party.

What kind of representation did the left wing have in the national leadership? Our analysis of the Magdeburg congress showed the most proportionate division in the party council, where the leftists held 30 per cent of the posts. In the vastly more important Reichstag fraction, however, they made up perhaps 25 per cent. The control commission claimed only one leftist, Lore Agnes, a hangover from the Nuremberg merger agreement. And, of course, on the all-powerful executive the opposition had no representation whatsoever.

In this discrepancy between its popular support and its voice in the party leadership lay the organizational dilemma of Left Social Democracy. Although the bloc enjoyed the backing of a very substantial minority in the party, perhaps even a majority at the peak of its strength, it was unable to influence the national policy of the SPD to any appreciable extent. As long as traditional organizational practices re-

107. These votes have been analyzed in detail above, pp. 78–83.

stricted intraparty democracy, there was no effective way to dislodge the entrenched leadership or alter its policies. Even if the Left Social Democrats had possessed a sizable majority of rank-and-file support they would have been condemned to this condition of political impotence in the SPD.

Yet to leave the party and set up a rival organization was scarcely a better solution. Enormous financial and practical difficulties stood in the way, and it would be much harder to win support outside the SPD than as an opposition within it. Finally, beyond all questions of feasibility, even the most radical Social Democrat would hesitate to take on the moral onus of having cracked the solidarity of the working class still further. The organizational conundrum of the left wing was at least as perplexing as that of the conservative leadership.

We have seen that at the 1931 congress, two years after the Magdeburg triumph, the growth of the opposition was not only halted but seriously reversed. The circumstances of this decline, and the new schism which followed it, will be discussed below.

Second Schism: The Socialist Workers' Party

Intraparty opposition to the SPD leadership seemingly would have increased in the general radicalization of German public opinion that followed the onset of the depression, even more so because of the party's "toleration" policy toward Brüning's constitutional dictatorship. Such an increase may well have occurred (there is no way of measuring it), but for Left Social Democracy as a united bloc the Brüning period brought all but complete disintegration. To understand the reasons, internal and objective, for this rapid disintegration, we must begin with a political dispute of the year 1931—the construction of Pocket Battleship B.

230

It is ironic that Pocket Battleship A furnished the Left Social Democrats with their best issue and their greatest support whereas its sister ship, coming two years later, gave the first impetus to their disintegration. Since October 1930 the SPD had "tolerated" (i.e. declined to overturn) the Brüning cabinet, for fear that a Hitler government would follow in its wake. The Left Social Democrats opposed this toleration policy with at least as much vigor as they previously had opposed the Great Coalition.[108] Such was the lineup when, in March 1931, the Reichstag had to vote on funds for Pocket Battleship B. At the SPD fraction caucus before the vote, a majority of approximately sixty deputies favored abstention, so as not to endanger the government's majority; forty deputies called for a straight negative vote. Although fraction discipline required that the minority submit, nine of the most militant left-wingers, led by Seydewitz and Rosenfeld, decided that here was an issue to be carried to the rank and file. With the party congress only two months off, the nine radicals violated discipline by voting against funds on the Reichstag floor. Nineteen other deputies absented themselves from the session to avoid the disciplinary dilemma.[109]

The Nine had badly miscalculated. At the Leipzig congress the conservative leadership played down the political issue of the dispute and emphasized the breach of discipline. Although a strong mood of discontent pervaded the congress, the opposition was hopelessly fragmented. The most moderate dissenters (whose spokesmen were Aufhäuser and Toni Sender), opposed to toleration under normal circumstances, felt the danger of Nazism was so great that Brüning had to be supported for the time being.[110] Another faction (Künstler

108. See, e.g., Max Seydewitz, "Der falsche Weg," *Der Klassenkampf, 4* (1930), 641–45.
109. Ibid., *5* (1931), 193, 198.
110. *Prot. 1931*, pp. 128–30, 142–44.

and Kirchmann) agreed with the Nine on the political issue but could not sanction their breach of discipline.[111] In the end Seydewitz and Rosenfeld could count on only a small portion of the total opposition strength; a resolution condemning their action passed 324 to 62, with 8 abstentions.[112] The toleration question was conveniently dispatched by leaving the decision up to the Reichstag fraction. At this congress Seydewitz also ran for party chairman, challenging the one-nomination system for the first time since 1913; he emerged with 54 votes.[113] The left opposition had been divided and conquered.

Emboldened by their success, the party leaders began to take a stricter attitude toward the left. Hitherto they had avoided provoking a split that might carry a third of the membership out of the party, but now it appeared that the most radical Left Social Democrats could be pared off without seriously endangering the unity of the movement. Meanwhile the leftist leaders, either unaware of the changed circumstances or resigned to a schism, continued their active opposition.

On July 1, 1931, *Der Klassenkampf* published a "Warning Cry to the Party," signed by Seydewitz, Rosenfeld, Ströbel, and Max Adler, which attacked the toleration policy and encouraged readers to send in expressions of agreement.[114] The party council chose to regard this action as an attempt to form a factional organization (Sonderorganisation) in the party and prohibited further collection of signatures.[115] The left-wingers ignored the prohibition and went on to create a new opposition weekly newspaper, *Die Fackel.* The execu-

111. Ibid., pp. 134–36, 145–47.
112. Ibid., pp. 187, 288, 299–300.
113. Ibid., p. 242.
114. *Der Klassenkampf, 5,* 385–86.
115. *Jahrbuch 1931,* p. 117.

tive demanded that this publication venture be given up; the demand was refused. The executive thereupon expelled Seydewitz and Rosenfeld on September 29, under the special statutory powers given it by the 1924 congress.[116] A series of further expulsions and resignations followed to complete the schism.

On October 4, 1931, left-wing representatives from all over the Reich met in Berlin to found the Socialist Workers' Party (Sozialistische Arbeiterpartei, SAP). They were reluctant to divide still further the loyalties of the German working class, and times were, as Seydewitz said, "most unfavorable" for a new organizational undertaking, but they saw no alternative. Seydewitz continued: "Had we done nothing the members might have gone over to the Communist Party and by November Rosenfeld and I might have been without any followers."[117] If prospects were not exactly rosy, there was still ground for limited optimism as numerous groups and grouplets coalesced into the new party during the following months. First came other organizations forced out of the SPD: the radical pacifist German Peace Society and the left-wing International Socialist Militant League (or Nelsonbund).[118] From the official SPD youth section the new party attracted a substantial minority.[119] The splinter groups of Georg Ledebour and Theodor Liebknecht also joined, as did a dissident right-wing Communist opposition group under Heinrich Brandler.[120] There were also a number of Trotsky-

---

116. Ibid., p. 107.
117. Quoted from "Formation of a Socialist Labour Party," *Labour Monthly, 8* (1931), 719.
118. August Siemsen, *Anna Siemsen, Leben und Werk* (Hamburg, n.d. [1952]), pp. 67–68.
119. *Jahrbuch 1931*, p. 108.
120. Ledebour, *Georg Ledebour*, pp. 12, 24–26; *Sozialistische Monatshefte, 38* (1932), 70.

ists (including Paul Fröhlich), and other ex-Communists.[121] With six Reichstag deputies from the old party, the SAP was guaranteed a voice in the national legislature.[122]

Ideologically, the Socialist Workers' Party made no radical break with the traditions of its predecessors. The toleration policy (which was really the coalition problem in a new disguise) remained the major bone of contention with the SPD. "As the principal difference [from the Social Democrats]," declared a spokesman at the founding congress, "I would like to place in the foreground our position toward the state and toward state power."[123] In the event of an attack by the Right on the democratic foundations of the Weimar Republic, the new party advocated that the proletariat seize power and establish a temporary dictatorship. As a solution to the economic depression, the SAP urged the socialization of large industry.[124] It was strongly internationalist and antimilitarist. For the immediate future the party set itself the goal of achieving a united front between the Social Democrats and Communists so that the German working class might renew the struggle against fascism with closed ranks.[125]

Organizationally, as one might expect, the SAP was ultrademocratic: proportional representation throughout party institutions, only elected delegates at congresses, a maximum

121. Siemsen, *Anna Siemsen*, p. 68; Anderson, *Hammer or Anvil*, p. 146.
122. These were Seydewitz, Rosenfeld, Ströbel, Portune, Ziegler, and August Siemsen. The party likewise boasted an impressive array of publications, from its daily, *Sozialistische Arbeiterzeitung*, and its weekly, *Die Fackel* (later *Sozialistische Wochenzeitung*), to its semimonthly theoretical organ, *Der Klassenkampf*.
123. Quoted in *Sozialistische Monatshefte, 38*, 70–71.
124. See Max Adler, et al., *Die Krise des Kapitalismus und die Aufgabe der Arbeiterklasse* (Berlin, 1931); Fritz Sternberg, *Der Niedergang des deutschen Kapitalismus* (Berlin, 1932).
125. *Der Klassenkampf, 5*, 641–48; Fritz Borinski, "Der revolutionäre Sozialismus der SAP," *Neue Blätter für den Sozialismus, 3* (1932), 98–103.

salary for secretaries equal to an average worker's wage, and all leaders and functionaries to be elected frequently and on a political basis.[126] Here the heritage of Eisenach once more asserted itself.

With the elections of July 1932 came the first test of the new party's popularity, and the results must have shocked even the least optimistic supporters. The SAP received nationally only 72,630 votes, or 0.2 per cent of the total. In one stroke all six deputies lost their seats. Even in Saxony, traditional stronghold of the left, only 0.7 per cent of the vote was captured.[127] The SAP had failed abysmally. "Most workers," as Evelyn Anderson has observed, "were by instinct reluctant to support a 'splinter' party that increased further the tragic rivalry and disunity within the movement."[128]

No longer having any serious political future, the party maintained a marginal existence down to the end of the Republic. The November 1932 elections further decreased its sliver of the national vote to 45,201, or 0.1 per cent.[129] But if they left German politics by the sectarian exit, the members of the SAP—as indeed Left Social Democrats generally— later distinguished themselves in the forefront of the underground resistance against Nazi totalitarianism.[130]

Thus two years after its impressive showing at Magdeburg, the Left Social Democratic opposition was scattered in several directions. We have already mentioned three of the resultant groupings: (1) those who reluctantly supported the toleration policy of the right wing, (2) those who opposed

126. Ibid., *3*, 100; Ernst Eckstein, "Das Statut der Sozialistischen Arbeiterpartei," *Der Klassenkampf*, *6* (1932), 104–06.
127. *Statistik, 434*, 8–10.
128. *Hammer or Anvil*, p. 146.
129. *Statistik, 434*, 79.
130. See Lewis J. Edinger, *German Exile Politics* (Berkeley and Los Angeles, 1956), pp. 70, 78–82, and passim.

this policy but wanted to carry on their opposition within the party,[131] and (3) those who split out into the SAP.

There remains to discuss a last and very significant group —those who transferred their allegiance to the Communist Party. Already at the 1931 congress one Left Social Democratic Reichstag deputy, Jacobshagen, declared himself for the KPD. He was followed a few months later by another deputy, Oettinghaus.[132] These desertions at the leadership level must have been duplicated many times among the rank and file. In the electoral region of Chemnitz–Zwickau, one of the Saxon strongholds of the Social Democratic left wing, the party lost 58,226, or 18 per cent of its voters, between 1928 and July 1932. The great majority of these must have gone over to the Communists, who picked up 74,294 votes in the same period.[133] The path between Weimar and Moscow became increasingly hard to follow.

Ultimately, then, the strength of Left Social Democracy was sapped by its disintegration into four different camps, each defensive about its own position and hostile to the rest. That this happened was due partly to internal factors: the death of Paul Levi, the most capable leader of the opposition; the tactical miscalculations of some of the left-wingers; the political astuteness of the conservative leadership. But objective factors played perhaps an even more important role. The anticoalition cornerstone of Left Social Democratic ideology had as its precondition, at least for many leftists, the stability of the Weimar Republic. After 1930 this stability no longer existed, and the defense of the Republic again assumed an immediate urgency. Then too, the unparalleled

131. This group remained a significant force within the party and gathered around a new monthly, *Marxistische Tribüne*, edited by Arkadij Gurland.

132. *Prot. 1931*, pp. 123–24; *Jahrbuch 1931*, pp. 107–08.

133. Calculated from figures in Horkenbach, *Das Deutsche Reich, 1918–1930*, p. 468; ibid., *1932*, p. 276.

political tensions, the agonizing alternatives, and the enormous weight of responsibility that faced socialists in the last years of Weimar were all bound to have a centrifugal effect on intraparty life.

The history of the Social Democratic left wing through its several pendular swings, from rival party to internal opposition back to rival party, can be summed up in a few words. Originating in the prewar left center and forced out of the old party over the war question, the opposition grouping first founded the USPD in 1917. After five years of ups and downs the Independents returned to the fold in 1922, only to re-emerge in the Saxon Conflict as a new opposition. In this shape the left wing grew steadily until it fell apart in the last years of the Republic, the new SAP being a much smaller edition of the earlier rival party.

If one were to assess the political influence this left wing had on the SPD, one would be forced to conclude that it was very small. Before the war there had been a triangle of forces within the movement—left, right, and center. Shifting tactical alliances among these forces had insured that no single one would be completely dominant. But after the political realignments of the early Weimar period, there remained only two of the original three—a preponderant right wing and a minority left wing. The latter consequently was condemned to permanent and ineffectual opposition. In the high command of the party the leftists had very few representatives, and the dominant conservative leaders were more apt to regard their advice with open contempt than to give it a place in policy decisions. Where compromises were made (and this was seldom) the right wing usually acceded to some radical verbal gesture, while the left wing made all the concessions of substance. Only in the Saxon Conflict did the opposition score something like a victory, and here only after two years of bitter factional fighting. The conservative leader-

237

ship of the Social Democratic Party was badly heckled by the rebellious minority, but its hegemony in party affairs was not seriously disturbed.

As a postscript to this chapter on the revolt against the organization we should note the existence of opposition from another quarter—the so-called "Young Turks." This was a small group of gifted young Social Democratic intellectuals, including Kurt Schumacher, Carl Mierendof, Julius Leber, and Theo Haubach, who coalesced in the early thirties and expressed themselves largely through the organ of the religious socialists, Eduard Heimann's *Neue Blätter für den Sozialismus*. The group was far more important for its intellectual contributions and for the Bonn SPD leader it produced (Kurt Schumacher) than as a faction within the Weimar party. It never enjoyed much mass support and could not make a serious bid for party power. A few of its leaders held Reichstag seats and Adolf Grimme, a sympathizer, was Prussian Minister of Education between 1930 and 1932.

It is difficult to place the Young Turks in the traditional political spectrum. Their socialism was reformist and nationalist, but they sought to revitalize the party and take the offensive politically in ways that did not sit well with the entrenched leadership. Above all they appreciated the force of irrationality, and especially irrational nationalism, in twentieth-century political life. Understanding the appeal and danger of Nazism, they did not share the faith in steady progress that was the cornerstone of reformist Marxism. Social Democracy, in their view, could outflank the Nazis only by abandoning the humdrum electioneering methods of the party bureaucracy and launching a vigorous new offensive, using the irrational and nationalist appeals exploited so successfully by Hitler—pageantry, symbolism, and demagogic speakers.

The Young Turk attitude toward the party leadership and bureaucracy can be deduced from the foregoing. It was as critical, from different premises, as that of the Left Social Democrats. Theo Haubach wrote in 1930:

> The realistic wing [of the party] frequently takes an express joy in pettiness, in tactical coups, often has a disastrous preference for small-minded chicanery, and at the same time a powerful aversion to great offensives and hard struggles. Ideologically this wing has seized upon those elements in socialist doctrine which strengthen a belief in historical inevitability and automatic progress. It has moved so far in the direction of liberalism that it constitutes a danger for the movement as a whole.[134]

Julius Leber's reflections on the Nazi victory of 1933 include a trenchant analysis of Social Democratic failings, and reveal clearly the tactical methods that the Young Turks would have preferred. Leber lamented that

> [The party] had scarcely any speakers left who were capable of mobilizing the masses. What it had were only report makers. While the National Socialist speakers heated and whipped their followers into a white-hot frenzy, Social Democratic speakers tormented their listeners so long with figures, statistics, and proofs that all enthusiasm ultimately was frozen over. Real popular agitators (Volksredner) no longer existed in Social Democracy.[135]

The nationalist and demagogic inclinations of the Young Turks made them in some respects parallel to the "national" socialist movements of Marcel Déat in France, Henrik de-Man in Belgium, and Sir Oswald Mosley in Great Britain.[136]

---

134. "Die Generationenfrage und der Sozialismus," *Soziologische Studien*, dedicated to Alfred Weber (Potsdam, 1930), p. 114.

135. *Ein Mann geht seinen Weg* (Berlin, 1952), p. 241.

136. Cf. Carl Landauer, *European Socialism* (Berkeley and Los Angeles, 1959), *2*, 1396.

The comparison does injustice to the Young Turks, however, since they never moved over into the fascist camp. With a fervent belief in democracy, they continued their struggle against Nazism even after 1933, an opposition that cost most of them their lives. Kurt Schumacher survived, after many years in a concentration camp, to become the first leader of a revived Social Democratic Party in postwar Germany.

7. Conclusion: The Middle-Aged Party

At the end of this involved study of the internal history of Weimar Social Democracy, what over-all trends can be discerned in the party's domestic affairs? Given such trends, what were their general causes? What effects did they have on Social Democratic politics? What was their implication for the future? To answer the first question, it would perhaps be admissible to employ the catchword description then current: Verbonzung, Verkalkung, Verbürgerlichung (literally: bossification, ossification, bourgeoisification).[1] If this description was flip and disparaging, it also penetrated to the heart of the matter. Used in a broad, nonpejorative sense and within the limits suggested below, these three terms may serve to describe the dominant trends within the Weimar SPD.

Verbonzung may be taken to include the whole range of oligarchical tendencies that we have observed in the preceding chapters. It was Robert Michels who first studied these tendencies in detail, elaborating them into a general "Iron Law of Oligarchy" in his famous *Zur Soziologie des*

---

1. Sigmund Neumann, in this connection, uses the terms, "Verbürgerlichung, Verbonzung, Unjugendlichkeit," which amount to the same thing (*Die deutschen Parteien, Wesen und Wandel nach dem Kriege* [Berlin, 1932], p. 28).

Parteiwesens in der modernen Demokratie, first published in
1910. In the preface to a 1925 edition, Michels commented
briefly on the developments of the intervening fifteen years:
"From constant and intensive concern with the most recent
history of political parties . . . I have concluded that the
tendencies hitherto scientifically established by me have increased monstrously in quantitative terms, without being essentially altered qualitatively."[2] Our findings, while they
make no pretense of establishing any scientific or iron laws,
tend basically to substantiate this judgment.

We have seen that virtually every reform of the party
statute delivered new formal powers to the executive, chiefly
in matters of finance, property rights, expulsions, and the
nomination of Reichstag candidates. As a by-product of the
Saxon Conflict it received authority to annul Land policies.
By means of the informal influence it exerted on the press,
on party secretaries, and elsewhere the executive possessed
an even tighter grip on party affairs than was specified in
the statute. Indeed, so strong was this grip that without im-
punity the SPD high command could conspire behind the
backs of the Saxon party members to set up a coalition that
they adamantly opposed, or even flaunt party legality openly
as in the mass expulsion of the antiwar opposition in 1917.

In the Weimar period the system of checks and balances
within the organization broke down almost completely. The
control commission was an anachronism, the party council,
a rubber stamp; and the congress could not act as an adequate
check, partly because of the influence the executive had in
its functioning, partly because of the way it was constituted.
One-fourth of this body was composed of national leaders,
and the rest were chosen only indirectly by the membership.
The right of the congress to elect officers was perfunctory,

2. (2d ed. Leipzig, Kröner, 1925), p. xxii.

and after 1925 its meetings were reduced to one every other year. The Reichstag fraction was permeated with executive and other high party officials, who together with like-thinking trade-union leaders safely controlled the decisions of that body. Significantly, one of the executive co-chairmen (Wels) presided over the congress; the other (Müller) over the Reichstag fraction.

Members of the executive, and party leaders generally, were elected and re-elected in a one-nomination system, and on the nonpolitical appeal of personal loyalty. As a consequence, the left opposition was underrepresented in all the institutions of national leadership. Even on occasions when hostility against the "bosses" ran very high, such as at the Magdeburg congress of 1929, the entrenched leadership simply could not be removed from office.

If not very sensitive to pressure from below, the SPD leaders *were* responsive to the wishes of their brother leaders in the trade-union hierarchy. Despite the supposed neutrality of the ADGB, its top officialdom was able, by means of strategic positions in the Social Democratic cabinets and the Reichstag fraction, and through formal and informal meetings with the executive, to exert a powerful influence on party policy. It is not wholly accidental that a letter from Leipart brought about greater changes in the draft of the Heidelberg Program than were made by the presumably sovereign party congress. Direct trade-union influence came, not up from below but across, as it were, from one oligarchy to the other.

Besides increased power, the word Verbonzung suggests a widening gap between the leaders and the led. The structural rearrangements of the 1919 statute, as we have seen, contributed heavily to this latter process since they transferred to the Land and regional machines most of the functions hitherto exercised by rank-and-file membership meetings at the electoral district level. But the separation sprang

243

not simply from these structural changes: Social Democratic leaders led utterly different lives than did their predominantly working-class supporters. Many were of bourgeois origin, and those who had begun their lives as workers (almost always skilled workers) had long ago exchanged their proletarian jobs for white-collar positions in the party or trade-union apparatus. Here, as they gained expert knowledge and practical experience, as they came into broader contact with the upper orders of society, as their working-class roots faded farther and farther into the background and automatic re-election guaranteed them life tenure in the socialist bureaucracy, the SPD leaders developed what Max Weber called "the physiognomy of prosperous innkeepers." They could rarely be called to account for their actions and tended to develop a contemptuous attitude toward criticism from below.

The oligarchical trend, however, was not completely unlimited. The remnants of a democratic organizational structure—the heritage of Eisenach—impeded its full development. Thus the Left Social Democrats had, if not adequate minority representation, at least room within the party household to agitate for their views and to criticize the conservative leadership. Leftist regional organizations were by and large able to send their spokesmen to the Reichstag and maintain their own press. The Saxon Conflict showed that the leaders could not permanently ignore the demands of an indignant membership. Because the heritage of Eisenach had not totally disappeared, a heritage which the bourgeois parties lacked completely, the SPD was possibly the least undemocratic of the major political parties in the Weimar Republic.

The second over-all trend, *Verkalkung,* has to do with the general stagnation and ossification of the movement. After half a century of seemingly inexorable growth, the German socialist movement ceased to expand. SPD electoral strength reached a peak in 1919 that it was not again to attain. The parallel high point for the membership and for the Free Trade Unions was 1922. Moreover, it no longer appeared that a major economic crisis would sweep the party into power, for the SPD now functioned like a government party, gaining votes in stable prosperous times and losing them in periods of widespread social unrest. The German Socialist movement had reached what came to be called the "one-third barrier": it had won over the support of about a third of the nation but apparently could go no farther.

The widening recognition that such a hurdle existed had a heavy impact on the movement. For if the one-third barrier could not be broken through, then all hopes of winning an absolute majority and carrying out a socialist transformation of society were utopian, and the party was doomed to become nothing more than the permanent parliamentary lobby for organized labor. At the core of the problem seemed to lie the failure of Marx's prophecy; the proletariat was actually shrinking in relation to other classes and no longer composed even 50 per cent of the German population. To cope with this threatening situation, the Social Democrats consciously endeavored to transform themselves into a people's party in order to make the widest possible electoral appeal. But, while not wholly unsuccessful, this effort failed to wrench the organization out of its doldrums. Apparently, as many votes were lost on the left as were gained on the right. The one-third barrier remained.

As the long advance of the SPD ground to a halt in the Weimar period, there appeared other signs of ossification. The older type of leader, the revolutionary agitator, had long since vanished and been replaced by the new type, the methodical and efficient bureaucrat. But now this generation of new-style leaders was growing old and in the process becoming more cautious and more reluctant to accept any unfamiliar ideas. The bureaucratic spirit seemed to permeate the entire apparatus, sapping its earlier vitality. Purely organizational work and preoccupation with the giant complex of ancillary activities took the place of political discussion and obscured the primary purpose of the party. As decisions tended increasingly to be made at the top of the pyramid, political interest at the bottom tended to slacken. Symptomatically, the Social Democratic press became less and less an arena for intraparty discussion and controversy, more and more an instrument simply for expounding an official party line.

The faithful, stable SPD membership, like its leaders, grew older and older without adequate replacement in the younger generation. The failure to recruit sufficient numbers of young people can be attributed partly to the general conditions of postwar Germany but partly to the policies of the adult organization. The strict paternal regime provided by the elders was bound to sit poorly with the boisterous and radical new generation. Youth leaders of promise could not but be dismayed by the prospects of long, routine apprenticeships in the party apparatus before they attained positions of importance. Left Social Democrats were able to win the allegiance of some of these discontented youths, but undoubtedly the Communists were the chief beneficiaries, as the age structure of their leadership, for example, has illustrated.

The tendency toward ossification did not continue totally without limitation or opposition. Increased Social Democratic popularity among the rural proletariat ran counter to the main trend. The drive to recruit middle-class support was an effort to break the ossifying process, as was the youth program of 1931, which attempted to give the party an emergency transfusion of new blood. While both these efforts showed partial success, neither was sufficient to restore to the movement its lost dynamic, as the Left Social Democrats and the Young Turks both recognized.

The last over-all trend, *Verbürgerlichung,* has been defined before. Objective Verbürgerlichung refers to the altered social composition of the party. We have seen that by the later Weimar period about 30 per cent of the Social Democratic vote and about 23 per cent of the party's membership came from the lower middle classes. Bourgeois intellectuals composed a third of the broad party leadership, while the two-thirds who claimed working class origins had been elevated by the movement to white-collar status (this latter development was not a new one).

Subjectively, the social attitudes and mores of the Social Democratic rank and file were undoubtedly affected by the general filtering down of middle-class values that occurred in this period, perhaps especially so because of the predominance of skilled and better-paid workers in the party. Moreover, the new petty bourgeois adherents of Social Democracy, won over by the people's-party appeal, obviously did not adopt a proletarian style of life but caused a further subjective Verbürgerlichung of the movement as a whole. Finally, the party leaders, because of their white-collar occupations, their positions of prestige, and their social contact with the upper classes were clearly the most verbürgerlicht of all.

The process of Verbürgerlichung was augmented by another simultaneous development: as new middle-class supporters were coming in by the front door, old proletarian supporters were leaving by the back door. We have seen that great numbers of Social Democrats, especially in the large industrial centers that formed the oldest strongholds of the movement, went over to the Independents between 1917 and 1920, and many of these continued their leftward journey into the KPD after Halle. During the inflation and later, during the depression, the Communists received fresh waves

247

of recruits from the SPD. As these overwhelmingly proletarian elements abandoned their old party, they left it still more to the influence of its nonproletarian minority.

Despite this tendency toward Verbürgerlichung, it must be said that the Social Democratic Party remained a predominantly working-class party. The middle-class elements constituted an important minority but a minority nonetheless. The powerful voice which the trade unions had in the formation of party policy, if nothing else, insured that the SPD would remain in the first instance the political spokesman of German labor.

Verbonzung, Verkalkung, Verbürgerlichung—if these were the dominant trends in the internal life of Social Democracy, to what extent should they be viewed as effects of the Weimar electoral system, to what extent attributed to other causes? This question merits consideration because, in the lengthy controversy over proportional representation, opponents of the system have held it responsible for the general decline of the SPD and other democratic parties. Thus the most notable scholarly critic of proportional representation, F. A. Hermens, has attributed the tendency toward bossism and stagnation almost entirely to the influence of that unfortunate system.[3]

Hermens' case appears strongest when he deals with the encouragement given to the oligarchic and bureaucratic tendencies. As we have seen, enlarged electoral units abetted the decline of intraparty democracy and decreased the contact between Reichstag deputies and their constituents. The party executive acquired more influence in the selection of candidates, as did the regional bureaucracies. The list system ignored individual personality, enhanced the importance of

3. *Democracy or Anarchy? A Study of Proportional Representation* (Notre Dame, 1941), pp. 51–66, 231–46.

the vote-getting apparatus, and helped party and trade-union bureaucrats obtain places in the Reichstag fraction, of which they constituted 61 per cent by 1930.

But Hermens goes too far when he includes the internal discipline of the fraction and its subordination to the party organization among the effects of proportional representation. Such observations may well apply to the bourgeois parties[4] but not to the SPD, which never possessed a tradition of parliamentary independence. The author cites two examples to prove his case: the reluctant submission of the Social Democratic Baden Landtag fraction to a congress directive in a matter concerning religious policy, and the expulsion of the twenty-three Saxon deputies in 1926 for refusing to carry out congress instructions for dissolution.[5] Neither of these illustrates bureaucratic or central control, since regional congresses issued the instructions. The latter seems particularly ill chosen since, as we have observed, the central SPD leadership supported the Twenty-Three through most of the dispute and only grudgingly bowed in the end to rank-and-file pressure from the Saxon membership. Hermens appears entirely unaware of the traditional subordination of Social Democratic deputies to the congress, as well as their tradition to vote as a unit, neither of which had the remotest connection with proportional representation. In fact, the SPD Reichstag and Landtag fractions enjoyed, if anything, greater rather than lesser independence during the Weimar years.

In their zeal to demonstrate the oligarchic and bureaucratic effects of proportional representation, critics have also ignored other causes of the same phenomena. Hermens

---

4. Ibid., pp. 55–56, 232–35. Hermens also tries to sharpen his contrast by putting forth the patently absurd view that all the parties were democratic prior to 1918, indeed "cannot but be democratic" under a constituency system (p. 51).

5. Ibid., p. 233.

writes, for instance, that the list system "created—particularly in the ranks of the largest Republican party, the Socialists—a type of party worker called . . . the *Funktionär*."[6] The creation of such officials in the SPD, of course, antedated the Weimar Republic by many years. In the broadest sense, the bureaucratic and oligarchic tendencies must be traced to the general requirements of electioneering in an era of mass democracy, not merely to a particular electoral law. We have noted that these patterns reveal themselves in countries where the constituency system is still used, as well as in Germany prior to 1918. In this respect, proportional representation must be viewed as a stimulant to already extant tendencies.

Hermens also sees the stagnation of the SPD as a product of the Weimar electoral system, and again with some justice. The bureaucratization of the party helped to sap its earlier vitality, lowered the quality of its leadership, and reduced its appeal especially to the younger generation.[7] But here as well, a single-minded view of causation grossly distorts the picture. The party attracted so few young people not merely because of its ossified hierarchy, but because the prosaic reformism and, indeed, the entire rationalistic structure of Social Democratic ideology was out of harmony with the dominant mood of the turbulent Weimar youth. And surely the taproot of the one-third barrier was the party's inability to extend its influence much beyond the ranks of the industrial proletariat—a sociological and psychological barrier that had little if anything to do with the electoral system. The similar inability of other European socialist parties to win absolute majorities prior to World War II attests to the universality of this problem.

Other aspects of Hermens' critique have even less merit when applied to the SPD. He argues that proportional repre-

6. Ibid., p. 235.
7. Ibid., pp. 235–42.

sentation tends to create radicalized Weltanschauungen-
parteien, parties with rigid and uncompromising ideologies.[8]
While he concedes that all the major German parties traditionally possessed this character, he refuses to recognize that
the Social Democrats, at least, clearly became more flexible
and compromising, rather than less so, during the years of
the Weimar Republic. In the same vein the author suggests
that proportional representation is responsible for "parties
of integration," and proceeds to describe the SPD's ancillary
paraphernalia as if it never existed before the war.[9]

Finally, the Weimar electoral system is alleged to have
caused a splitting of parties because it offered a Reichstag
seat to any group capable of mustering 60,000 votes.[10] The
history of Weimar socialist parties offers scant support for
this allegation. Three rival parties already existed when the
new system was introduced in 1919, and a few years later
in 1922 we find, not proliferation, but a reduction to two,
the SPD and the KPD! All subsequent splits and splinters
in both camps failed to produce a single significant or lasting
political party. The most ambitious of these splinters, the
Socialist Workers' Party, discussed above, initially took away
six Reichstag deputies from the SPD, but in the following
elections, conducted during the depth of the depression and
under electoral procedures supposed to encourage splinter
parties, all six lost their seats. The SAP was left without any
representation and therefore without any direct influence on
legislation or the formation of cabinets.

While proportional representation removes the major dis-
ability which minor parties suffer under the constituency
system, its positive encouragement to them has been greatly

8. Ibid., pp. 243–44.
9. Ibid., pp. 33–35.
10. Ibid., pp. 15–19, 221–31.

exaggerated. In the Weimar experience, although the number of parties on the ballot sometimes exceeded thirty, never were more than fifteen represented in the national legislature. And by strange coincidence, this exactly equals the number of parties represented in the 1912 Reichstag elected under the old system (even after deducting six national minority parties that no longer existed in Versailles Germany).[11] In 1912 the largest six parties accounted for 88.6 per cent of the total vote; in 1928, after ten years of proportional representation and when the votes for minor parties had leveled off at the peak of their dispersion, the largest six still held 80.3 per cent—hardly a disastrous loss.[12] And moreover, in 1912 a coalition government, in order to command a Reichstag majority, would have required the support of at least four parties (excluding the Social Democrats, who at that time did not enter coalitions); in 1928 it required only three (SPD, Z, DVP). Clearly, the splitting tendencies of proportional representation were neither so pronounced nor so catastrophic as has been claimed.

The trend toward Verbürgerlichung in the SPD is not treated by Hermens, partly because its causes are basically unrelated to the electoral system and partly, one suspects, because this phenomenon goes counter to the stereotype of rigidified party development he seeks to present. The roots of Verbürgerlichung, as we have studied them, lie in the professionalization of the Social Democratic leadership, in

11. Enid Lakeman and James D. Lambert, *Voting in Democracies* (London, 1955), pp. 183–85. Lakeman and Lambert present in this volume the most up-to-date defense of proportional representation and include many useful statistics.

12. Calculated from statistics in Koppel S. Pinson, *Modern Germany* (New York, 1954), pp. 572–75. The fatal radicalization of German public opinion beginning in 1930 should not be confused with dispersion, since it actually brought a bipolar concentration of the vote, delivering 92 per cent to the six largest parties by July 1932.

the attraction of nonproletarian elements and, more vaguely, in the gradual acceptance by German workers of middle-class standards of taste and value.

In general, the critics of proportional representation have tended to lump indiscriminantly the genuine effects of that system with the seemingly necessary consequences of mass organization in a bureaucratic era, with the general character of political life in an age of ideology, with the inherent limitations and peculiarities of a multiparty system, with the political effects of the Great Depression, and with various other factors. Any balanced description of the causes of Social Democratic Verbonzung, Verkalkung, and Verbürgerlichung must be painted on a much broader canvas.

What effects did these three dominant trends in the internal life of Weimar Social Democracy have on the party's politics? It would be possible to answer this question adequately only in a detailed political history of the SPD, where specific events could be taken up at length. Even then it would be hazardous to attribute actions and policies to these general trends in too positive a manner. They exerted an influence, to be sure, but an underlying influence, responsible not so much for each specific decision as for a certain mood or mentality in the party.

Nor should this influence be examined in the abstract, outside the context provided by the general political position of the SPD in the Weimar Republic. The great schism which, between 1916 and 1922, separated the Social Democratic and Communist movements, not only left the conservative wing in complete control of the SPD but also created a new external situation for that party. For the first time in its history the SPD was faced with a major party on its left; like the German armies, it now had to fight a two-front war. And as the KPD developed from its Luxemburgist roots into a full-blown Stalinist party, totalitarian in both ideology and organization, the SPD recoiled from it in increasing horror. In this recoil from the enemy on the left, the party moved farther to the right, definitely renouncing the revolutionary aspects of its Marxist heritage and proclaiming itself, as Bernstein had hoped, a "democratic socialist party of reform." The reformist philosophy became the clear and official doctrine of the SPD.

The appearance of the Communist Party was not the only circumstance that altered the political situation of Social Democracy and pushed it in a conservative direction. A least equally important was its defensive role in Weimar politics. The party had gained important victories in the November Revolution: a democratic republic, an improved position for the trade unions, an extended system of social welfare. But the Weimar SPD never received a solid mandate for further change; on the contrary, there arose a powerful opposition to the original gains of November. The task of the party, at least in the eyes of its leaders, was to conserve and consolidate its gains, rather than to press aggressively forward with new demands. It was, seemingly by the nature of the situation, a conservative role.

Within this broad political context, one may say that the three internal trends described above reinforced the increasing conservatism of the Social Democratic Party. They worked in harmony with the general drift, encouraging and abetting it, rather than slowing it down or having no effect at all.

The oligarchical tendencies which we have discussed under the rubric, Verbonzung, produced in the leadership of the SPD a staff of middle-aged career bureaucrats. Their long experience in performing the petty details of party administration imbued them with a keen appreciation of the concrete and practical, combined with a deep distrust of the novel. They preferred to stick to the routine forms of political activity familiar to them rather than experiment with untested tactics, methods, or ideas. And so highly did they value the vast organization they had helped construct that, where risks to it were involved, their actions became distinctly timid and hesitant. The trade-union leaders, having similar career histories, only reinforced the inclinations of the party leaders, especially so since the successful activity of the trade-union branch required a stable, responsible, predictable political branch. The leaders of Weimar Social Democracy were conservative not only by conviction, then, but by background and temperament as well.

The great power of these leaders and their independence from below insured that they would follow a conservative line without reference to changes of mood in the rank and file. Several times during the years of the Republic—in the aftermath of the Kapp Putsch, the great inflation, the pocket battleship crisis of 1929, the depression—mass sentiment in the party was radicalized without effecting any changes in the policy or personnel of the high command. And, in general, the oligarchical practices that underrepresented Left Social Democracy kept party policy to the right of the real center of gravity in the movement. Thus the tendency toward bossism added to the conservative drift.

Ossification likewise contributed to this process. As Social Democracy became an older and more settled movement, as its members and leaders gradually aged, there undoubtedly resulted a certain loss of aggressiveness and vitality. Many older Social Democrats at all levels of the organization must have felt that their generation had accomplished enough in the great victories of the November Revolution: they had earned their pension. This feeling found no adequate counterbalance in the vigor of a rising generation.

But perhaps more directly important in political influence was the general stagnation of the SPD before the one-third barrier. For if expansion could not be renewed, then the long-range aims of the movement could never be realized. Then the party's policy in the here and now could only be to defend existing gains and perhaps win a few new concessions. With each electoral disappointment, socialism must have seemed more remote and visionary, and the conservative policies of the leadership more realistic and unavoidable.

Finally, the conservative influence of the propensity toward Verbürgerlichung must be weighed. The SPD leaders who had been removed from the frustrations and insecurities of working-class employment and given white-collar positions in the party apparatus thereby lost their vested interest in social change. Their personal revolution had already been accomplished. With the social changes of the November Revolution, the deepest grievances of many Social Democratic leaders against the old order were removed. They naturally became less anxious to overturn the society that accorded them such prestige.

The political Verbürgerlichung implicit in the remodeling of the SPD as a people's party likewise must be understood as a move to the right. In order to attract the votes of peasants and the new middle class, the party soft-pedaled the doctrine of class struggle and the traditional Marxist terminology, abandoned socialist plans for agriculture, offered backhanded support for agricultural protection, and so forth. The more the SPD tried to win over petty bourgeois and marginal voters, the more moderate and unoffending its program and behavior had to become.

Through these several channels, then, the internal processes here analyzed abetted the great transformation of German Social Democracy. In this classic metamorphosis the SPD evolved from an idealistic and expansive social movement, aimed at the total reorganization of society, into a settled minority party representing the political interests of German labor. Social Democracy, in a word, passed from youth to middle age.

In 1945 when the party emerged again after twelve years of Nazi dictatorship, its middle-aged characteristics were even more pronounced. In fact the first decade or so after World War II witnessed no profound changes in the internal life of Social Democracy. There was no revitalization of intraparty democracy; stagnation and ossification remained; the movement became even less proletarian and anticapitalist.[13] But at present historic changes appear to be taking place.

Throughout the postwar period, Social Democrats have recognized stagnation as their number-one problem. They have sought desperately for some means of rejuvenating the party cadres and breaking permanently through the one-third barrier. The first method tried was that of Kurt Schumacher, who got a chance to put his Young Turk ideas into practice during the early postwar years. But a strong nationalist appeal, even sparked by Schumacher's great personal charisma, failed to produce the desired majority among war-weary and disillusioned Germans. The riddle of the one-third barrier remained.

After Schumacher's death in 1952 there was an interval of several years during which other ideas congealed. A relatively small Left Social Democratic element sought to rejuvenate the movement through radicalization. It was an impulse from the moderate wing of the party, however, that initiated the process of doctrinal rethinking which resulted in the Bad Godesberg Program of November 1959.

13. See Klaus Schütz, "Die Sozialdemokratie im Nachkriegsdeutschland," *Parteien in der Bundesrepublik* (Stuttgart and Düsseldorf, 1955); and Richard Petry, "Die SPD und der Sozialismus," *Frankfurter Hefte, 9* (1954), 663–76.

This program represents, in essence, a second and more ambitious attempt to transform the SPD into a genuine people's party by "modernizing" both its underlying assumptions and its specific demands.[14] Socialist values derive not exclusively from Marxism, the new program recognizes, but are "rooted in Christian ethics, humanism and classical philosophy." The party would impose no ideological strait jacket on its supporters, asking only minimum agreement on a specific program of demands. Among these demands one no longer finds socialization of the means of production. Only if large concentrations of property "hinder the establishment of a just social order" or threaten "sound economic power relationships" would the SPD think public ownership "suitable and necessary." Efficient small and medium-sized enterprises would specifically be encouraged. Economic regulation would be restricted: "As much competition as possible—as much planning as necessary." In these and other ways, the traditional demands of the party have been modified. There remains, of course, a strong emphasis on social reform. But Social Democracy, the new program proclaims, has ceased to be a party of the working class and has become a "party of the people." Critics of this doctrinal transformation assert that the SPD is no longer a socialist party; defenders claim that its socialism has merely been modernized.

The recent period has also witnessed the rise of certain younger and more vigorous leaders. Foremost among these is Willi Brandt, mayor of West Berlin, and Social Democratic candidate for chancellor in the 1961 elections. With this

14. The Bad Godesberg Program has been printed in *Jahrbuch der Sozialdemokratischen Partei Deutschlands, 1958/1959* (Hannover and Bonn, 1960), pp. 373–86. An abridged English translation can be found in *The Socialist Call, 28* (1960), 12–16. For commentary on the program and on the present position of the SPD, see Lewis J. Edinger and Douglas A. Chalmers, "Overture or Swan Song: German Social Democracy Prepares for a New Decade," *The Antioch Review, 20* (1960), 163–75.

combination of a new program and new leaders, the SPD has high hopes for the future.

Although the alterations of 1958–60 clearly make the SPD a more conservative party in terms of the traditional political spectrum, and should lead to even more Verbürger-lichung, they may bring startling changes of much greater consequence. Revitalization of the movement, with active grass-roots participation, could reverse the old oligarchic trend. Most important, however, the stagnation that characterized the Weimar period and the first fifteen years after World War II may be shaken off. Rejuvenated and enlarged by an influx of nonproletarian supporters, the SPD could perhaps finally crash through the one-third barrier to victory at the polls.

Should this happen, and barring major catastrophes, the SPD might begin to play a new kind of role in German politics. As a broad party of social reform—the left flank of an evolving two-party system—it might alternate in power periodically with the Christian Democratic Union. If Social Democracy succeeds in drinking at the fountain of youth, future historians may well see the entire period between 1914 and 1960 as one of general and profound metamorphosis, preliminary to this new emergence.

Sources

In studying the internal history of Weimar Social Democracy, the richest sources are the two party publications most concerned with domestic affairs. Used in combination, I have found the *Protokoll über die Verhandlungen des Parteitags der Sozialdemokratischen Partei Deutschlands* (Berlin, published for the years 1919–22, 1924–25, 1927, 1929, 1931) and the *Jahrbuch der deutschen Sozialdemokratie* (Berlin, published for the years 1926–31) to be inexhaustible fountains of information. The congress proceedings that appear in the *Protokolle* offer an otherwise unobtainable picture of the party with its hair down, without the mask of official unanimity. The internal divisions can best be analyzed in the voting patterns of the congress. The *Protokolle* also reproduce the party's statutes, programs, resolutions, etc., as well as the minutes of the women's conferences. Moreover, for the years before 1926, these volumes contain the reports of the Reichstag fraction and the executive, the latter being especially useful for the student of internal affairs. Within each executive report are to be found the reports of the party council and control commission, together with a detailed financial accounting and information on the condition of the press and all the ancillary organizations. After 1926 this material appeared in the *Jahrbücher,* along with reports from the various Länder, occasional sociological surveys, and other information. These two SPD publications have been my most fecund source.

The parallel *Protokoll über die Verhandlungen des Parteitags der Unabhängigen Sozialdemokratischen Partei Deutschlands* (Berlin, published for the years 1917–20) furnished the same sort of information for the Independents as does the *Protokoll des Kongresses der Gewerkschaften Deutschlands* (Berlin, published for the years 1919, 1922, 1925, 1928, 1931) and the *Jahrbuch des allgemeinen deutschen Gewerkschaftsbundes* (Berlin, published for the years 1922–31) for the trade unions. The principal results of the triennial union congresses are conveniently summarized in Salomon Schwarz, *Handbuch der deutschen Gewerkschaftskongresse* (Berlin, 1930).

Reference works which have proved helpful include the annual volumes of *Schulthess' Europäischer Geschichtskalender* (Munich, 1860 et seq.), where one can find a detailed chronology of public events in Germany. A similar but more abbreviated chronology appears in Cuno Horkenbach, *Das Deutsche Reich von 1918 bis heute,* 4 vols. (Berlin, 1930–33), together with a wide variety of valuable statistics and biographical data on the leading personalities of the period. For Reichstag deputies, I have gathered information from the official *Handbuch der verfassunggebenden Deutschen Nationalversammlung* (Berlin, 1919), followed by the periodically published *Reichstags-Handbuch* (Berlin), as well as its unofficial equivalent, *Kürschners Volkshandbuch Deutscher Reichstag* (Berlin). One can find abundant statistical data on Reichstag elections in the *Statistik des Deutschen Reiches* (Berlin, 1873 et seq.), and in Wilhelm Dittmann, *Das politische Deutschland vor Hitler, Nach dem ämtlichen*

Material des statistischen Reichsamtes in Berlin (Zurich, 1945).

The socialist movement produced a large number of periodicals, many of which are useful to the student of the SPD's internal development. *Neue Zeit* (Stuttgart, 1883–1923), succeeded by *Die Gesellschaft* (Berlin, 1924–33), was the SPD's official theoretical monthly and contains innumerable reports and interpretative articles on party affairs. Unofficial socialist publications sometimes prove more valuable than party organs: *Neue Blätter für den Sozialismus* (Potsdam, 1930–33), put out by a group of Protestant socialist intellectuals, has some particularly perceptive thinking about the movement. The same is true of the older Revisionist monthly, *Sozialistische Monatshefte* (Berlin, 1897–1933), which also contains a handy periodic summary of developments in the socialist movement. The organs of Left Social Democracy, *Sozialistische Politik und Wirtschaft* (*Levi Korrespondenz*) (Berlin, 1924–28), followed by *Der Klassenkampf* (Berlin, 1927–32), are important both for their criticism of affairs in the SPD and as documents of the emerging left wing. Detailed reports on the trade unions can be found in the official ADGB weekly, *Correspondenzblatt* (Hamburg, Berlin, 1891–1923), which was replaced after the inflation by *Gewerkschafts-Zeitung* (Hamburg, Berlin, 1924–33). In this period there also appeared an ADGB monthly devoted to more general questions, *Die Arbeit* (Berlin, 1924–33). Two other periodicals concerned with social questions should be mentioned: *Archiv für die Geschichte des Sozialismus und der Arbeiterbewegung* (Leipzig, 1910–30), and *Archiv für Sozialwissenschaft und Sozialpolitik* (Berlin, Tübingen, Leipzig, 1888–1933).

Although they have been of only secondary value in this study, there is an impressive number of autobiographies, memoirs, letters, and so forth, written by Social Democratic leaders: Eduard Bernstein, *Erinnerungen eines Sozialisten* (Leipzig, 1930); Otto Braun, *Von Weimar zu Hitler* (New York, 1940); Otto Buchwitz, *50 Jahre Funktionär der deutschen Arbeiterbewegung* (Berlin, 1950); Friedrich Ebert, *Schriften, Aufzeichnungen, Reden. Mit unveröffentlichten Erinnerungen aus dem Nachlass* (Dresden, 1926), and *Kämpfe und Ziele* (Dresden, 1927); Albert Grzesinski, *Inside Germany* (New York, 1939); Paul Hirsch, *Der Weg der Sozialdemokratie zur Macht in Preussen* (Berlin, 1929); Wilhelm Hoegner, *Der schwierige Aussenseiter* (Munich, 1959); Karl Kautsky, *Erinnerungen und Erörterungen,* ed. Benedikt Kautsky, Quellen und Untersuchungen zur Geschichte der deutschen und österreichischen Arbeiterbewegungen, *3* (S-Gravenhage, 1960); Wilhelm Keil, *Erlebnisse eines Sozialdemokraten* (2 vols. Stuttgart, 1947); Julius Leber, *Ein Mann geht seinen Weg. Schriften, Reden, und Briefe von Julius Leber,* herausgegeben von seinen Freunden (Berlin, 1952); Minna Ledebour (ed.), *Georg Ledebour, Mensch und Kämpfer* (Zurich, 1954); Paul Loebe, *Erinnerungen eines Reichstagspräsidenten* (Berlin, 1949), expanded in a second edition under the title, *Der Weg war lang* (Berlin, 1954); Hermann Müller, *Die November Revolution, Erinnerungen* (Berlin, 1931); Gustav Noske, *Erlebtes aus Aufsteig und Niedergang einer Demokratie* (Offenbach/Main, 1947), and *Von Kiel bis Kapp, Zur Geschichte der deutschen Revolution* (Berlin, 1920); Philipp Scheidemann, *Memoiren eines Sozialdemokraten* (2 vols. Dresden, 1928); Toni Sender, *The Autobiography of a German Rebel* (New York, 1939); and Carl Severing, *Mein Lebensweg* (2 vols. Cologne, 1950).

All these titles clearly fall into the category of original sources. The traditional distinction between primary and secondary material, however, soon breaks down in dealing with a subject such as this. Numerous works written *about* some aspect of Weimar Social Democracy are written *by* contemporary authors with the aim of affecting its policies. It seems wisest, therefore, to proceed from this point topically, citing primary, secondary, and in-between works all without distinction.

The only historical survey of the SPD organization is Wilhelm Schroeder's brief *Geschichte der sozialdemokratischen Parteiorganisation in Deutschland,* Abhandlungen und Vorträge zur sozialistischen Bildung, *4–5* (Dresden, 1912). The value of this book is enormously enhanced by the inclusion of all the party statutes from 1863 to 1912. I have been unable to obtain two manuscript dissertations on the organizational history of the prewar party: K. Ackermann, "Organisatorische Streitigkeiten in der deutschen Sozialdemokratie, 1890–1914" (diss. Heidelberg, 1932); and D. Bronder, "Organisation und Führung der sozialistischen Arbeiterbewegung im Deutschen Reich, 1890–1914" (diss. Göttingen, 1952). The collective work by Fritz Bieligk, *et al., Die Organisation im Klassenkampf,* 2. Buch der Roten Bücher der "Marxistischen Büchergemeinde" (Berlin, n.d. [1931]), although the contributions are uneven in quality, provides a thorough discussion of most of the problems treated in this dissertation. Its Left Social Democratic bias is in many ways an advantage since it permits the authors a frankness not possible for the conservative wing.

On the leaders of the SPD there exist a number of biographies, few of which transcend the limitations of simple eulogy: Paul Kampffmayer, *Fritz Ebert, ein Lebensbild* (3d ed. Berlin, 1924); Max Peters, *Friedrich Ebert, Erster Präsident der Deutschen Republik* (Berlin, 1954); Hans Steffen, *Otto Braun* (Berlin, 1932); Erich Kuttner, *Otto Braun* (Leipzig, 1932); Hans Menzel, *Carl Severing* (Berlin, 1932); Wenzel Jacksch, *Die Fackelträger, Hans Vogel, Gedenkblätter* (Offenbach/Main, 1946); F. Wesemann, *Kurt Schu-*

macher, Ein Leben für Deutschland (Frankfurt/Main, 1952); Otto Bach (ed.), *Rudolf Wissell* (Berlin, n.d.); Ernst Haase, *Hugo Haase, sein Leben und Wirken* (Berlin, n.d.); and August Siemsen, *Anna Siemsen, Leben und Werk* (Hamburg, n.d.). For Weimar trade-union leaders, one may consult Theodor Leipart, *Carl Legien, Ein Gedenkbuch* (Berlin, 1929); and Paul Ufermann (ed.), *Alwin Brandes* (Berlin, 1949).

To study the party leadership sociologically one should still begin with Robert Michels' prewar classic, *Zur Soziologie des Parteiwesens in der modernen Demokratie* (Leipzig, 1911), translated by Eden and Cedar Paul as *Political Parties, A Sociological Study of the Oligarchical Tendencies of Modern Democracy* (Glencoe, Ill., 1915). Further discussion of the same general topic may be found in Leonard Nelson, *Demokratie und Führerschaft* (Berlin, 1932). I have been unable to obtain J. Siemann, "Soziologie der sozialdemokratischen Führerschicht, 1918–1933" (diss. Göttingen, 1955). Parallel studies of trade-union leaders are Philipp A. Koller, *Das Massen- und Führerproblem in den freien Gewerkschaften,* Ergänzungsheft XVII des Archiv für Sozialwissenschaft und Sozialpolitik (Tübingen, 1920); and Theodor Cassau, *Das Führerproblem innerhalb der Gewerkschaften* (Berlin, 1925). Also see Alexander Schifrin, "Parteiapparat und Parteidemokratie," *Die Gesellschaft, 7* (1) (1930), 505–28; "Kritik an der Organisation," ibid., *8* (2) (1931), 166–78; and "Der Streit um die Parteidemokratie," ibid., *8* (2), 472–77; together with a reply by Kurt Laumann, "Zur Problem der Aktivierung der Partei," ibid., *8* (2), 460–71. Carl Mierendorff explores the problem of "Wieviel 'Bonzen' gibt es?" in *Neue Blätter für den Sozialismus, 2* (1931), 142–43, while Felix Riemkasten makes a rightist attack on the SPD leadership in his biting novel, *Der Bonze* (Berlin, 1930).

Sociological studies of the Reichstag members are: Walter Kamm, *Abgeordnetenberufe und Parlament*, Sozialwissenschaftliche Abhandlungen, *4* (Karlsruhe, 1927); and Adolf Borell, *Die soziologische Gliederung des Reichsparlaments als Spiegelung der politischen und ökonomischen Konstellation* (diss. Giessen, 1933). The researcher may also consult Walther Lambach, *Die Herrschaft der Fünfhundert* (Berlin and Hamburg, 1926); Richard Lewinsohn, *Das Geld in der Politik* (Berlin, 1931); James K. Pollock, *Money and Politics Abroad* (New York, 1932); and Klemens Kremer, *Der Abgeordnete zwischen Entscheidungsfreiheit und Parteidisciplin* (Munich, 1952).

The party press is considered in Ludwig Kantorowicz, *Die sozialdemokratische Presse Deutschlands, Eine soziologische Untersuchung* (Tübingen, 1922); Elfriede Fischer, *Grundlagen der Interpretation der Politik der deutschen Sozialdemokratie durch die sozialdemokratische Presse* (diss. Heidelberg, 1928); and Kurt Koszyk, *Zwischen Kaiserreich und Diktatur, Die sozialdemokratische Presse von 1914 bis 1933,* Deutsche Presseforschung, *1* (Heidelberg, 1958). On the Reichsbanner, see Friedrich Otto Hörsing, "Reichsbanner Schwarz-Rot-Gold," *Volk und Reich der Deutschen,* ed. Bernhard Harms (Berlin, 1929), *2,* 178–94; *Das Reichsbanner Schwarz-Rot-Gold,* Beiträge von Paul Loebe, Philipp Scheidemann, Wilhelm Sollmann, u.a. (Frankfurt/Main, 1924); and Ernst Posse, *Die politischen Kampfbünde Deutschlands,* Fachschriften zur Politik und Staatsbürgerlichen Erziehung (Berlin, 1930).

The standard history of the SPD youth movement is Karl Korn, *Die Arbeiterjugendbewegung* (2d ed. Berlin, 1923). Also see Willy Münzenberg, *Die sozialistische Jugendorganisation vor und während des Weltkrieges* (Berlin, 1919); Theo Haubach, "Die Generationenfrage und der Sozialismus," *Soziologische Studien,* dedicated to Alfred Weber (Potsdam,

1930); and Bruno Neumann, "Wandlungen des Jungsozialismus," *Die Gesellschaft,* 3 (2) (1926), 514–20. Broader studies of Weimar youth can be found in Viktor Engelhardt, *Die deutsche Jugendbewegung als Kulturhistorisches Phänomen* (Berlin, 1923); Günther Dehn, *Proletarische Jugend, Lebensgesinnung und Gedankenwelt der grossstädtischen Proletarier-Jugend* (Berlin, 1929); and E. Günther Gründel, *Die Sendung der jungen Generation* (Munich, 1932).

On the German electorate I have found Heinrich Striefler, *Deutsche Wahlen in Bildern und Zahlen* (Düsseldorf, 1946) extremely good. Rudolf Heberle, *From Democracy to Nazism, A Regional Case Study on Political Parties in Germany* (Baton Rouge, 1945) presents a superb analysis of Schleswig-Holstein; also see Otto Schrag, *Die Homogenität der Parteienzusammenstellungen im Reich und in den Ländern* (diss. Heidelberg, 1933); Arthur Dix, *Die deutsche Reichstagswahlen 1871–1930 und die Wandlungen der Volksgliederung* (Tübingen, 1930); and Emil Eichhorn, *Parteien und Klassen im Spiegel der Reichstagswahlen* (Halle, 1925); Meinrad Hagman, *Der Weg ins Verhängnis* (Munich, 1946); Günther Franz, *Die politischen Wahlen in Niedersachsen, 1867 bis 1949* (3d ed. Bremen-Horn, 1957); and Alfred Milatz, "Das Ende der Parteien im Spiegel der Wahlen 1930 bis 1933," *Das Ende der Parteien, 1933,* eds. Erich Matthias and Rudolf Morsey (Düsseldorf, 1960). For Social Democratic voters specifically, there are: R. Blank, "Die soziale Zusammensetzung der sozialdemokratischen Wählerschaft Deutschlands," *Archiv für Sozialwissenschaft und Sozialpolitik,* 20 (1905), 507–50; and Hans Neisser, "Sozialstatistische Analyse des Wahlergebnisses," *Die Arbeit,* 7 (1930), 654–59. The voting habits of German women are explored in Hans Beyer, *Die Frau in der politischen Entscheidung, Eine Untersuchung über das Frauenwahlrecht in Deutschland,* Soziologische Gegenwartsfragen, 2 (Stuttgart, 1933);

K. Panitz, "Wie wählen die Frauen," *Neue Zeit, 39* (1) (1921), 242–45; and Max Schneider, "Die deutsche Wählerin," *Die Gesellschaft, 4* (2) (1927), 364–70. The new middle class, wooed by the SPD in its efforts to become a people's party, is analyzed in Emil Lederer and Jakob Marschak, "Der neue Mittelstand," *Grundriss der Sozialökonomik, 9* (1) (1926), 120–41; Siegfried Kracauer, *Die Angestellten aus dem neuesten Deutschland* (Frankfurt/ Main, 1930); and Rudolf Küstermeier, *Die Mittelschichten und ihr politischer Weg* (Potsdam, 1933). Emil Lederer explores the relationship of this group to Social Democracy in "Die Umschichtung des Proletariats," *Die neue Rundschau, 40* (1929), 145–61, as does Theodor Geiger in "Panik im Mittelstand," *Die Arbeit, 7* (1930), 637–54, and "Die Mittelschichten und die Sozialdemokratie," ibid., *8* (1931), 619–35.

The rural aspects of the people's-party question may be studied in K. Krüger and F. Baade, *Sozialdemokratische Agrarpolitik* (Berlin, 1927), and Wolfgang Hirschberg, *Landwirtschaftskrise und Sozialdemokratie* (diss. Heidelberg, 1929). Alexander Gerschenkron presents a masterful political analysis of the entire agricultural scene in *Bread and Democracy in Germany* (Berkeley and Los Angeles, 1943).

Henrik deMan is the principal writer on *Verbürgerlichung;* see his *Untersuchung zur Psychologie des Sozialismus* (Jena, 1927), translated by Eden and Cedar Paul as *The Psychology of Socialism* (New York, 1927); and "Verbürgerlichung des Proletariats?" *Neue Blätter für den Sozialismus, 1* (1930), 106–18. Also see Hans Speier, "Verbürgerlichung des Proletariats," *Magazin der Wirtschaft, 7* (1931), 591–96, 633–38; and Theodor Geiger, "Zur Kritik der Verbürgerlichung," *Die Arbeit, 8* (1931), 534–47.

There are a few works that treat the sociological problems of the SPD in a broader perspective: Robert Michels, "Die deutsche Sozialdemokratie, Parteimitgliederschaft und soziale Zusammensetzung," *Archiv für Sozialwissenschaft und Sozialpolitik, 23* (1906), 471–556; Boris Goldenberg, *Beiträge zur Soziologie der deutschen Vorkriegssozialdemokratie* (diss. Heidelberg, 1932); Theodor Buddeberg, "Das soziologische Problem der Sozialdemokratie," *Archiv für Sozialwissenschaft und Sozialpolitik, 49* (1922), 108–32; and Werner Sombart, *Der proletarische Sozialismus,* (10th ed. 2 vols. Jena, 1924). On the proletariat as a social class, one may consult Goetz Briefs, "Das gewerbliche Proletariat," *Grundriss der Sozialökonomik, 9* (1) (1926), 142–240; Jakob Marschak, "Zur modernen Interessendifferenzierung," *Soziologische Studien,* dedicated to Alfred Weber (Potsdam, 1930), and Theodor Geiger, "Zur Theorie des Klassenbegriffs und der proletarischen Klasse," *Schmollers Jahrbuch, 54* (2) (1930), 185–236. Attempts to explain social psychology of the working class appear in Heinz Marr, *Proletarisches Verlangen, Ein Beitrag zur Psychologie der Massen* (Jena, 1921); and Robert Michels, "Psychologie der antikapitalistischen Massenbewegungen," *Grundriss der Sozialökonomik, 9* (1) (1926), 241–359. An excellent and detailed statistical analysis of the entire German social structure, based on the 1925 occupational census, may be found in Theodor Geiger, *Die soziale Schichtung des deutschen Volkes,* Soziologische Gegenwartsfragen, *1* (Stuttgart, 1932).

There is an ample literature on the history and sociology of the trade unions. Perhaps the best short introduction is Theodor Cassau, *Die Gewerkschaftsbewegung, Ihre Soziologie und ihr Kampf,* Soziale Organisationen der Gegenwart, *8* (Halberstadt, 1925). A more detailed official treatment can be found in the joint effort, Adolf Braun, *Die Gewerkschaften vor dem Kriege,* and Richard Seidel, *Die Gewerkschaften nach dem Kriege,* published together as *Die Gewerkschaften, Ihre Entwicklung und ihre Kämpfe* (2 vols.

Berlin, 1925). Also see Karl Zwing, *Soziologie der Gewerk-schaftsbewegung* (Jena, 1927), and his *Geschichte der deutschen freien Gewerkschaften* (2d ed. Jena, 1926), which constitute volumes *1* and *5* in the Gewerkschafts-Archiv-Bücherei. Likewise: Robert Goetz, *Les syndicats ouvriers allemands après la guerre, idéologies et réalités* (Paris, 1934); Jack Schiefer, *Geschichte der Deutschen Gewerkschaften* (Aachen, 1946); Wolfgang Abendroth, *Die deutschen Gewerkschaften* (Heidelberg, 1955); Otto Heilborn, *Die freien Gewerkschaften seit 1890* (Jena, 1907); and Paul Umbreit, *Die deutschen Gewerkschaften im Weltkriege*, Sozialwissenschaftliche Bibliothek, *1* (Berlin, 1917); and Fritz Opel, *Der Deutsche Metallarbeiter-Verband während des ersten Weltkrieges und der Revolution*, Schriftenreihe des Instituts für wissenschaftliche Politik in Marburg/Lahn, *4* (Hannover and Frankfurt/Main, 1957).

The political development of the unions and their relationship to the SPD has been the subject of several good studies. A recent survey is Wolfgang Hirsch-Weber, *Gewerkschaften in der Politik, von der Massenstreikdebatte zum Kampf um das Mitbestimmungsrecht*, Schriften des Instituts für Politische Wissenschaft, *13* (Cologne, 1959). Heinz Josef Varain, *Freie Gewerkschaften, Sozialdemokratie und Staat, Die Politik der Generalkommission unter der Führung Carl Legiens (1890–1920)*, Beiträge zur Geschichte des Parlamentarismus und der politischen Parteien, *9* (Düsseldorf, 1956) can be used together with a fairly reliable Communist account of the same period, Paul Merker, *Sozialdemokratie und Gewerkschaften, 1890–1920* (Berlin, 1949). For our period there is a useful microfilmed Ph.D. dissertation: Gerard Braunthal, "The Politics of the German Free Trade Unions during the Weimar Period" (Columbia Univ., New York, 1954: University Microfilms Publication 6584, Ann Arbor, Mich.), part of which has been published as "The German

Free Trade Unions during the Rise of Nazism," *Journal of Central European Affairs, 15* (1956), 339–53. The trade-union historian, Richard Seidel repeats only the official shibboleths in his brief *Gewerkschaften und politische Parteien in Deutschland* (Berlin, 1928). Also see: John L. Snell, "Socialist Unions and Socialist Patriotism in Germany, 1914–1918," *American Historical Review, 59* (1953), 66–76; Walter Pahl, "Gewerkschaften und Sozialdemokratie vor 1933," *Gewerkschaftliche Monatshefte, 4* (1953), 720–24; Franz Neumann, *European Trade Unionism and Politics* (New York, 1936); Lothar Erdmann, *Die Gewerkschaften im Ruhrkampf* (Berlin, 1924); and two articles by the last author, "Gewerkschaften und Sozialismus," *Die Arbeit, 2* (1925), 657–74, and "Nation, Gewerkschaften, und Sozialismus," ibid., *10* (1933), 136–52. A convenient review of trade-union developments since World War II may be found in Otto Kirchheimer, "West German Trade Unions," *World Politics, 8* (1955–56), 484–514.

Very little has been written about the USPD or Left Social Democracy. Eugen Prager, *Geschichte der USPD, Entstehung und Entwicklung der Unabhängigen Sozialdemokratischen Partei Deutschlands* (Berlin, 1921) is the standard, rather out-of-date history of the former. Also see Lenore O'Boyle, "The German Independent Socialists During the First World War," *American Historical Review, 56* (1951), 824–31; Karl Liebknecht, *Klassenkampf gegen den Krieg* (Berlin, n.d.); G. Zinoviev, *Zwölf Tage in Deutschland* (Hamburg, 1921); Heinrich Cunow, "Die Auflösungsprozess der U.S.P.," *Neue Zeit, 39* (1) (1921), 105–10, and his "Zur Fusion der U.S.P. mit der K.A.G.," ibid., *40* (2) (1922), 25–28. About the Left Social Democrats one can learn but little from Max Schippel, "Der sächsische Parteiradikalismus," *Sozialistische Monatshefte, 22* (1926), 308–11; Georg Decker, "Opposition," *Die Gesellschaft, 7* (1) (1930), 196–204;

and Franz Petrich, "Kritik der Opposition, Antwort an Decker," ibid., 7 (1), 454–61. Fritz Borinski writes a trenchant criticism of the SAP in "Der revolutionäre Sozialismus der SAP," *Neue Blätter für den Sozialismus, 3* (1932), 98–103.

For the political views of the Left Social Democrats, one must go to their press. They also published a series of five slim volumes for their book club which were called Rote Bücher der "Marxistischen Büchergemeinde": Max Adler, et al., *Die Krise des Kapitalismus und die Aufgabe der Arbeiterklasse* (Berlin, n.d. [1931]); Fritz Bieligk, et al., *Die Organisation im Klassenkampf* (Berlin, n.d. [1931]); Theodor Hartwig, et al., *Unsere Stellung zu Sowjetrussland* (Berlin, 1931); Anna Siemsen, *Auf dem Wege zum Sozialismus* (Berlin, 1932); and August Enderle, et al., *Das rote Gewerkschaftsbuch* (Berlin, 1932). Fritz Sternberg treats the economic crisis in *Der Niedergang des deutschen Kapitalismus* (Berlin, 1932). Also see three pamphlets put out by the SAP: *Wer hat die SPD gespalten?* (Berlin, 1931); *Was will die SAP?* (Berlin, 1931); and *Die Tolerierungspolitik der SPD* (Berlin, 1931).

To bring in contemporaneous developments in the KPD, one should read: Ossip K. Flechtheim, *Die Kommunistische Partei Deutschlands in der Weimarer Republik* (Offenbach/Main, 1948); Ruth Fischer, *Stalin and German Communism, A Study in the Origins of the State Party* (Cambridge, Mass. 1948); Eric Waldman, *The Spartacist Uprising of 1919,* Marquette German Studies, 1 (Milwaukee, 1958); Arthur Rosenberg, *A History of Bolshevism from Marx to the First Five Years' Plan,* trans. Ian F. D. Murrow (London, 1939); Franz Borkenau, *The Communist International* (London, 1938), published in the United States as *World Communism, A History of the Communist International* (New York, 1939); and B. Lazitch, *Les partis communistes d'Europe,*

1919–55 (Paris, 1956). The sociological relationship between the KPD and the SPD remains one of the least explored areas of German socialist history. Some information may be obtained from Siegfried Bahne, "Die Kommunistische Partei Deutschlands," *Das Ende der Parteien, 1933,* eds. Erich Matthias and Rudolf Morsey (Düsseldorf, 1960); Kaasch, "Die soziale Struktur der KPD, 1928," *Die Kommunistische Internationale, 9* (1929), 1050 ff.; and Walter Rist, pseud., "Die KPD in der Krise," *Neue Blätter für den Sozialismus, 2* (1931), 434–45. Even less helpful are Curt Geyer, *Der Radikalismus in der deutschen Arbeiterbewegung, Ein soziologischer Versuch* (Jena, 1923); and Alfred Meusel, "Der Radikalismus," *Kölner Vierteljahrshefte für Soziologie, 4* (1924–25), 44–68.

With regard to the Social Democratic Party, there remain to be cited the general histories of the movement and monographs on particular political aspects. Evelyn Anderson, *Hammer or Anvil, The Story of the German Working-Class Movement* (London, 1945) is a brief but excellent survey of the whole sweep of SPD history down to 1945, with most of the attention devoted to the Weimar period. Also see a recent popular survey: W. Matull, *Werden und Wesen der deutschen Sozialdemokratie* (Berlin, 1957), as well as a compendium of dates, F. Osterroth, *Chronik der sozialistischen Bewegung Deutschlands* (Berlin, 1957). A pedestrian official history of the prewar period has been written by Richard Lipinski, *Die Sozialdemokratie von ihren Anfängen bis zur Gegenwart, eine gedrängte Darstellung für Funktionäre und Lernende* (2 vols. Berlin, 1927–28). Franz Mehring's classic *Geschichte der deutschen Sozialdemokratie* (4 vols. in 2, Stuttgart, 1897) is still the most detailed account of the years before 1890. For the next period see G. A. Ritter, *Die Arbeiterbewegung im Wilhelminischen Reich, 1890–1900* (Berlin, 1959), as well as Peter Gay, *The Dilemma of Demo-*

cratic Socialism, Eduard Bernstein's Challenge to Marx (New York, 1952). The best single volume yet to be written on the SPD is Carl E. Schorske's brilliant and incisive *German Social Democracy, 1905–1917, The Development of the Great Schism* (Cambridge, Mass. 1955). Several monographs have appeared recently on special problems of prewar Social Democratic politics: Milorad M. Drachkovitch, *Les socialismes français et allemand et le problème de la guerre 1870–1914* (Geneva, 1953); Gerhard Schulz, *Die deutsche Sozialdemokratie und die Entwicklung der auswärtigen Beziehungen vor 1914* (Berlin, 1952); Albrecht Lotholz, *Die Haltung der Sozialdemokratie in den Heeres- Flotten- und Weltmachtsfragen, 1890–1914* (Freiburg, 1955); Reinhard Höhn, *Sozialismus und Heer* (2 vols. Berlin, 1959); and Hans Ulrich Wehler, *Sozialdemokratie und Nationalstaat, Die deutsche Sozialdemokratie und die Nationalitätenfragen in Deutschland*, Marburger Ostforschungen, *18* (Würzburg, 1962).

The years of war and revolution have been treated in several studies: Hermann Heidegger, *Die deutsche Sozialdemokratie und der nationale Staat, 1870–1920, unter besonderer Berücksichtigung der Kriegs- und Revolutionsjahre*, Göttinger Bausteine zur Geschichtswissenschaft, *25* (Göttingen, 1956); Edwyn Bevan, *German Social Democracy During the War* (London, 1918); Johann Meenzen, *Aussenpolitik und Weltfriedensordnung der deutschen Sozialdemokratie, 1914–18* (Hamburg, 1951); A. Joseph Berlau, *The German Social Democratic Party, 1914–1921* (New York, 1949); Heinz Schürer, *Die politische Arbeiterbewegung Deutschlands in der Nachkriegszeit, 1918–1923* (diss. Leipzig, 1933); Walter Tormin, *Zwischen Rätediktatur und sozialer Demokratie, Die Geschichte der Rätebewegung in der deutschen Revolution, 1918/19,* Beiträge zur Geschichte des Parlamentarismus und der politischen Parteien, *4* (Düsseldorf, 1954); and Rudolf Coper, *Failure of a Revolution, Germany in 1918–1919* (Cambridge, Mass. 1955).

The only works dealing specifically with the Weimar period of SPD history are Siegfried Marck's brief *Sozial-demokratie, Die geistige Struktur der politischen Parteien Europas, 4* (Berlin, n.d. [1931]), and a Communist analysis in Eugen Varga (ed.), *Die Sozialdemokratischen Parteien, Ihre Rolle in der internationalen Arbeiterbewegung der Gegenwart* (Hamburg, 1926). Paul Weidmann has reprinted the Gotha, Erfurt, and Görlitz programs in his analytic dissertation, *Die Programme der Sozialdemokratischen Partei Deutschlands von Gotha bis Görlitz* (diss. Hamburg, 1926). Also see Reimund Klinkhammer, *Die Aussenpolitik der Sozialdemokratischen Partei Deutschlands in der Zeit der Weimarer Republik* (Freiburg, 1955). For the role of the SPD in Prussia, see Earl R. Beck, *The Death of the Prussian Republic, A Study of Reich–Prussian Relations, 1932–1934,* Florida State University Studies, 31 (Tallahassee, 1959); and Hajo Holborn, "Prussia and the Weimar Republic," *Social Research, 22* (1956), 331–42.

The exile period between 1933 and 1945 is the subject of Lewis J. Edinger's excellent *German Exile Politics, The Social Democratic Executive Committee in the Nazi Era* (Berkeley and Los Angeles, 1956), which can be used with Erich Matthias, *Sozialdemokratie und Nation, Ein Beitrag zur Ideengeschichte der sozialdemokratischen Emigration ... 1933–1938* (Stuttgart, 1952). Klaus Schütz has written on the SPD in the Bonn Republic: "Die Sozialdemokratie im Nachkriegsdeutschland," *Parteien in der Bundesrepublik, Schriften des Instituts für politische Wissenschaft, 6* (Stuttgart and Düsseldorf, 1955); also see Richard Petry, "Die SPD und der Sozialismus," *Frankfurter Hefte, 9* (1954), 663–76; and Lewis J. Edinger and Douglas A. Chalmers, "Overture or Swansong: German Social Democracy Prepares for a New Decade," *The Antioch Review, 20* (1960), 163–75.

To set German Social Democracy in the broader stream of European socialist politics, one may consult: Rudolf Schlesinger, *Central European Democracy and Its Background* (London, 1953); Adolf Sturmthal, *The Tragedy of European Labor, 1918–1939* (New York, 1943); Lewis L. Lorwin, *The International Labor Movement, History, Politics, Outlook* (New York, 1953). For the history of the International, see especially James Joll, *The Second International, 1889–1914* (New York, 1956), and Maria Sokolova, *L'Internationale Socialiste entre les deux guerres mondiales* (Paris, 1954). The history of the Weimar SPD is particularly well treated in Carl Landauer, *European Socialism* (2 vols. Berkeley and Los Angeles, 1959). Finally, there remains G. D. H. Cole's monumental *A History of Socialist Thought* (5 vols. in 7, London, 1953–60).

The best work on Weimar political parties is Sigmund Neumann, *Die deutschen Parteien, Wesen und Wandel nach dem Kriege,* Fachschriften zur Politik und staatsbürgerlichen Erziehung (Berlin, 1932), which the author has brought up to date in his contribution, "Germany: Changing Patterns and Lasting Problems," in *Modern Political Parties, Approaches to Comparative Politics,* ed. Sigmund Neumann (Chicago, 1956). Also see: Ludwig Bergsträsser, *Geschichte der politischen Parteien in Deutschland* (10th ed. Munich, 1960); Rainer Barzel, *Die deutschen Parteien* (Geldern, 1952); and Herbert Sultan, "Zur Soziologie des modernen Parteisystems," *Archiv für Sozialwissenschaft und Sozialpolitik, 25* (1926), 91–140. Thomas Nipperdey has studied the prewar organization of the parties in "Die Organisation der bürgerlichen Parteien in Deutschland vor 1918," *Historische Zeitschrift, 185* (1958), 550–602, and has expanded this to cover the SPD in *Die Organisation der deutschen Parteien bis 1918* (Düsseldorf, 1961). The behavior of the individual parties in the crisis of 1933 is carefully analyzed in Erich Matthias and Rudolf Morsey (eds.), *Das Ende der Parteien, 1933,* Veröffentlichung der Kommission für Geschichte des Parlamentarismus und der politischen Parteien (Düsseldorf, 1960). Other individual party studies are few: Karl Bachem, *Vorgeschichte, Geschichte und Politik der deutschen Zentrumspartei* (9 vols. Cologne, 1927–32); Karl Buchheim, *Geschichte der christlichen Parteien in Deutschland* (Munich, 1953); and Werner Liebe, *Die Deutschnationale Volkspartei, 1918–1924* (Düsseldorf, 1956). The problem of proportional representation is treated in Johannes Schauff (ed.), *Neues Wahlrecht* (Berlin, 1929); F. A. Hermens, *Democracy or Anarchy? A Study of Proportional Representation* (Notre Dame, 1941); Maurice Duverger, *et al., L'Influence des systèmes électoraux sur la vie politique* (Paris, 1950); and Enid Lakeman and James D. Lambert, *Voting in Democracies* (London, 1955).

For non-German organizational and sociological comparisons, I have found particularly helpful: R. T. McKenzie, *British Political Parties, The Distribution of Power within the Conservative and Labour Parties* (London, 1954); and Maurice Duverger (ed.), *Partis politiques et classes sociales en France* (Paris, 1955). Among the general studies of political parties, the following are very insightful: Neumann's *Modern Political Parties* cited above; Maurice Duverger, *Political Parties, Their Organization and Activity in the Modern State,* trans. Barbara and Robert North (London, 1954); G. E. Lavau, *Partis politiques et réalités sociales* (Paris, 1953); and Seymour M. Lipset, *Political Man, The Social Bases of Politics* (New York, 1960).

Finally, among the various histories of the Weimar Republic, the following bear mention: Erich Eyck, *Geschichte der Weimarer Republik* (2 vols. Erlenbach-Zurich, 1954–56); S. William Halperin, *Germany Tried Democracy, A*

278

Political History of the Reich from 1918 to 1933 (New York, 1946); Arthur Rosenberg, *A History of the German Republic, 1918–1930,* trans. Ian F. D. Murrow (London, 1936); Theodor Eschenburg, *Die improvisierte Demokratie der Weimarer Republik* (Laupheim, 1957); Ferdinand Friedensburg, *Die Weimarer Republik* (Frankfurt/Main, 1957); Wilhelm Hoegner, *Die verratene Republik* (Munich, 1958); Karl Dietrich Bracher, *Die Auflösung der Weimarer Republik, Eine Studie zum Problem des Machtverfalls in der Demokratie,* Schriften des Instituts für politische Wissenschaft, *4* (2d ed. Stuttgart and Düsseldorf, 1957). A Social Democratic interpretation of the period may be found in Friedrich Stampfer, *Die ersten 14 Jahre der Deutschen Republik* (2d ed. Offenbach/Main, 1947); a Communist version in Paul Merker, *Deutschland Sein oder nicht Sein?* (2 vols. Mexico, 1944–45).

For bibliography on Weimar Social Democracy, one should consult Charles Gulick, *et al.* (eds.), *History and Theories of Working-Class Movements, A Selected Bibliography* (Berkeley, 1955), and *Bibliographie zur Geschichte der deutschen Arbeiterbewegung* (Leipzig, 1955), as well as two recent bibliographical review articles: Helga Grebing, "Die deutsche Sozialdemokratie seit 1914," *Politische Studien, 9* (1958), 849–59; and William Harvey Maehl, "Recent Literature on the German Socialists, 1891–1932," *Journal of Modern History, 33* (1961), 292–306.

Index